TIP OF THE ICEBERG

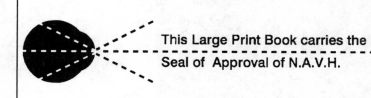

This Large Print Book carries the
Seal of Approval of N.A.V.H.

TIP OF THE ICEBERG

MY 3,000-MILE JOURNEY AROUND WILD ALASKA, THE LAST GREAT AMERICAN FRONTIER

MARK ADAMS

THORNDIKE PRESS
A part of Gale, a Cengage Company

A Cengage Company

Farmington Hills, Mich • San Francisco • New York • Waterville, Maine
Meriden, Conn • Mason, Ohio • Chicago

LIBRARY OF CONGRESS CIP DATA ON FILE.
CATALOGUING IN PUBLICATION FOR THIS BOOK
IS AVAILABLE FROM THE LIBRARY OF CONGRESS

ISBN-13: 978-1-4328-5533-8 (hardcover)

Published in 2018 by arrangement with Dutton, an imprint of Penguin
Publishing Group, a division of Penguin Random House LLC

Printed in the United States of America
1 2 3 4 5 6 7 22 21 20 19 18

For Lauren, Kerry, Jason, and Sarah —
travel companions from way back

I told him he must reform, for a man who neither believed in God nor glaciers must be very bad, indeed the worst of all unbelievers.

— John Muir, *Travels in Alaska*

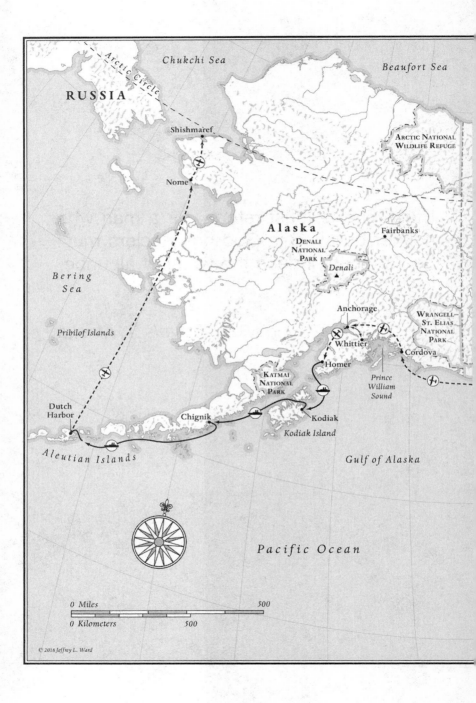

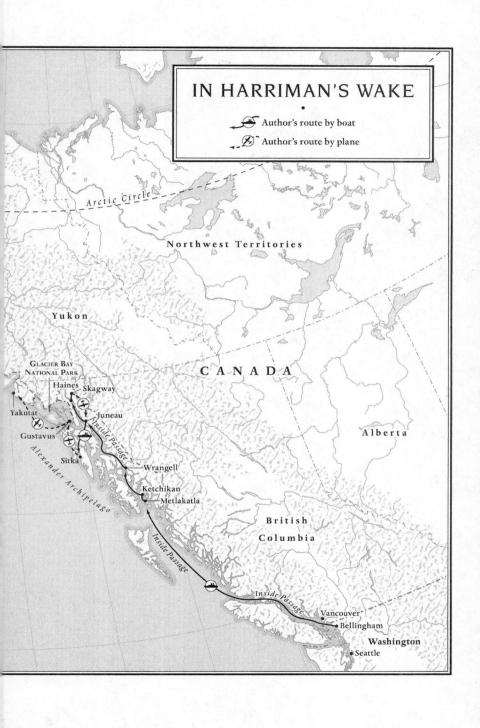

AUTHOR'S NOTE

The figure of three thousand miles in this book's subtitle was calculated on paper with a pencil and ruler, and includes water, air, and ground travel. In other words, it could be off by a little, or by a lot. "My 3,286.4 Mile Journey Around Wild Alaska, Roughly Half of Which Occurred on the Sea and Should Therefore Probably Be Tallied as Nautical Miles" might be more accurate, but it wouldn't fit on this book's spine. Any young Scouts working on cartography badges may notice that if you count all the sea miles from Bellingham, Washington, to Dutch Harbor, Alaska, that number is also, coincidentally, about three thousand.

Also, a few minor identifying details in this story, including some names, have been changed because not everyone I've written about knew they were going to be characters in a book.

PROLOGUE

Glacier Bay National Park

Our two-person kayak skimmed the surface of Glacier Bay's glassy water, the bow pointed like a compass needle at the rocky lump of Russell Island. The sun was out, always a pleasant surprise in Southeast Alaska, and a light mist lingered around the island's upper half. We'd been paddling for about an hour, but I had no idea how far we'd come or how far we had left to go. My sense of scale hadn't yet acclimated to the vastness we'd entered — water, sky, and mountains were all I had to work with. Aside from the splash of our paddles and the occasional taptapping of sea otters cracking open mussels, all was quiet.

"Will there be anyone else on Russell Island?" I asked David Cannamore, who was seated behind me. David was a former college athlete who guided kayakers around Glacier Bay National Park and Preserve all day, every day during the summer. He paddled with the metronomic grace of a professional tennis player volleying against a ball machine and accounted for perhaps 80 percent of our forward progress.

"I seriously doubt it," David said. "I've camped a lot of places in this park, but never on Russell Island. There probably aren't even any bears there."

Bears were just one subject I'd never given much thought to back in New York City that seemed to come up again and again in Alaska. Others included the five varieties of Pacific salmon, the structural integrity of permafrost, recipes for moose meat, the declining quality of rubber boots, and a simmering resentment toward Washington, DC, that fell under the general rubric of "federal overreach." Glaciers were another popular topic. As David and I paddled across the silent immensity of Glacier Bay, we were surrounded on all sides by the park's namesake rivers of ice flowing down from the mountains. Their frozen innards glowed a phosphorescent blue that eclipsed the cloudless sky above. A few times every hour, the giants discharged ice from their wrinkled faces — *crack, rumble, splash* — one of nature's most spellbinding performances.

According to the slightly damp map I kept

pulling out of a pocket beneath my life vest, the glaciers of Glacier Bay were doing something else, too. They were melting, and had been doing so for some time. There was no better evidence of this than Russell Island. In 1879, the then unknown conservationist John Muir had first scouted the bay in a dugout canoe guided by Tlingit Indians. Russell Island marked the furthest reach of his journey, for it was embedded in two hundred feet of solid ice, a pebble crushed beneath the leading edge of a glacier that flowed back up beyond the horizon into Canada. For the next twenty years, Muir returned repeatedly to Glacier Bay and its ever-changing landscape. On his seventh and final visit, in 1899, Muir estimated that the ice wall had retreated four miles. Russell Island was surrounded by open water.

Wavy lines on my map, each labeled with a year, demarcated the former extent of Glacier Bay's namesake ice in decades past. These were the shrinking borders of an empire under siege, evidence that in the century following John Muir's visits, the frozen kingdom whose praises he'd sung had been dissolving like a popsicle in the sun. Muir Glacier, named to honor the writer who literally put Glacier Bay on the map and almost singlehandedly created the market for scenic Alaska cruises, had withdrawn more than twenty miles since 1879.

For many people, especially environmentalists who revere John Muir as a nature prophet, this glacial retreat is obvious evidence of global warming. Which makes sense until you stop to ask why the ice had begun melting before the gasoline-powered automobile was invented. In some places along Alaska's coast, including Glacier Bay, one can find glaciers that are *growing.* More than a century after Muir's investigations, a lot of things were behaving unpredictably in Alaska, not just the glaciers but also animals, plants, weather, and — considering my sudden desire to go kayaking and camping in America's most remote wilderness — me.

Small white bergs drifted past as we paddled, reminders that the tranquil water beneath us could chill the life out of you in a few minutes. I'd already heard plenty of stories about outdoor adventures in Alaska that had quickly turned into outdoor tragedies. A group of six fishermen casting these same frigid waters not far from shore a few weeks earlier had leaned over to admire a catch and overturned their boat. The four who survived the cold shock were hypothermic when rescued. You didn't turn your back on Alaska.

From a distance, Russell Island had looked like a good place for a prison colony. When David and I landed, we found a perfect deserted isle with a panoramic view: two rows of dark mountains tapering toward a massive white block of ice. We set up camp in a patch of tall grass above the beach. David cooked a simple dinner, careful to keep even the tiniest scrap of food a hundred yards away from our tents in case any hungry bears came through. He'd grown up in Alaska and had encountered plenty of bears, and he didn't seem too concerned about the megafauna threat level on Russell Island. He'd seen none of the usual signs of bear activity: claw marks, scat, the large divots they dig out to sleep in.

"If you get up before the morning's first cruise ship comes through, have a good look around," David told me before we crawled into our tents for the night. "At that hour there probably won't be anyone but us for twenty miles in any direction."

Sunlight spilled into the fjord just after 4:00 A.M. — daybreak in Southeast Alaska in June — and illuminated the glacier at the head of the bay. When my great-grandparents were holding hands as teenagers, that ice had engulfed the spot where I stood. I sat on a rock that had been deposited by the glacier's hasty retreat sometime between John Muir's first visit, in 1879, and his last, in 1899, pulled out my map, and tried once again to untangle the changes that had taken place in that span.

When I looked up, I saw immediately that David's observation about our morning solitude needed a clarification. We were definitely the only humans on Russell Island, and probably the only people for many miles in any direction. But we weren't exactly alone.

CHAPTER ONE:
A VISIT TO MR. MERRIAM

Washington, DC

On March 25, 1899, a gentleman from New York City arrived unannounced at the Washington, DC, office of natural historian C. Hart Merriam. At age forty-three, Merriam had already been practicing science seriously for three decades, dating back to some unauthorized taxidermy performed on his sister's dead cat. In 1872, on summer break from high school, he had served as naturalist on an expedition to America's newly christened Yellowstone National Park and published his findings in a fifty-page government report. He had since earned and abandoned an MD degree, cofounded the National Geographic Society, and identified dozens of bird and mammal species.

Merriam did not, however, recognize the name of the mysterious stranger who'd interrupted his typically hectic workday. Edward H. Harriman, as any close observer of Wall Street would have known, was on the verge of becoming one of the most famous — and, in the trust-busting years to come, infamous — entrepreneurs of the late Gilded Age. In the years prior to setting foot in Merriam's office at the U.S. Division of Biological Survey, at 14th and Independence, Harriman had taken control of the underperforming Union Pacific Railroad. The previous summer, the new chief executive had personally inspected more than six thousand miles of track, examining "every poor tie, blistered rail, and loose bolt," according to one superintendent. The complete modernization Harriman ordered for the Union Pacific had left his railroad in rapidly improving shape and its chief executive physically exhausted. For the summer of 1899, Harriman's physician — who joined him in Merriam's office — was ordering him to take a sabbatical.

Harriman, whose quicksilver mind terrified his underlings and allowed him to see opportunities invisible to others, had conceived something much more ambitious than a couple of months of tennis and lemonade at his country estate. His plan was to outfit a large steamship as his private yacht and survey the coast of Alaska. In the previous fifteen years, it had become possible to book package tours up the Inside Passage, as the waterways of the British Columbia coast and Alaska panhandle had come to be known. A steady flow of well-to-do excursioners had been lured by newspaper and magazine stories raving about Alaska's glaciers. One particularly adventurous writer had done more than all others combined to promote the territory's frozen wonders: John Muir.

Harriman was bringing along his wife and children, as well as a few guests and an ample crew, but his ship had the capacity to carry many more. He sought Merriam's help in rounding up a team of America's top experts in the natural sciences to accompany them. "He thought that there should be two men of recognized ability in each department," Merriam later recalled. "Two zoologists, two botanists, two geologists and so on." Harriman expected to depart from Seattle in just two months.

Harriman's rough itinerary combined familiar elements of the newly fashionable northern Grand Tour with exploration into points unknown. His steamship would sail up the Inside Passage and visit its best-known spots: lawless Wrangell; Skagway, epicenter of the Klondike Gold Rush; the old Russian capital, Sitka; and Glacier Bay, perhaps the biggest draw of all, thanks to the ecstatic nature rhapsodies that Muir published in America's most popular magazines. But one of the secrets to Harriman's success was ignoring limits set by others. *His* Alaska course would extend thousands of miles further, continuing west toward the Bering Sea, scouting Prince William Sound, Kodiak Island, the Aleutians, and beyond, obscure places where large swaths of territory were labeled UNKNOWN on maps and scientific discoveries were waiting for anyone who stepped on shore. Thanks to railroad men like Harriman, the wild American West had been all but subdued in less than a hundred years. In 1805, Lewis and Clark had witnessed herds of buffalo so large their movements shook the ground. By 1899, that same species faced extinction. The true American frontier now lay in the wilderness to the north. As the historian Maury Klein puts it, "Harriman's idea of rest was to organize, underwrite, and direct what became the last major scientific expedition of the nineteenth century."

Seated in his office, Merriam was polite but dubious about Harriman's offer. Whoever had steered Harriman to Merriam had chosen wisely, though. The scientist, son of a congressman, was exceedingly well connected. He made quick inquiries, which confirmed that the railroad man was not only serious but probably incapable of joking. Cartoonists delighted in depicting Merriam, who wore round spectacles and combed his hair into a tall pouf, as an administrative owl. He was wise enough to see that he might have stumbled across the most elusive of creatures: a scientific expedition with no fixed budget. When Harriman visited Merriam's home that night and insisted that in addition to covering all costs he would allow the team Merriam selected free rein to conduct their own research, Merriam was convinced that Harriman's northbound Noah's Ark was no rich man's boondoggle.

"To be a member of it would be the event of a lifetime," he realized.

CHAPTER TWO:
ALL POINTS NORTH

New York City

Next to the cluttered desk in my office, I keep a small collection of manila folders labeled with the names of destinations I would like to write about one day. Inside each folder are scraps of paper — bar napkins covered in semi-legible hieroglyphics and yellowed newspaper clippings pertaining to a particular place. In the folder marked ALASKA, there's a piece of hotel stationery on which I scribbled something an Alaskan friend once told me. Three basic types of people live in Alaska, he said. There are the Native Alaskans, who've been there since time immemorial. There are people who have come north running *toward* something, usually a chance to do something unpleasant to make a lot of money quickly, such as gutting fish twelve hours a day or operating a welding torch in minus-forty-degree temperatures. And there are those who are running *away* from something, like a bad marriage or fluoridated water.

Travel writing is an odd and pleasant way to make a living, one that has enabled me to fast-forward to the sort of life people profiled in *Forbes* often anticipate once they've made a Harriman-worthy fortune. I wander the world meeting interesting people; I write books; and when not on the road, I spend so much time around the house that my children sometimes feel obligated to tell friends that I really do have a job. Over the years, I have learned that the most interesting questions to answer about a place are rarely the most obvious ones: where to go, when to do so, what to eat, who to go with, or even how to get there. The essential question about travel is: Why? Perhaps you've dreamed of Kenya ever since seeing *Out of Africa* as a child, or want to meet your distant relatives in Ireland, or long to see a lemur in the wild. A journey *away* from something — work, stress, societal norms that frown on drinking before 10:00 A.M. — is a vacation. A journey *toward* something — a trip with an objective — is an expedition. There are a handful of spectacular places I've put off visiting (and writing about) for years because I never found a good enough reason to go. Until recently, Alaska was one of them.

Outside of my professional travel obligations, I like a plain old relaxing vacation as much as anyone, and was in the midst of one not long ago when I found myself in the slightly seedy Seattle neighborhood of Pioneer Square, staring up at a totem pole. The presence of a totem pole at a busy intersection in Seattle wasn't especially noteworthy — they're only marginally less common than stoplights — though I was surprised to encounter standing beneath this one a friendly young U.S. national park ranger in his Smokey Bear hat. The pole, he enthusiastically informed me, was actually a duplicate. The original had been obtained in 1899 by a group of prominent local business leaders who'd sailed north to Alaska's Inside Passage to steal one from a Native village. The Pioneer Square pole thieves seem to have stolen their idea, too, the ranger went on. They'd been inspired by the ballyhooed return to Seattle of the Harriman Expedition.

As it happens, one of the qualifications of my unusual job is knowing a thing or two about the history of exploration. An entire bookcase in my office is crammed with accounts of journeys to the far corners of the

26

earth. The existence of the Harriman Expedition was news to me, though, a gap in my knowledge that grew into embarrassment once I got a look at the league of extraordinary gentlemen Hart Merriam assembled in 1899. His selections had participated in almost every important American expedition since the Civil War. The obvious first choice was William Healey Dall, the dean of Alaskan explorers, who'd begun visiting the northern wilderness when it was still Russian and had written *Alaska and Its Resources,* perhaps the most influential book ever published on the territory. Grove Karl Gilbert, veteran of multiple Rocky Mountain campaigns, was thought by many to be the greatest American geologist who ever lived. Henry Gannett's brilliant innovations in geography led him to be known as "the Father of American Map Making." George Bird Grinnell, editor of the influential *Forest and Stream* magazine, had founded the Audubon Society and was arguably the most respected outdoorsman in the country. Some expeditioners were already good friends. Others knew one another only by reputation. Everyone knew Merriam.

Not all prospective members were academic specialists. Aside from taking the rest his doctor had prescribed, Harriman seemed to have two primary goals for his summer in Alaska. He wished to return from his adventures with a trophy bear, so two taxidermists and a scout were hired to accompany the group. Harriman also, in the Carnegie-esque spirit of the age, hoped to render a philanthropic service by enabling scientists in various fields to survey the wonders of Alaska, enlarge their collections of specimens, and share their findings with an American public that had developed a passion for the natural history museums that were proliferating around the country. Merriam expanded the team to include three artists and a young photographer, Edward S. Curtis, who had guided Merriam and Grinnell to safety after they'd gotten lost while hiking on Mount Rainier in 1898. Rounding out the roster was a pair of America's best-known authors in a genre — nature writing — that was growing in popularity as America's wilderness vanished. One was John Burroughs, famous for his best selling essays on birds and flowers, who signed on to write the expedition's official history.

The second author was both an obvious invitee and a reluctant one. John Muir was perhaps America's leading writer on the relatively new subject of wilderness protection, a movement that within a few years would come to be known as conservation. He had visited Alaska six times and was generally acknowledged as the top expert on its glaciers. His 1879 canoe trip through the Inside Passage is one of the most famous voyages in American exploration. (Muir's first encounter with Glacier Bay is the heart of his classic *Travels in Alaska,* a copy of which I *did* have in my office bookcase.) He had also founded the Sierra Club, to defend California's dwindling wild places against men like Harriman, practitioners of what Muir called "gobble gobble economics." Unfamiliar with Harriman, and perplexed by his unusual offer, Muir dragged his feet until his friend Merriam convinced him that the ship would be making stops in Alaskan locations that even Muir had yet to explore.

With his legacy in mind, Harriman paid Hart Merriam to edit what became twelve beautifully printed volumes of writings and photographs by the expedition members. Taken as a whole, the *Harriman Alaska Series* serves as a sepia snapshot of Alaska's natural riches in 1899: bears and whales and fjords and snowcapped peaks. Most striking of all, due largely to Muir's influence, are the hundreds of glaciers, many newly discovered and each as distinct in words and pictures as a snowflake under a microscope.

Since 1867, when the United States purchased the half million square miles of what had been called "Russian America," the territory has had a split personality. Alaska is the Last Frontier, land of sublime wild beauty. It is also, in the words of author and eco-activist Edward Abbey, "the last pork chop," a natural larder waiting to be raided. Alaska has been shaped by three gold rushes, each of which left behind a fundamentally different place. The first was the soft gold rush of fur, starting in the mid-eighteenth century, which opened the Great Land to the ships of Europe's most powerful nations. The second was the hard gold rush of the 1890s, which drew thousands of new non-Native residents north for the first time. The scientists assembled by Hart Merriam witnessed the unintended consequences of unregulated exploitation in Alaska — species driven to extinction, pristine lands and waters contaminated, Native cultures destroyed — and recorded these effects in the *Harriman Alaska Series* as well.

Alaska's third and biggest boom was the liquid gold rush that began with the construction of the Trans-Alaska Pipeline in the

1970s. Around the time I learned of the Harriman Expedition's existence, news stories began to report that, after nearly forty fat years, Alaska's third rush was reaching a crisis point just as its others had. The state's oil reserves were dwindling, and the price per barrel had collapsed, crippling the regional economy. Alaska faced a difficult choice: double down and open protected wilderness areas for drilling, which climate scientists argued was the opposite of what should be done in light of alarming warming trends; or move on to the Next Big Thing, whatever that might be, as the state always had.

It seemed I finally had my reason to visit Alaska — my answer to the question "Why?" I could follow in the Harriman Expedition's wake and compare what Hart Merriam's all-star team of experts had recorded with what was happening now. How to do so was another matter. Alaska is essentially a small continent: big enough to hold Texas, California, and Montana (the second-, third-, and fourth-largest states) and still have room left over for New England, Hawaii, and a couple of metropolises. It contains seven mountain ranges and ten peaks taller than any in the Lower 48. Its waterfront accounts for *half* of all the coast in the United States.

Louisiana has four times as many miles of paved roads. Except for a few of the larger cities and towns, most places in Alaska — and almost every place visited by the Harriman Expedition — can be reached only by boat or airplane. You can't even drive to Juneau, the state capital.

Because of these obstacles, Alaska has always been as much a seafaring culture as Polynesia. The great majority of its recreational visitors today make the journey the same way they would have in 1899: on ships. Each summer a million cruise ship passengers make the same scenery hajj as the Harriman Expedition. The most recent data I could find showed the Inside Passage had catapulted over Las Vegas and Orlando to become America's number-one tourist destination.

I'd never before traveled any serious distance by water, and the idea seemed appealing, a throwback to a time of steamer trunks and straw boaters, a golden age before TSA pat-downs and punitive baggage fees. If I'd been in the market for an Alaska vacation, an Inside Passage cruise would've worked fine. But as was the case with Harriman, my ambitions were a little more grand.

There was another option. Alaska has its

own coastal transportation network, the Alaska Marine Highway System, created to deal with its unique needs. Most of the state's residents live near the sea. The Marine Highway's purpose is to move people and vehicles long distances to remote places for a reasonable price. Alaska's ferries have as much in common with Greyhound buses as with anything offered by Norwegian Cruise Line, but what they lack in amenities they make up for in flexibility. With a little patience, Dramamine, and maybe a few time-saving shortcuts, it appeared to be possible to ride the three thousand miles from Washington State to Dutch Harbor, in the Aleutians, in about two months, the same time the Harriman Expedition took.

Not just a vacation, I told myself, pulling Muir's *Travels in Alaska* off the shelf, but an expedition. It could even, as Muir's pal Hart Merriam might say, be the event of a lifetime.

CHAPTER THREE:
FIRST-CLASS MEN

Westbound on the Harriman Special

Harriman and most of his invited specialists left Grand Central Station by train on the twenty-third of May 1899, in several private carriages that included a dining car, two sleepers, and a plush smoker stocked with fine cigars and a five-hundred-volume library on all topics related to Alaska. Harriman kept a private car for his own use. His guests, accustomed to the shoestring budgets of government-funded expeditions, luxuriated in the hospitality made possible by capitalism. The painter Frederick Dellenbaugh, who had run the uncharted Colorado River with explorer John Wesley Powell in large rowboats, marveled at the hot and cold running water in his stateroom and the choices of entrée with dinner — baked bluefish, prime roast beef, roasted Philadelphia capon. As Harriman's guests settled in for their weeklong cross-country

34

journey, the host passed through his train cars to get acquainted.

Like Merriam, several of the men on the train had never heard of their small, mustached host prior to receiving his invitation. He did not exude warmth. "Every feature of his countenance manifested power, especially his wonderful eyes, deep and frank yet piercing, though likely at first sight to keep people at a distance," observed John Muir. In addition to being an innovative thinker, a genius with numbers, and a fierce competitor, Harriman was something of a late bloomer, whose name would not become synonymous with business until the coming decade. He had dropped out of school at fourteen to take a job as an office boy on Wall Street. By age twenty-two he had worked his way up to a seat on the New York Stock Exchange. In 1881, he was part of a syndicate that purchased a small, decrepit railroad in upstate New York, which Harriman arranged to resell for a profit. Not until 1898 did he acquire his first major railroad, the Union Pacific.

Harriman was known for his ability to digest huge amounts of information quickly, which allowed him to impose order and efficiency on situations that might easily spin into chaos, such as corralling a shipload of scientists whose individual worlds revolved around mollusks or birds or rocks and expecting them to spend two months harmoniously in close quarters. Once Harriman had taken the measure of a subordinate and found him adequate, however, he was an eager delegator of authority. As the special train chugged toward Chicago, Harriman "announced that it was not his desire to dictate the route to be followed, or to control the details of the work," Merriam wrote. Instead, he appointed his guests to serve on a variety of committees of the sort one might have in a business organization. These he deputized to make decisions about the expedition's specific itinerary.

After crossing the Mississippi, the passengers aboard the special train observed mounting evidence of the taming of the West: fenced farms, coal mines, networks of train tracks. "In places the country looks as if all the railroad forces of the world might have been turned loose to delve and rend and pile in some mad, insane folly and debauch," John Burroughs wrote. Settlements remembered as pinpricks on a map a few years prior had grown into full-fledged towns and cities. Omaha was hosting the Greater America Exposition, to which Harriman's guests were escorted on a private trolley. In Boise, where the local paper declared Harriman "the man of the hour in railroad circles," the team was met at sunrise with a parade sponsored by the chamber of commerce. Merriam suggested that Shoshone Falls, in Idaho's Snake River Canyon, might make a nice day trip. Harriman wired ahead, "ordering horses, a stagecoach, and two buggies to be brought up by rail," according to historians William Goetzmann and Kay Sloan. No expense needed to be spared, as Harriman was making money faster than he could spend it. For the fiscal year that ended June 30, 1899, the Union Pacific would earn a net profit of fourteen million dollars.

As the Harriman special train rolled through the Rockies, a smaller coterie of guests, including Muir, had embarked from California to meet the others in Portland, where a dinner was being held at the city's finest hotel. The final leg of their rail journey was eased by Harriman's sometime rival J. P. Morgan, who had ordered the tracks of his Northern Pacific Railroad cleared. In Seattle, photographer Edward Curtis and his assistant, D. G. Inverarity, completed the party. As the Harriman Alaska Expedition prepared to depart Seattle on the thirty-first, its detail-oriented patron stood in the gray Northwest drizzle keeping an eye on the tons of strange cargo being loaded onto the *George W. Elder:* the baggage and scientific equipment of all his guests, hunting rifles and ammunition, a complete photo dark room and slide projector, a piano, the five hundred books on Alaska, cigars, brandy, champagne, and, according to Burroughs, "eleven fat steers, a flock of sheep, chickens, and turkeys, a milch cow, and a span of horses."

Harriman had assembled a company of men who would come to be known as some of the founders of American conservation, at the very moment when a movement to protect America's natural beauty was forming. Paradoxically, Harriman states in the first paragraph of the first volume of the *Harriman Alaska Series* that his interest in Alaska had been piqued by the opportunity to kill a Kodiak bear. What may seem incongruous more than a century later was at the time entirely consistent. Though urban environmentalists tend to avoid the subject, the roots of their movement are inextricably intertwined with hunting.

Perhaps the leading example of this duality was George Bird Grinnell. Grinnell in 1899 was best known as the editor of *Forest and Stream,* a magazine for sportsmen that championed the preservation of habitat. His pedigree as an outdoorsman was extraordinary. When he was a boy, his family had lived on the bucolic north Manhattan estate of the late naturalist and bird artist John James Audubon, where he was tutored by Lucy Audubon, John's widow. During the 1870s, Grinnell had made several trips west — assisting on some of the first dinosaur fossil hunts (guided by "Buffalo Bill" Cody) and serving as the naturalist on General Custer's 1874 Black Hills Expedition. (He declined Custer's invitation to join the doomed 1876 campaign that ended at Little Big Horn.) With each return trip west, Grinnell saw that populations of large animals were dwindling due to overhunting. Traveling through Nebraska in 1870, historian Michael Punke writes, "Grinnell's train had twice been halted by herds of buffalo." Two years later, he rode with the Pawnee on one of their last great buffalo hunts. By 1879, not a single bison was to be found in the state of Colorado.

In response to similar threats to wild bird populations, Grinnell founded the Audubon Society, which he briefly ran from the *Forest and Stream* offices. He also used the magazine to advocate for law enforcement against poaching in existing national parks and the formation of new ones. (Montana's Glacier National Park, which was established in 1910 and recently welcomed its 100 millionth visitor, was largely Grinnell's creation.) When Grinnell gave a lukewarm review to the book *Hunting Trips of a Ranchman,* the author, twenty-six-year-old New York State assemblyman Theodore Roosevelt, stormed into the editor's office to rebut the criticisms. A friendship followed, and two years later, in December 1887, Grinnell and Roosevelt decided to form the Boone and Crockett Club. The club's members, each of whom was required to have killed at least three kinds of trophy animals, would use their political influence to promote preservation of wild places, not least because that was where big game lived.*

The creeping panic felt by men like Grin-

---

* Hart Merriam, who was a Boone and Crockett member, was another amalgam of hunter and animal advocate. During his brief career as an MD, according to his biographer Keir Sterling, Merriam owned "three descented skunks" who often accompanied him on house calls. "At home, when he was working in his office, the skunks teased him by pulling off his shoes," according to Sterling.

nell and Roosevelt was due not only to the diminishing numbers of animals to shoot. In 1893, the historian Frederick Jackson Turner announced that, according to the latest census data, the American frontier had disappeared. For decades, hardy pioneers had gone west to conquer the wilderness. Nature, like the Native Americans, was treated as an enemy to be subdued. Turner argued that the frontier experience had shaped the American character, with its love of freedom and rugged individualism. Europe suffered willingly under kings and emperors. The United States demanded democracy. With the frontier gone, Turner and others wondered, what would become of America?

Except the American frontier hadn't disappeared. It had simply moved north. The territory of Alaska was so distant and vast that, as the superintendent of the same 1890 census on which Turner had based his pessimistic hypothesis pointed out, it presented "difficulties in the way of enumeration scarcely conceivable in the older portion of the country." Not only were the contents of this immense northern enigma unknown, but no one was even certain how to begin measuring them. The first glimmer of a new ecological awareness may have been dawning in response to the end of the Wild West, but that urge to save the wilderness had been sparked by the threat of scarcity. Alaska was so big and so wild that its natural resources were assumed to be inexhaustible and ripe for exploiting. As the *Elder* cruised northward, campaigns that would test the limits of those resources were well under way.

Chapter Four:
The Two Johnnies

Seattle

The more than one thousand islands of the Alexander Archipelago — "so numerous," John Muir once wrote, "that they seem to have been sown broadcast" — make up the French braid that extends down from the bulk of the forty-ninth state's cranial landmass. They are actually the mountaintops of a submerged range that extends south, aboveground, all the way to the Cascades. If a voyage up the Inside Passage often feels more like floating down a river canyon than sailing upon the open seas, it is because in both instances you're sailing between two walls of rock. Just to be certain, though, I booked the first leg of my journey on the MV *Kennicott,* one of only two Alaska ferries accredited for ocean travel.

The 126 persons aboard the newly refurbished *George W. Elder* set sail on May 31, along with their assorted livestock and poultry. Per Harriman's exacting standards, the ship was in fine shape. Built of iron, 250 feet long with a fresh white paint job, the *Elder* gleamed like Alaskan snow beneath the plume of black coal smoke that she exhaled from her smokestack. She had two decks for staterooms and crew quarters. Above them sat the hurricane deck, with its pilothouse and a small brass cannon. In addition to the dining room and library, Harriman had arranged for a salon where lectures could be given, board games played, religious services offered, and magic-lantern slides of each day's discoveries projected. A large derrick stood sentinel over all, in anticipation of lifting a trophy bear on board.

The specialists settled in, two men in each stateroom. The air was convivial, with several opportunities per day to mingle. John Burroughs, the official chronicler of the trip, was feeling a bit out of sorts. At sixty-two, he was accustomed to life at his "hermit's retreat" in the Catskill Mountains. This was his first trip not just to Alaska but west of the Mississippi. Burroughs was not a great traveler, prone to seasickness and melancholy. He is a likely suspect as the anonymous perpetrator who nicknamed the ship the *George W. Roller* at the first sign of turbulence. Muir, whose cabin was nearby, was only a year younger but retained his boyish enthusiasm for adventure. The two men were perhaps America's leading nature essayists and knew each other well. They were sometimes paired together as "the two Johnnies," and in one photograph from the trip, their matching long beards give the impression of Father Time looking into a mirror. The two also shared an appetite for teasing with some bite. Muir once reacted to a letter from Burroughs explaining that current circumstances would not allow him to join a voyage to Europe by telling another friend that "the 'circumstances' are his wife." In the Harriman Expedition's official history, Burroughs noted, "In John Muir we had an authority on glaciers, and a thorough one — so thorough that he would not allow the rest of the party to have an opinion on the subject."

Whereas most of the scientists aboard the *Elder* signed into the logbook with their academic or government titles, Muir identified himself as "author and student of glaciers." In both cases, his expertise was largely self-taught, a lifelong act of rebellion against his father, Daniel, a fanatical Calvinist who required his eldest son to memorize Bible verses daily. If John made a mistake reciting the day's selection, Daniel gave him a thrashing. By the time he was eleven, when the Muirs moved from Dunbar, Scotland, to the wilderness of Wisconsin, John knew all of the New Testament by rote and most of the Old Testament, too. No enterprising devil ever found idle hands among the Muir children. "Old man Muir works his children like cattle," one Wisconsin neighbor observed. When the family needed a new well, John spent months chiseling through eighty feet of sandstone. Decades later, after he'd fought some of the most vicious battles in early conservation history, he could single out just one thing on earth that he hated without reservation: cruelty.

Though he is now revered as a nature druid, Muir was technologically gifted as a young man, a habitual tinkerer and inventor. At age twenty-two, he caused a stir at the state fair in Madison with one of his creations, an alarm clock that not only woke deep sleepers but tilted their beds, tipping them out onto their feet. (Muir heeded his father's order not to read the newspaper, so that reports of his brilliance would not inflame his vanity.) He enrolled in Wisconsin's new state university, where his love of botany and the mechanics of the natural world soon blossomed into a fascination with science.

After two years of university instruction and a long, solitary ramble around the Great Lakes collecting plants, Muir landed a job in an Indianapolis carriage-parts factory, where his mechanical skills helped him to rise quickly to supervisor. In March 1867, Muir was attempting to remove the belt from a circular saw. A file he was holding slipped and flew into his right eye. "When he opened the eyelid, the liquid filling the space between the lens and the cornea dripped into his hand," according to Muir biographer Donald Worster. By day's end, sympathetic blindness had left him sightless in both eyes.

While convalescing, Muir thought about a plan he'd secretly been nursing for years: to retrace the botanic peregrinations of the German scientist Alexander von Humboldt, who had been the first to comprehensively survey the flora and fauna of Central and South America. Among Humboldt's radical ideas was that the species of the world were inextricably linked in a vast web, part of a single living organism. The natural order was not fixed, as scientists since Aristotle had argued, but dynamic. Only one species held the power to irrevocably disrupt the natural world: *Homo sapiens.*

Muir's blindness was temporary. He resolved to take a long journey through the tropics just as his hero Humboldt had, to replenish his soul with "wild beauty." In his bag he carried a change of underclothes, a few books, and a small notebook. Any stranger who happened to peek inside its front cover would have found this Humboldtian address inscribed there:

John Muir
Earth-Planet
Universe

In the fall and winter of 1867 and 1868, Muir walked more than a thousand miles through the postwar American South as he worked through a cosmic conundrum. Daniel Muir's dogmatic Christianity held that God had created man in his own image and given him dominion over the fish of the sea, the fowl of the air, and every creeping thing that creepeth upon the earth. John Muir always had a weakness for animals; as a boy, he'd accidentally choked a cat to death while attempting to remove a bird trapped in its mouth. "Nature's object in making animals and plants might possibly be first of all the happiness of each one of them, not the creation of all for the happiness of one," he reasoned. To Muir, nature was not humankind's servant. Nature and God were one. Within a year of settling in California, in 1868, he'd already formulated what would become the core of his philosophy: "When we try to pick out anything by itself, we find it hitched to everything else in the Universe."*

The shrinking of the American frontier had the effect of broadening the market for nature writing. Muir, who spoke in captivating paragraphs and thought nothing of scaling cliffs alone, found the act of composition almost too terrifying to contemplate. Slowly, he adapted his lyrical gifts to the printed page. In 1875, his byline appeared for the first time in a national publication, *Harper's New Monthly Magazine.* The article, which dealt with a subject on which he was

* Muir's thinking was influenced by the Transcendentalists, especially Ralph Waldo Emerson and Henry David Thoreau, who held that the divine exists in nature and that all things are connected. Emerson met Muir in Yosemite Valley in 1871 and was delighted to find a mountain man living the philosophy he'd formulated at his desk in Concord. "He is more wonderful than Thoreau," he said afterwards.

becoming something of an expert, was titled "Living Glaciers of California."

CHAPTER FIVE:
FERRY TALES

Aboard the Kennicott

My own expedition began with a train to a plane to a bus, which deposited me next to a boat in Bellingham, Washington, on the last Saturday afternoon in May. Bellingham is where the southernmost Alaska Marine Ferry terminal is located, and turned out to be a lot closer to Vancouver than to Seattle, which I'd flown into. At three in the afternoon, a very long line of vehicles was already waiting to drive aboard the MV *Kennicott*. According to my reservation, the vessel was scheduled to disembark at six. The ticket agent at the ferry terminal said our departure had been delayed three and a half hours due to low tides further up the coast. The Marine Highway had neglected to inform passengers about the new departure time, so a lot of unhappy vehicle owners, many of who were Alaskans returning home, having driven several hours already, were walking from car to car commiserating about the waste of their time. (Alaskans, one quickly learns, have an especially low opinion of bureaucracy.) Fortunately for me, Bellingham is the sort of cute seaside town whose economic engine runs on leisure activities, so I whiled away a few hours browsing in the bookstore, sipping beer, and purchasing a few last trip essentials.

Boarding the *Kennicott* felt less like setting sail on an all-inclusive Caribbean cruise than it did punching in for work at a shipyard. Cars and trucks rolled onto the ship alongside pedestrians. A significant percentage of passengers carried coolers and grocery bags. You were supposedly limited to a hundred pounds of carry-on weight, but no one I met had ever heard of anyone checking. Perhaps half the people in line wore baseball hats and boots. The predominant color scheme was camouflage, which seemed to be the navy blue of Alaska. Had a voice come over the public address system asking anyone who'd reached the finals of a Willie Nelson look-alike contest to report to the ticket office, the crowd would have thinned by about a third. Most of the passengers seemed to be men traveling solo, but there were some retired couples and a few young families. I'd reserved a roomette and waited in line at the purser's desk to get my keys and rent a set of sheets and a towel.

Not everyone was willing to shell out the fifty dollars a night for a bed. By the time I located a wall map to find my room, squatters with sleeping bags had occupied all the booths in the cafeteria. Hardier folks had duct-taped tents to the floor of the outdoor observation deck, which took on the look of an REI refugee camp. I shared the elevator to the sundeck level with a gray-haired couple who seemed to be in a festive vacation mood. The man, who wore a goatee and a beret, used a gnarled six-foot walking stick to push the elevator buttons. "See, I told you it would come in handy," he told his wife with satisfaction.

With its soothing beige-and-baby-blue color scheme, linoleum floors, and faint smells of cleaning products and machine oil, the *Kennicott* reminded me of a giant floating Laundromat. My roomette was identical to a two-person sleeper on Amtrak, about eight feet long by six feet wide. Two pleather-covered seats faced each other, with a low Formica table in between, as if in preparation for a chess match. These folded down to make a narrow bed; another bunk was strapped against the wall above. A communal bathroom with showers was located at the end of the hall. The view from my single porthole looked out onto the ankles of some fellow passengers and their cigarette butts. Together with the two pints of pale ale I'd consumed, the *Kennicott* engine's soft hum had a soporific effect. I folded down the table, arranged my bed, and marveled at how the roomette managed to be both womblike and sterile. Within minutes, I drifted off.

Perhaps half an hour later, I was awakened by pounding on the wall above my head and screaming. I looked out the porthole and ascertained from the relative calm of the assembled ankles that we were not on fire. We hadn't even left the dock. The noise was coming from the room next door and apparently was one end of a cell phone call. Most of what I could make out consisted of the same profanity repeated over and over, followed by a litany of a *Kennicott* roomette's shortcomings.

"WHERE'S MY [FORNICATING] PRIVATE BATHROOM?"

"WHERE'S MY [FORNICATING] TV?"

"WHY DID I HAVE TO PAY THREE [FORNICATING] DOLLARS FOR [FORNICATING] SHEETS AND

SOAP?" (This was actually a valid complaint, since the sheets were thin and scratchy, and my bar of soap had clacked like a poker chip and cracked in two when I dropped it on the linoleum floor. My neighbor's final criticism was timely, and certainly a complaint never heard aboard the *Elder*.)

"DID YOU KNOW THERE'S NOT EVEN A BAR ON THIS BOAT?"

For years, the bars on Alaska marine ferries had been one of the fleet's most famous and appealing features, a place where sourdoughs (longtime residents of the state), cheechakos (newcomers), and visitors could mingle and get acquainted. On his way north in the book *Going to Extremes,* Joe McGinniss tosses back cocktails with a high-ranking state official and an ex-hippie coke addict. Unfortunately, a steep decline in the price of oil had left Alaska with an enormous budget deficit, and the money-losing ferry bars were an early victim of the state's newfound austerity. From what I'd read, much deeper cuts were still to come.

Passengers could still purchase wine and beer in the cafeteria, which was open until midnight. I assume this was my neighbor's course of action, because when I got up early the next morning and stepped into the hall, his keys were dangling from his doorknob. For a moment I considered tossing them into the sea as a thank-you gift for waking me the night before, but this seemed contrary to the open-minded spirit of an expedition. Instead I walked down to the showers and had a pleasant conversation with a nude halibut fisherman. He happily accepted one of the halves of my cracked soap.

The air outside on the deck was cold. I took the stairs down to the cafeteria, which opened at 4:00 A.M. (staffed by the same guy who'd served beer until midnight, who was now chopping iceberg lettuce for the salad bar), and bought a cup of coffee. Between the retro decor and the lack of cell service, which led most people to stare out the window, read a book, or do crossword puzzles, it could've been 1998. Mostly, people passed the time by talking to strangers.

When I arrived in the cafeteria, at around four thirty, two men were standing apart, staring out the large windows into the day's first light, which revealed what most views along this stretch of the British Columbia coast do: a thickly forested shoreline obscured by a gauzy drizzle, dotted with occasional homes and lighthouses. Soon enough, the three of us were drawn together by whatever invisible force compels men to talk about directions.

"I think those lights might be Powell River," said one. "I used to fish up here some."

"Could be," said the other. "Sure would be nice to know where we were." He turned and asked if I had any ideas.

"I'm sort of enjoying not knowing where I am for once," I said, and meant it. I couldn't have pegged our location within a hundred miles if I'd wanted to.

We sat down at a round table and sipped our coffees. Doug was a retired fishing guide who was moving to the Alaska town of Homer with his wife; they had a good portion of their worldly possessions, including their dog, stashed in a truck on the car deck below us. The other fellow, Beau, was a retired California state hydrologist who'd shaped much of his life around traveling. When his kids were younger, he'd planned a special trip for each, purchasing a box of books about the upcoming destination for father and child to read and then discuss as they spent months together in a camper van. I assumed Beau's children didn't forget to call on Father's Day.

"This journey on the ferry up the Inside Passage is probably my favorite in the world," he said. He'd made it several times already.

It takes thirty-eight hours to sail from Bellingham to Ketchikan, the first stop in Alaska. Thirty-hours is an ideal amount of time for ferry travel, roughly akin to the rhythms of attending an out-of-town wedding minus the ceremony. You get an optional night of fun (if so inclined), a full day of socializing, and a final morning to revisit with anyone you especially like, or to hide out if you've embarrassed yourself. The cafeteria served three mediocre hot meals a day, none of which would cause a stir in a high school lunchroom, which, if you squinted, we could have been sitting in. People cruised the room holding orange plastic trays, looking for a welcoming smile as an invitation to join someone's table.

Because the mood was generally festive and entertainment options were limited, the usual social taboos were suspended. Anyone could, and did, walk up and talk to anyone else. It probably didn't hurt that customers were allowed one free refill of coffee, and consumption wasn't policed unless someone abused the privilege. An air force pilot in her mid-twenties sat down at our table and explained what it was like to handle a C-130. ("You could land one in a parking lot if you had to — that's what it's designed for.") A guy from Northern California who'd just sold his winery explained why life as a vintner was less glamorous than it seemed. ("You're still a farmer, you're just a farmer who grows grapes.") Doug's wife arrived and gave a brief sample of her singing voice, and she and Doug asked Beau — who now consulted in organic farming — about the best gardening strategy in Alaska's brief growing season. (Answer: a greenhouse, sunk a few feet into the ground to access warmer soil.) Beau's college roommate Paul, temporarily his bunkmate again in a roomette, arrived shortly before lunch and recounted the effect his sister posing as a *Playboy* centerfold had on his college years, in the early 1970s. "As you'd imagine, the subject did come up occasionally," he said.

Some people, like me, were eager to have their first look at Alaska, but many more were excited to be returning. One navy veteran, in a Jimi Hendrix T-shirt and a baseball cap bearing the name of a ship he'd served on long ago, said, "I've been Outside for five years," using the Alaskan term (usually capitalized in print) signifying the other forty-nine states. "It feels good to be almost home."

Mile after mile of hilly green shoreline unspooled through the windows. Every few hours, an announcement came over the public address system saying that passengers were allowed down to the car deck, to let their dogs out for a bathroom break or to grab something from their vehicles. The contents of the car deck underscored the utilitarian mission of the ferries: to get stuff to places in Alaska that had no road access — a front-end loader on a flatbed, a couple of boats, small commercial trucks. (It is possible to get from Seattle to Anchorage via the Alcan Highway, but the estimated drive time is forty-two hours. Seattle to New York, twice the distance as the crow flies, is forty-one hours.) Some vehicles were headed for those towns — Haines, Skagway — where the Alaska road system begins. Most of them were modern covered wagons: cars and pickups and a couple of U-Hauls loaded down with all of someone's personal property, belonging to people like Doug, headed to new territory.

One such pioneer was Stan, a chubby guy from Ohio who wore the jersey of his favorite NFL quarterback all three days I saw him.

Stan borrowed Beau's atlas and pointed out the spot where he'd purchased an old gold mine. His plan was to use a backhoe to dig up bucketfuls of earth that he could then sluice for precious metals. His finger indicated a spot just south of Denali National Park, which seemed a bit isolated. For Stan, this was a major selling point.

"I hate the Lower 48," he said. "I'm tired of paying taxes, tired of paying to raise other people's kids." (Alaska, thanks to oil revenues, has no income tax and no statewide sales tax.) He had little patience for anyone who believed in climate change or the "amateur experts" who worried about it. "What really happens is the glaciers melt into the ocean, which starts the ice age process all over again," he said, citing as his source a PowerPoint presentation he'd seen at a convention for people in the power plant business, from which he had recently taken early retirement. Not that he was very hopeful about the future anyway, since he was fairly certain that Armageddon was coming and had stockpiled plenty of guns and freeze-dried food at his new homestead. Stan was the only person on the *Kennicott* whom I saw reprimanded for taking more than one free coffee refill.

"Man, I can't wait to get to Alaska," he said finally.

That feeling, anyway, was universally shared.

CHAPTER SIX:
THE GREAT LAND

In the Northern Pacific

Climate change may be a touchy subject in Alaska, but anthropologists generally agree that a drastic shift in temperatures facilitated the populating of North America. During the Late Wisconsin glacial period, beginning roughly twenty-five thousand years ago, so much water was captured in ice sheets that sea levels fell to more than three hundred feet lower than they are today. (Florida was twice its current width; the Aleutian Islands were a scimitar-shaped peninsula.) What is now the seafloor between Siberia and Alaska was exposed as a thousand-mile-wide strip of land known as the Bering Land Bridge. There is much debate over exactly how the first immigrants arrived in the Americas — it's possible that they crossed from Siberia on foot or hugged the coast in boats — but Alaska was likely humanity's primary point of entry to the

Americas.

The first place in the New World to be settled was the last to be located by Europeans during the Age of Exploration. Following Columbus's first transatlantic crossing, in 1492, the Spanish had claimed much of the Americas within thirty years. The Portuguese completed the first circumnavigation of the globe in 1522. Yet more than two hundred years would pass before the first known white men landed in Alaska.

Shortly before his death in 1725, Russian emperor Peter the Great sponsored an expedition that he hoped might answer one of the great remaining questions of world geography: Was Asia connected to North America? Siberian natives had shared stories of a "great land" to the east. Peter selected Vitus Bering, a Dane serving as an officer in the Russian navy, to lead an expedition to find out whether these tales were true, and if so to search for any evidence of European settlements that would preclude a Russian land claim. Bering's first major excursion, in 1728, demonstrated that Asia was separated from other landmasses by the strait that now bears his name, but failed to find any significant new territory. It was 1741 before his second expedition departed from Siberia. Bering helmed one of two ships, and the other sailed under the command of Aleksei Chirikov, an officer from the 1728 voyage. After much fruitless nautical meandering, the ships became separated in a storm on June 20. Bering sailed into the Gulf of Alaska, and on July 16 one of his crew spotted the snowy eighteen-thousand-foot peak of Mount St. Elias. Around the same time, Chirikov sent eleven sailors ashore south of Glacier Bay in a longboat. His men were never seen again. A second party of four was dispatched and also vanished. Chirikov, having lost a sizable portion of his crew, sailed toward home.

Bering, meanwhile, landed briefly on Kayak Island, where the expedition's naturalist, Georg Wilhelm Steller, recorded a single jay that resembled one he had seen in a book about the Carolinas — evidence that they had indeed found the Americas. On the attempted return home, with winter coming on, Bering's ship ran aground. The captain was one of nineteen who died before the spring thaw, of scurvy. Forty-six survivors sailed back to Kamchatka the following summer in a boat built from the wreckage of their ship. With them they carried a cargo of exquisite furs. "The immediate result," wrote William Dall in an essay adapted from a history lecture he'd delivered to his *Elder* shipmates, was "to stimulate every inhabitant of the region who could leave Kamchatka to push out and secure riches."

Among the skins with which the crew of the second expedition returned were sea otters, whose luxurious warmth made them extremely valuable. Russian trappers quickly began to make their way east along the Aleutian Islands, exhausting the population of sea mammals at each stop. Their treatment of the native population, the Aleuts, was savage. Men were enslaved as hunters. Women were raped. Children were taken hostage, their ransoms often paid in furs. Diseases against which the Alaskans had no immunity were introduced, with devastating results. The Aleut population fell by more than 80 percent in three decades.

Whispers of Russian discoveries in Alaska filtered back to Western Europe through the court at St. Petersburg. The Spanish, who rather ambitiously had claimed all lands touching the Pacific Ocean, had concentrated their colonial activities in South and Central America. Sensing a new threat, they founded missions at sites further up the coast, including San Diego and San Francisco.

Great Britain was the other major European power on the North American continent, and it had staked a competing claim to most of the Pacific coast from Mexico to Alaska. Spain had the advantage of settlements. Britain possessed the world's finest navy and one of history's greatest sea captains, James Cook. During two round-the-world voyages, Cook had mapped the South Seas, including the previously unknown lands of Australia and New Zealand. On July 2, 1776, the same day delegates to the Second Continental Congress voted in Philadelphia to declare independence from Great Britain, Cook set sail from Plymouth, England, on his third great voyage.

Cook's primary mission was to find the Northwest Passage, a hypothetical water route around the North American landmass that would vastly shorten sea voyages from Europe to the Orient. (Prior to the opening of the Panama Canal, Asia-bound ships could sail only via Cape Horn, or eastward around the Cape of Good Hope.) With two vessels, the *Discovery* and the *Resolution,* Cook sailed east via Tahiti, encountering in his path the previously unknown Hawaiian Islands. He and his crew mapped the Pacific Northwest Coast from just north of Washington State to the Bering Sea, bringing into focus for the first time the actual geographic outline of Alaska. Cook would never hear the acclaim for his discoveries, however — he was killed in a skirmish with Native Hawaiians in 1779.

An officer on Cook's voyages, George Vancouver, expanded on his mentor's cartography with a series of journeys along the Alaskan coast from 1792 to 1794. Vancouver had been instructed to determine once and for all whether a Northwest Passage led from the far North Pacific to Hudson Bay. On July 12, 1794, while probing the inlets of the Alexander Archipelago, a group of Vancouver's men in longboats, led by Lieutenant Joseph Whidbey, encountered the mouth of Glacier Bay. They were unable to enter, however, because their path was blocked by what Vancouver later described as "compact and solid mountains of ice, rising perpendicularly from the water's edge."

Vancouver was a fussy, unpleasant man in a silly wig but also an extraordinarily precise mapmaker. The charts assembled by his crew are works of art, and more resemble Albrecht Dürer's woodcuts than the rudimentary atlases of Russian America that came before. So fine was their work that, eighty-five years later, when John Muir began his explorations in Alaska, it had not been improved upon. Vancouver's surveys were no longer entirely accurate, however. For by the time Muir arrived, the mountains of ice seemed to have vanished.

Chapter Seven: "Civilizing the Savages"

Annette Island

The *Elder* continued up the hazy coast of British Columbia, working its way slowly north as it squeezed between Vancouver Island and the mainland. John Burroughs, famous for his gentle descriptions of the bucolic Catskills, was overwhelmed by his first attempts to capture the jagged Pacific coast in prose. "The edge of this part of the continent for a thousand miles has been broken into fragments, small and great, as by the stroke of some earth-cracking hammer," he wrote. "Silver threads" of meltwater poured forth from the thick spruce and hemlock. The *Elder* made frequent stops for scientific sorties. An attempted hike to one waterfall proved that the rainforest, which rolled by with such lovely monotony from the comfort of a steamship, was, on foot, as impassable as anything explorers encountered in the Amazon jungle. The soggy climate prevented the kinds of wildfires that would clear undergrowth elsewhere. Giant thorned plants impaled the hands of hikers, who slipped on mosses as thick as fallen snow. "Traversing Alaska forests must be a trying task even to deer and bears," Burroughs wrote.

William Dall, who had made the same sea journey fourteen times in his thirty years of exploring Alaska, cautioned his fellow passengers that the lush scenery they were passing paled in comparison with what lay ahead. If anyone knew what to expect, it was Dall. Shortly before the *Elder* crossed from Canada into Alaskan territory, he gave a lecture relating some of his adventures. At twenty-one, he had been a member of a scientific party that researched the possibility of stringing a telegraph line across Alaska by way of the Yukon. The group leader's sudden death left Dall in charge, a role that required him to endure two winters in conditions that dropped below minus sixty degrees Fahrenheit. Dall spent the 1870s leading geographic surveys along the Alaskan shoreline that took him to the end of the Aleutians. By the time the *Elder* arrived in Alaskan waters, the territory contained a Dall Island, a Dall Ridge, and a Dall River, all named in the explorer's honor, and was populated with Dall sheep. Twenty years earlier, Dall had even named the *Elder*'s first stop in Alaska, Annette Island, after his new bride.

By 1899, Annette Island was better known throughout the United States than almost any other place in the District of Alaska. It was the site of a well-publicized experiment in assimilating Alaska's natives into American society. The *Elder*'s chaplain, Dr. George F. Nelson, described the process as "civilizing the savages." When the *Elder* docked on the morning of Sunday, June 4, a party of Natives greeted the group and escorted them to the home of the minister behind this experiment, William Duncan.

Duncan was an Episcopalian missionary known for his work among the Tsimshian Indians of British Columbia. In 1862, he had founded a community called Metlakatla with a small nucleus of his new converts. "Duncan's intent behind this move was to isolate them from the influences of their unconverted relatives and the vices introduced by the traders, such as alcohol and prostitution," writes the Tsimshian historian Mique'l Dangeli. Metlakatla's population grew quickly as other Tsimshian sought to escape a smallpox epidemic.

Duncan drew up a list of rules to help the

Tsimshian adapt to the unstoppable incursion of Western society. Children were required to attend school and receive religious instruction. Ancient traditions were banned, including face painting, non-Christian supernatural beliefs, and the use of shamans and medicine men. He was especially firm about outlawing alcohol. The Anglican Church's insistence that Duncan use wine as a sacrament in religious rituals initiated the final schism that sent Duncan to Alaska. When Duncan founded New Metlakatla (the "New" was soon dropped, to some confusion) on Annette Island in 1887, the reverend orchestrated a publicity blitz in the Lower 48 that celebrated his successes in transforming what he considered the tribe's primitive behavior.

The Harriman team was given a tour of the town, which George Bird Grinnell compared to "an old-fashioned New England hamlet in its peaceful quiet." The streets, he noted, were broad and straight. The houses had neat gardens and fences. Most of the team members were escorted to the town's large church, where the entire village of nearly one thousand Tsimshian seemed to have turned out for worship. Duncan gave a sermon in the native language, which the local residents apparently listened to rapturously. Burroughs's impression of the local tongue was one of "a vague, guttural, featureless sort of language."

The expeditioners were terribly impressed with Duncan's accomplishment. "It took many years for Mr. Duncan to change these Indians from the wild men that they were to the respectable and civilized people that they now are," Grinnell wrote in an account of the visit. "Whatever they are today Mr. Duncan has made them."

Grinnell was among the most sympathetic whites when it came to the plight of America's persecuted natives; he had written deep anthropological studies of the Indians of the Great Plains and had been adopted by the Pawnee. And yet when the *Elder* arrived in Alaska, neither he nor anyone else seems to have bothered to ask the Tsimshian their side of the story. Perhaps they were in too great a hurry, because the expeditioners obviously missed something. The stated vision of the Metlakatla museum dedicated to Duncan's legacy is to "nurture a constructive dialogue" on the founder's work and to "actively promote our community's healing from this history."

One person aboard the *Elder* who had spent a lot of time among Southeast Alaska's natives was John Muir. Without their guidance, he never would have seen the territory's most spectacular glaciers, let alone popularized them. The *Elder* likely wouldn't have been in Alaska at all.

CHAPTER EIGHT:
THE SECRET HISTORY

Anchorage

The Tsimshian were relatively late arrivals
to Southeast Alaska. For thousands of years,
the islands of the Alexander Archipelago
had been primarily the territory of the Tlingit. (A third group, the Haida, arrived from
the south in the eighteenth century.) The
Annette Island end of the Alaska panhandle
is at roughly the same latitude as Edinburgh.
The warm Kuroshio Current flows north
from Japan and west across the Pacific
Ocean, bringing moderate temperatures and
biblical amounts of precipitation. Most of
the Inside Passage is temperate rainforest.
Tlingit culture developed in concert with
such a rich environment. Sturdy spruce,
hemlock, and cedar were used to build long-
houses, carve totem poles, and craft dugout
canoes. The sea provided an inexhaustible
source of protein, especially salmon. Fishing rights to specific areas were carefully

managed by individual families.

Tlingit society at the start of the nineteenth century was made up of approximately sixteen tribes, called *kwaan*. The clan system within each tribe was matrilineal — inheritance and clan identity were passed down through mothers. Europeans who traded with the Tlingit, whose networks extended deep into the Alaskan interior, noted that women were the primary negotiators and drove harder bargains than men. War was common among tribes, and holding slaves was a major sign of status. The Tlingit were famous for their potlatches, multi-day feasts held to display wealth, honor the dead, or settle debts.

Once the Russians arrived in the Alexander Archipelago, change came quickly. According to Robert Fortuine's *Chills and Fever,* a smallpox epidemic in the 1830s wiped out at least one-quarter and perhaps more than half of the panhandle's native population in a few years. Russia's minimal administrative efforts were dedicated primarily to deterring the entrance of fur-trading rivals, especially the British. When the United States purchased Alaska, in 1867, the Natives were confused. The Tlingit insisted that the Russians had been their guests and thus owned no land to sell.

Under the Treaty of Cession, ratified by Congress prior to the handover, white residents of the territory were made naturalized citizens if they remained at the end of three years. "Uncivilized native tribes" would be subject to all laws and regulations but were denied "all the rights, advantages, and immunities of citizens of the United States." They were barely tolerated guests in the home they'd occupied for thousands of years.

"A history of conditions in Alaska from 1867 to 1897 is yet to be written, and when written few Americans will be able to read it without indignation," William Dall wrote shortly after returning from the Harriman Expedition. In the absence of territorial government, the U.S. Army, exhausted from the recently concluded Civil War, was given the duty of maintaining order. In 1869, three Tlingit villages at Kake were shelled with artillery, in retribution for the killings of two trappers. After a brief period during which the Treasury Department's customs collectors were the only government authority in Alaska, the U.S. Navy was placed in charge, with similar bad results. In 1882, the Tlingit residents of Angoon demanded compensation for the accidental killing of their shaman. The navy sent a warship to bombard their village. Salmon canneries set up operations wherever they pleased and robbed clans of their traditional food source. The discovery of gold pushed Natives from their ancestral lands. "They take our property, take away ground, and when we complain to them about it, they employ a lawyer and go to court and win the case," one Tlingit leader testified before the district governor in 1884. "We are very poor now. The time will come when we will not have anything left." Children were orphaned by disease, and alcoholism ran rampant. Tlingit society fell into chaos.

Into this vacuum of authority stepped the Christian missionaries. When the Presbyterian cleric Dr. Sheldon Jackson arrived at the rough-and-tumble settlement of Fort Wrangell in 1877, he found a seedy boomtown, filled with gold miners, gamblers, drinkers, and prostitutes. (The "Fort" was later dropped from the town's name by the U.S. Post Office.) But he also found in Wrangell a group of Tsimshian woodcutters who had been evangelized by William Duncan at the original Metlakatla, in British Columbia. They, in turn, had begun to spread the Word to the Tlingit. Using Wrangell as their base of operations, Jackson and his missionaries launched an ambitious campaign to save the Native peoples of Alaska through temperance and education. If they destroyed what the Christians considered a pagan culture in the process, that was not just the price of survival, but an added benefit.

There were a number of Alaska-related subjects I wanted to get up to speed on quickly, so a couple of months before I left on the *Kennicott,* I made a reconnaissance trip to Anchorage and Fairbanks to pick the brains of several experts. My first stop was a visit with Diane Benson, a Tlingit assistant professor of Alaska Native studies and rural development at the University of Alaska at Fairbanks (UAF). Her Tlingit name is L'xeis'. I'd asked her to help me fill in the black hole of history from the Native perspective at the time the *Elder* arrived.

"I've always been fascinated by this period, because there's so much transition, so much devastation," Benson told me during a long lunch. We were seated in a booth at a Mexican restaurant near the university's Anchorage campus. Benson recommended I clean my palate of guacamole before attempting the correct pronunciation of Tlingit, which requires placing the tongue behind the front teeth.

Many Alaskans have multiple jobs; it's not uncommon to learn that the person foaming milk for your cappuccino is also a carver-fisherman-bookkeeper. Benson's résumé was eclectic even by local standards: She had hauled nets on a commercial salmon boat, driven tractor trailers on the Alaska Pipeline, worked as a newspaper reporter, run an all-Alaska talent agency, written and starred in a popular one-woman show about an Alaskan civil rights pioneer, and, prior to her academic career, run unsuccessfully for both U.S. Congress and lieutenant governor as the Democratic candidate.

"My grandparents and great-grandparents were alive when the Harriman Expedition arrived in 1899," she told me. "People were just trying to find a way to survive this onslaught. There was a whole push to acculturate and assimilate." Sheldon Jackson was a tireless advocate for providing education for Native children when few people were looking out for their interests. He just thought their languages were "too heathen and sin-ridden to express civilized Christian thought," according to historians Nora Marks Dauenhauer and Richard Dauenhauer. In what now looks like a pretty flagrant violation of the separation of church and state, Jackson was named superintendent for education in Alaska. His personal distaste for Native languages was codified into law under the Organic Act of 1884. Even people's names were changed. "My grandfather had a perfectly good Tlingit name that they couldn't pronounce, so he became George Dick," Benson said.

Life under military control had been anarchy for Alaska's Natives, but under the Organic Act things didn't improve much. As noncitizens, Natives had almost no legal rights. Their property could be seized, and they could be jailed without trial. "I worked on the pipeline the first three years, so I have a pretty good idea what lawless looks like," Benson said. "Who's going to ensure justice in the event of a crime? Who's going to step in if somebody comes and takes away your child or your land? Nobody. One of my grandfather's sisters was taken away and probably sold into slavery." Under Jackson's system, children were also sent away to boarding school, where speaking a Native language elicited swift punishment. Deadly waves of smallpox and other diseases swept through Native communities well into the twentieth century. Faced with extermination or assimilation, most Natives chose the latter. Entire generations grew up not learning their traditional language or culture. "My great-grandmother refused to learn English," Benson said. Today the situation is commonly reversed — a Native community will have a few octogenarian members who speak their language fluently and are trying to pass it along to their great-grandchildren before it vanishes.

"So Alaska in 1899 is a disrupted place, made all the more disrupted by the Great Death, that final sweep of epidemic," Benson said. "It impacted the choices my family made. I can hardly speak about it without weeping." The period of death and destruction "was kind of the final blow for our reliance on our shamans. And that created a huge depression, in a sense, an emotional depression."

Jackson's direct influence on Alaskan culture is still being debated, just like that of William Duncan at Metlakatla. I met one ninety-five-year-old Tlingit elder who said that being sent off as a boy to the Sheldon Jackson School in the late 1920s was the greatest thing that ever happened to him. Jackson's indirect role in preserving the state's wilderness is less well known. While making one of his frequent stops on the lecture circuit at a national convention of Sunday school teachers held at Yosemite Valley on June 7, 1879, Jackson found himself paired with a disheveled amateur who spoke on the topic of California's glaciers. Whatever vague plans John Muir had to explore the north evidently were accelerated by Jackson's descriptions of Alaska's natural wonders. A few weeks later, both men were aboard a steamship ultimately bound for Wrangell. Jackson would be saving souls. Muir had no set plans other than to see some glaciers and perhaps find something worth writing about.

CHAPTER NINE:
SURVIVAL OF THE WETTEST

Ketchikan

About thirty minutes from Ketchikan, houses started to appear on the shore, sporadically at first and then close enough together that one neighbor could spy on the next one's barbecue. Probably half of the *Kennicott*'s passengers went out on the front deck to snap photos of our arrival. From a mile or so out, most of what we could see was three enormous cruise ships, each several times the size of the *Elder.* Their white masses walled off Ketchikan's downtown and contrasted with the deep green mountains that stood behind, their summits obscured in mist. Seaplanes buzzed in and out like dragonflies.

I was particularly fascinated by the bow activity of the *Kennicott* deckhands, who were arranging thick ropes with the care of python wranglers. Mine was the interest of a long-retired professional, since I had some experience in that line of work. For several summers during college and graduate school, I'd worked on tour boats that cruised up and down the Chicago River and onto Lake Michigan. Whenever I worked an especially long day on the water — we sometimes ran trips from 7:00 A.M. until 2:00 A.M. the next morning — I'd get home and fall into bed, only to feel the mattress rocking from side to side.

Had there been a deckhand emergency in which the lives of everyone on the *Kennicott* depended on finding someone who could tie knots such as a monkey's fist or a cleft hitch, I probably could've stepped in. The only other lesson about working on a boat that had stuck with me was that the waterfront tends to have the same moths-to-the-flame effect on weirdos that Alaska does. One of my fellow deckhands was a World War II veteran who couldn't read or write and frequently handed me slips of paper with five- or six-digit numbers scrawled on them, insisting that this was the phone number of his doctor and getting indignant when I asked if perhaps he'd copied it down wrong. Another, who went by the name Slim, was an ex-convict who'd killed two brothers in the early sixties. Twenty years later, he'd been paroled for participating in a government malaria-vaccine-testing program. We knew this because Slim carried his prison release papers with him everywhere in a gym bag, along with a very large knife that he called his "shiv." He once pulled it on my sister, who also worked there, when he thought she'd messed up his pizza order.

The novice seaman E. B. White met a lot of guys like Slim belowdecks on a steamship cruise that brought him to Ketchikan in 1923. He'd departed Seattle expecting to find "a land of deep snow, igloos, Eskimos, polar bears, rough men, fancy women, saloons, fighting sled dogs, intense cold, and gold everywhere." To his unpleasant surprise, he found in Ketchikan not the Alaskan winter wonderland of his dreams but "a warm, mosquitoey place smelling of fish." For decades, salmon canning was the primary business in town, and when the *Elder* steamed through in 1899, tiny Ketchikan consisted of a salmon cannery and a few buildings, not worthy of a stop when world-famous Metlakatla was just twenty miles to the south. Before long, Ketchikan had established itself as Alaska's "First City," not because it had the territory's largest population (which it did by the 1920s) but because it was the first port of call for cruise ships coming up the Inside Passage. More recently, it was the almost home of the infamous Bridge to Nowhere, a four-hundred-million-dollar project to replace the ferry that runs from the airport (which, because level ground is hard to come by near Ketchikan, is located on a nearby island), most of it to be paid for with federal earmarks.

Ketchikan is now the sixth-largest city in Alaska, about eight thousand people crowded into a fairly tight space along the coast. Houses clung to the slope above like ivy. When the *Kennicott* pulled up to the dock, I walked the mile or so along the waterfront toward the center of town.

There was a time when Ketchikan was the wettest city in America, in the alcoholic sense. "In the eighties, we had the highest percentage of liquor licenses per capita in the country," Dave Kiffer, a local historian and city council member, told me. Nowadays most of the drinkers were day visitors from the cruise ships, who thronged the Front Street shops selling jewelry, sweatshirts, and other mementos. From what I could tell from looking through the windows of congested stores, the sale of useless junk to transients was the biggest driver of Ketchikan's economy. I asked Kiffer about a rumor that all the waterfront shops were secretly owned by the cruise companies. "I've been trying to answer that same question for ten years," he said.

Among other things, Ketchikan is home to the southernmost district headquarters of the Tongass National Forest. The Tongass is one of those things — like the book and movie *Into the Wild* — that seems unquestionably wonderful to many of us who live Outside but is viewed more skeptically by Alaskans. The Tongass was the creation of Theodore Roosevelt, who never set foot in Alaska but was good friends with Merriam, Grinnell, and Burroughs and devoured the volumes of Harriman Expedition reports as soon as they appeared in print. Less than a year into his presidency, following the assassination of William McKinley, Roosevelt set aside the Alexander Archipelago Forest Reserve in 1902. A few years later, he expanded the area to include most of the Alaska panhandle, today's seventeen-million-acre Tongass National Forest.

A national forest is not a national park. It is public land overseen by the U.S. Department of Agriculture, set aside to be managed. Conservation is only one purpose. In the Tongass, old-growth forests were one of the resources to be administered. Bernhard

Fernow, the Cornell University forestry expert aboard the *Elder,* was doubtful that logging the trees of Southeast Alaska would ever be financially viable. "The conditions under which lumbering on the rugged slopes would have to be carried on are extremely difficult," he explained in an essay from the second *Harriman* volume. What neither Fernow nor Roosevelt foresaw was the arrival of technology, such as the chain saw, that would make clear-cutting possible. From the 1950s until the 1990s, large pulp mills operated throughout Southeast Alaska. The closing of Ketchikan's mill in 1997, the result of declining prices and environmental lawsuits, took five hundred of the town's jobs. It did not, however, completely end the practice of clear-cutting, whose ugly evidence is visible on mountainsides throughout the Inside Passage, scaly patches of eczema amid the lush greenery.

Singling out one enemy for environmentalists to protest against is harder than figuring out who owns all the souvenir shops. Often, the villain wears a white hat. When I arrived in Ketchikan, the Alaska Mental Health Trust, which provides services to those in need, was hoping to sell its logging rights to Deer Mountain, the scenic green backdrop to every wide-angle tourist photo of Ketchikan. Other timber rights were held by Vietnam veterans' groups, native tribes, and the University of Alaska.

After the timber business dwindled in the nineties, Ketchikan went all in on tourism. Brochures now touted visits to totem carvers and flightseeing trips and the Great Alaskan Lumberjack Show. On Creek Street, there is an old-timey museum in a former house of prostitution. The sign outside billed it as the place WHERE MEN AND SALMON BOTH CAME TO SPAWN, which I hope is the last tourist slogan I ever see related to ejaculation.

Ketchikan is still extremely wet by precipitation standards, receiving an average of 141 inches per year, some of which fell on my head as I searched for a place to eat that wasn't thronged with cruise ship guests. Rain is such a constant in Southeast Alaska that everyone I met seemed to own a pair of knee-high brown XtraTufs, whose ubiquity and versatility make them roughly analogous to cowboy boots in Texas. (Should you find yourself stumped for conversational topics while in the company of Alaskans, ask for their opinion about whether XtraTuf quality declined when the company outsourced manufacturing to China.) A good pair of rubber boots is a wise long-term investment. Unlike much of the world, which will be facing drought and famine in the not too distant future according to current climate change models, the Inside Passage is actually expecting an increase in precipitation by the year 2100.

CHAPTER TEN:
SECOND THOUGHTS

Metlakatla

In a lot of ways, Metlakatla is the opposite of Ketchikan. While Ketchikan has mushroomed since 1899, Metlakatla's population has grown only slightly since the original 826 settlers arrived in canoes. There are no restaurants or knickknack shops, alcohol is prohibited, and the closest thing to a tourist attraction is the Duncan Cottage Museum, which is the founder's preserved home. Museum director Naomi Leask had offered to show me around and talk about Duncan ("controversial to say the least"), but as I boarded the MV *Lituya* for the forty-five-minute ride south from Ketchikan, she texted that she had some last-family business, leaving me with the afternoon in Metlakatla to spend alone. It was Memorial Day, and the only riders aboard the *Lituya* were me, two other walk-on passengers, and two drivers who sat behind the steering wheels of battered vans parked on the outdoor car deck. We arrived at the Metlakatla terminal, everyone disembarked, and I stood in the parking lot trying to find a cell signal. In my haste to make the ferry, I'd neglected Naomi's advice to call a taxi beforehand. I was fourteen miles from the island's only town, on a road that, as far as I could tell, was utilized solely to drop off and collect people at the ferry, which would not be operating for another two days. As it would frequently in Alaska, my phone informed me decisively that I had NO SERVICE. On the map pinned above my desk at home, the distance I'd be traveling from the southeastern boundary of Alaska to the Aleutians was twice as long as my forearm. I'd made it less than the length of my thumbnail and I was already stuck.

Just as I hoisted my pack and was preparing to start walking to town, an SUV pulled into the lot. The driver opened the door, and I saw immediately that she was the sort of dedicated smoker I hadn't seen since childhood — not only turning sidesaddle, lighting up, and taking a deep drag on a long, skinny cigarette before her feet hit the ground but wearing a white sweatshirt with ash burns down the front. "You need a ride to town?" she asked. She'd come to collect her son, who at that moment emerged from the restroom. Her name was Kristin. I told her I'd come to see Naomi, and she nodded her head and stubbed out her smoke. She guessed Naomi might've been busy with her new baby; she'd just given birth a few days earlier. "This is a small town — everybody's more or less related somehow and everybody knows everybody's business," she said as we pulled away.

Kristin and her son gave me a quick tour of Metlakatla: the "cannery," which I eventually figured out means any sort of fish-processing plant in Alaska; the marina, filled with commercial fishing vessels; the credit union; and a surprising number of churches for an island with a population of fourteen hundred. One of the largest buildings was the William Duncan Memorial Church, a replica of the original, which I'd seen in Harriman photos. The street grid was the same as Duncan had laid out. Cheery cottages of the sort you might see in a New England seaside town stood next to abandoned houses, some filled with junk to a degree that would've impressed the Collyer brothers. My hotel, the only one on the island, was actually half of someone's house. I walked in the front door and was greeted by a very old man sitting in a recliner and watching *Tora! Tora! Tora!* In his hand he held a new-looking iPhone, which he was scrolling through searching for something; the fonts had been enlarged to the size of the letter *E* atop an eye chart. I asked if he knew where the manager was.

"WHAT?" he shouted, cupping his hand to his ear.

"IS THERE ANYONE HERE I CAN TALK TO?"

"You need to call Shirley," he said, handing me the phone.

"Is Shirley the manager?"

"Shirley is my friend. I want her to come visit."

I tried to call Shirley, who didn't answer. I apologized loudly and left my bag in the hall to get something to eat.

Naomi had told me that the Mini Mart would be the only place in Metlakatla to buy food on a national holiday, so I walked down Milton Street, past the school and the community center, where a small crowd had gathered for a Memorial Day observance. The girl working the counter at the Mini Mart greeted me as "Mr. Mark the writer from New York" when I ordered my halibut and chips. She was Naomi's sister-in-law. Naomi had phoned ahead to make sure I found the place.

After lunch, I started to walk back to the hotel and paused at a traditional dance celebration outside the community center. Maybe seventy-five people had gathered to watch a trio of drummers and a group of Tsimshian dancers dressed in traditional red-and-black robes. Metlakatla is the only one of Alaska's 229 Native communities that is also an Indian reservation, and while everyone was perfectly friendly, I couldn't escape the feeling, as I watched the performance, that I'd invaded a private gathering. I scanned the audience for any other out-of-place faces until I found one, belonging to U.S. Senator Lisa Murkowski. No one seemed to find this at all unusual; indeed, several people told me later that in Alaska, even people in remote villages expect their national elected officials to come through town regularly. As I watched Murkowski politely clap along to the beat, a fellow came up alongside and asked if my name was Mark.

"Naomi just texted me — she wanted to know if you'd found the Mini Mart," he said. "She should be back around five."

In Duncan's careful cultivation of Metlakatla's image in the press, the phrase "model Christian community" appears again and again. Duncan maintained in photographs what was essentially a nineteenth-century Instagram feed documenting every step of the community's growth, from the arrival of the first canoes to the cutting of trees to build his cathedral.

I met Naomi outside Duncan's house. She arrived pushing a stroller with her preschool-age daughter in it. Her husband, John, held the new baby, who was very cute. "Good sleeper, too," John said. "Unlike her sister." Naomi unlocked the front door and we walked through the small rooms, some neatly stacked with Duncan's old furniture. Glass-front cases held relics with hand-printed signs taped to them that said things like OLD MEDICINES — PLEASE DO NOT HANDLE ANYTHING. "This was built in 1891, modeled on a traditional longhouse," the multifamily dwelling common among the indigenous peoples of the Pacific Northwest, Naomi said.

In some ways, Duncan was more flexible than Sheldon Jackson about incorporating native customs and culture. Perhaps most significant was his willingness to give religious services in the Tsimshian language, Sm'algyax. Which is not to say that he is fondly remembered by all.

"I'll be out working in the front yard and

people passing by will make nasty comments," Naomi said. "Some people refuse to set foot in here. Others, you can't say a bad word about him." I tried to probe a little to see where Naomi's own feelings lay, but she maintained strict professional impartiality. She did, however, make occasional offhand comments such as "Well, we *have* found papers in which he says he doesn't want anyone to get above a fourth-grade education."

There is a great photo of Duncan in his office, surrounded by neat stacks of ledgers. Not a single religious icon is in sight, and he looks as if there is no place he would rather be. "Everything was super planned out and organized," Naomi told me. "You had to sign a contract saying you left your old culture behind." Duncan supervised the building of the cannery and the sawmill that would help subsidize Metlakatla. But the line between efficiency expert and control freak wasn't always clear. As with the Tlingit, Tsimshian names were honors that indicated things like status in the community and fishing rights. Duncan made them take new ones. Naomi showed me a glass case of old, rusty keys. "He kept the keys to everything," she said. "If we disobeyed him, he'd shut the water off." Whites who attempted to set foot on the island were arrested. Duncan spent much of the final twenty years of his life fighting the construction of a government school, his behavior growing more erratic and authoritarian until his death, in 1918.

Between his religious-utopia tendencies and his dictatorial ones, Duncan was starting to sound less like the savior portrayed by the Harriman team than Jim Jones, of Jonestown infamy. "Naomi, forgive me for saying so, but he sounds a bit like a cult leader," I said.

"Some people have said that," she said evenly.

Naomi and her family gave me a very brief ride back to my hotel. I returned to the Mini Mart and bought a bag of pretzels for dinner. Naomi's sister-in-law waved from behind the takeout counter. The next morning, I walked a couple of minutes to the floatplane dock, bought a ticket back to Ketchikan, and was airborne before my coffee had cooled enough to drink. From the air one could see thousands of ghostly trees, stripped of their bark, bumping up against the shoreline. As we'd gotten into her car at the ferry terminal, Kristin the smoker had told me a Sm'algyax word describing white things that show up on the beach unexpectedly. It can refer to either timber or people, she said, and laughed.

CHAPTER ELEVEN:
DEVIL MAY CARE

Wrangell

The ferry trip from Ketchikan north to Wrangell was only six hours, but those hours transpired roughly between 1:00 and 7:00 A.M. A cabin seemed like an unnecessary indulgence. I decided instead to pursue a low-budget option I'd heard about aboard the *Kennicott,* favored by those travelers for whom saving money trumped comfort: I'd sleep on a chaise lounge in the solarium. The best strategy, I was told, was to line up early at the ferry terminal and run on board to grab a deck chair as if staking a claim in the Oklahoma Land Rush. My taxi arrived at the Ketchikan ferry terminal well before midnight. No throng waited in the rain to board the *Matanuska,* only a few ticket holders. The boat was dark and quiet. I groggily crossed the car deck and climbed the staircase, hoping to find an empty lounger.

The flaw in my frugal sleeping plan was

immediately apparent: The *Matanuska,* smaller than the *Kennicott,* lacked both solarium and deck chairs. Its economy-class voyagers were instead sprawled out on the floor of the public lounge, nestled between rows of seats similar to those in a movie theater. The hard floor was covered with a thin layer of indoor/outdoor carpeting. Wise travelers had brought inflatable pads to cushion against the steel and earplugs to block out the snoring old men and one colicky baby who sounded like she was undergoing a difficult exorcism. I crawled into the thin polyester cocoon of my sleeping bag liner and tossed and turned, occasionally opening my eyes to find a teenage girl, also horizontal, staring at me from under a seat two feet away. At four, I gave up and went down to the cafeteria for a cup of coffee.

I stared out the window at the green clumps of what John Burroughs described as "small spruce-tufted islands" passing by. A few early risers filtered in. One guy, who looked to be in his twenties, sat at the next table examining the contents of the various pockets that covered his clothing from knees to clavicles. He stood up and turned to leave, then turned back again. "Almost forgot my wedding ring," he said, plucking a small silver band off the tabletop. "That would be bad. My *almost* wedding ring, I mean. I'm getting married in April." His name was Kenny, though he said that "down south" — in other words, any latitude lower than Ketchikan — he was sometimes known as "Irish." Something about him signaled Alaska-ness: perhaps the combination of his easy demeanor and XtraTuf boots. It might also have been the large tattoo of the state map inked on the side of his neck, with ALASKA scrawled across it in script. He'd just had the shading touched up at a friend's parlor in San Diego, which gave the state a nice 3-D effect.

I had heard that Wrangell was, to put it bluntly, kind of a dump. "The Wrangell village was a rough place," John Muir once wrote. "No mining hamlet in the placer gulches of California, nor any backwoods village I ever saw, approached it in picturesque, devil may care *abandon.*" (This quote is such a point of perverse civic pride that it is reproduced on the wall of the local history museum.) Wrangell was a gold rush town and attracted the sorts of unsavory characters one would associate with prospecting. Two years before the Harriman Expedition docked there, Wyatt Earp spent about a week as acting marshal before escaping. "Wrangell was another Tombstone," wrote his wife, Josephine, "full of boomers, con men, gamblers, ladies of the night, gunmen, pickpockets, and all sorts of flotsam from every corner of the earth." My *Lonely Planet* guide diplomatically described Wrangell as the "least gentrified" stop on the marine ferry route.

Kenny saw things differently. "Wrangell is a nice little place," he said. He lived in Ketchikan with his fiancée, who made good money in the summer working double shifts as a waitress in restaurants catering to cruise ship passengers. A lot of Alaskans managed their lives like hibernating animals, working insane hours during the months when daylight was plentiful — so plentiful that every hotel room I stayed in had blackout curtains worthy of the London Blitz — and catching up on sleep in the winter. Kenny was going up to Wrangell to work as a deckhand on his buddy's salmon boat, which he'd just inherited from his father. "Just the two of us," he said. "I'm telling you, this boat is like a Cadillac. Some boats, when you need to take a dump, you grab a bucket, fill it with seawater, do your business, and toss it overboard. This one's got a galley *and* a shower." He was a little worried about the upcoming salmon season. Early reports indicated that fish numbers were low, and his earnings were a percentage of the catch. One summer he'd made ten grand in a few busy weeks.

A woman in a jacket festooned with Disney characters approached the table unsteadily, asking for a light. She might've been thirty; she might've been fifty. Her face had the bloated agelessness of the not quite functioning alcoholic just before everything goes to hell. Kenny stood up and gently steered her out onto the deck, saying something about how they could both use a breath of fresh air. A few minutes later, he returned and said, in a low voice, "That's something you need to look out for in these small towns. I'm no stranger to bars, but some of these people, especially the Natives like that lady, they just drink all day and all night. If you start listening to them, they'll never leave you alone."

On a map, Wrangell Island looks like a sparrow taking flight in the direction of Denali. Its namesake town is located on the underside of the beak. From what I could see through the drizzle, as we squeezed between Zarembo Island and Etolin Island (combined size, slightly smaller than Oahu; combined population, fifteen), overdevelopment wasn't a major issue in these parts.

When our impending arrival was announced, Kenny and I walked past the purser's office and down the stairs to the car deck. Kenny stopped at the security locker to reclaim a rifle he'd checked. The gun reminded me to ask about a subject that had begun to worry me: bears. Bears, I was starting to learn, are like the weather in Alaska. Occasionally they're good, usually they're bad, in certain conditions they might kill you. Were bears something I needed to worry about in Wrangell?

"Wrangell is a blue-collar town full of fishermen who love to hunt and don't have a hell of a lot to do half the year," Kenny said, patting his gun case. "I don't think bears are going to be a problem."

My hotel was visible from the ferry's exit ramp, so I hoisted my pack like a merchant marine taking shore leave, declined Kenny's offer to meet in a couple of hours for an eye-opener at the Marine Bar, and strode off to crawl under the covers. The owner's e-mail instructions said she'd leave my reserved room unlocked, so I walked in and was about to heave my pack on the bed when a shirtless man stepped out of the bathroom. I can't say for sure which of us was more surprised, but it suddenly seemed like a good idea to grab a bite to eat before trying to sort things out. I mumbled an apology and walked toward what I guessed was the business district.

I hadn't gone far down Church Street when I found myself standing in front of a pretty white clapboard building, the First Presbyterian Church. This was its second iteration, the original having burned in 1929. That church had been under construction when John Muir cadged a place to sleep on its floor on his first night in Wrangell, back in 1879. (Unlike me, Muir liked sleeping on hard surfaces.) He had not gotten along well with Sheldon Jackson and his party of Presbyterian missionary officials, who called him "that wild Muir" while aboard the steamship *California* as it carried them up the Inside Passage. But by the time Muir arrived, Wrangell was Jackson's town, and it was the minister's name that the visitor dropped like a password to open the church door.

CHAPTER TWELVE:
THE SUMMER OF '79

Fort Wrangell

The *Elder* spent only a few hours in Wrangell after its stop in Metlakatla, but Muir already knew the town intimately. It had been his base of operations for the 1879 excursions as well as subsequent travel stories that would establish the Inside Passage as a destination. When Muir disembarked in Wrangell on July 14, 1879, Sheldon Jackson introduced him to S. Hall Young, one of his missionary associates in Alaska. Young recalled his first glimpse of "a lean, sinewy man of forty, with waving, reddish brown hair and beard, and shoulders slightly stooped." Unlike the missionaries on the *California,* Young fell under Muir's thrall the moment he shook his hand.

"From the first," Young recalled decades after their first meeting on the Wrangell docks, "I began to recognize him as my Master who was to lead me into enchanting regions of beauty and mystery, which without his aid must forever have remained unseen by the eyes of my soul."

That Muir connected so quickly with a missionary ten years his junior isn't entirely surprising. He was, of course, fluent in the language of spirituality, from his father's compulsory Bible studies. But Muir was also someone who, like so many people who've been drawn to Alaska since Wrangell's gold rush heyday, marched to the beat of his own drummer. In the years following the pipeline project of the 1970s, which served as a homing beacon for single men with undefined career goals and questionable social skills, the male-to-female ratio was large enough to inspire a dating platitude still repeated by Alaskan women today: "Alaska, where the odds are good, but the goods are odd." Muir certainly could have been categorized as odd goods when he arrived in Wrangell in 1879. For starters, he did not seem to have what might be considered a real job. S. Hall Young recalled his new friend being introduced as "Professor Muir, the Naturalist," but the Californian had no credentials. When not occupied roaming the mountains of the Sierra, Muir made his living in San Francisco as a freelance writer of adventure and nature tales. (A notoriously unsteady vocation then as now.) Only a month before departing for Alaska, Muir had finally gotten engaged to Louie Strentzel, at the age of forty-one.

Within days of arriving in Wrangell, Muir "inadvertently caused a lot of wondering excitement among the whites as well as the superstitious Indians" when he scaled a hill on the north end of town during a late-night rainstorm and built an enormous bonfire. Its plume, he wrote, shot up "a pillar of flame thirty or forty feet high." His intent was "to see how the Alaskan trees behave in storms and hear the songs they sing." A group of Tlingit converts, perhaps drawing parallels to the pillar of fire that guided the Israelites out of Egypt, knocked on Hall Young's door at 2:00 A.M. seeking spiritual guidance. Young explained that Muir had started the fire simply because that was the sort of thing he enjoyed doing. This seemed only to cause more confusion. The natives "ever afterwards eyed Muir askance, as a mysterious being whose ways and motives were beyond conjecture."

And yet, for all his quirks, Muir was almost universally regarded as brilliant, engaging, magnetic, and charming. His piercing eyes, one of them offset slightly by

111

the carriage-parts accident, conveyed his optimism and boyish enthusiasm. "From cluster to cluster of flowers he ran, falling on his knees, babbling in unknown tongues, prattling a curious mixture of scientific lingo and baby talk" is how Young described Muir encountering a favorite species of blooming flower. He was above all things a great talker. His speech on glaciers at the Yosemite event where he met Sheldon Jackson "fairly electrified his audience," a hundred of whom had followed him afterwards on a hike, according to the *San Francisco Chronicle.*

The bad reviews I'd gotten for Wrangell seemed to have been influenced by Muir's original thumbs-down. The only visible evidence of lawlessness was abandoned lots filled with rusting pickups, boats, and household appliances. One impromptu dump site sat next to the neatly groomed grounds of one of Wrangell's nicest churches. "That's what happens when you've got a car worth two hundred dollars and it'll cost you a thousand to ship it out of here," a Wrangellian told me. Mount Dewey, the four-hundred-foot-high hill where Muir lit his towering inferno, was just a few minutes' walk from my hotel, via zigzagging residential streets and wooden stairs. Nailed to a tree at the top of the trail was a "no fires" pictogram, which I hoped was the work of a Muir fan with a sense of humor. Beyond the harbor, the view probably hadn't changed much in centuries — green lumps of small islands clustered like a family of sea turtles. In the distance, the higher elevations were dusted with snow, the first I had seen.

Wrangell's downtown was small and geared toward the local marine economy rather than Inside Passage cruise ships. A sign outside the Elks Lodge at the main intersection advertised steak night on Saturday. The supermarket was closed on Sunday. Politically, Wrangell was a dark crimson spot within a deep red state. At the diner where I ate breakfast following my run-in with the seminude man at the hotel, the TV sets were tuned to a low-budget network somewhat to the right of Fox News, and the counter held stacks of *Guns & Ammo* and *Soldier of Fortune*. I flipped through a three-year-old issue of *North American Whitetail* and brushed up on bowhunting techniques as I ate my oatmeal. One of the most contentious presidential races in U.S. history was brewing down south, but in Wrangell the only posters hung in store windows hyped the contest between Kyla and Alex for queen of the 4th of July Celebration.

It was only after a few days in Wrangell — a quirk in the ferry schedule had left me with an extra-long layover — that I realized why everything seemed familiar. Wrangell was like those small western towns, now almost completely vanished, that my family used to stop in during multi-day drives out to national parks in the 1970s. Even my hotel, the Wrangell Extended Stay and Trading Post, had the sort of name that could only be used whimsically nowadays outside of Alaska, perhaps for a mustache wax emporium that served home-brewed rye whiskey. It was certainly the first establishment I'd stayed in that had a sign in the front window advertising the proprietors' interest in buying animal skins. WANTED: BEAVER IN THE ROUND ALSO MINK, OTTER AND WOLF PUT UP. ("In the round" and "put up," I now know, refer to skinning and drying techniques.) The owners, Mike and Lydia Matney, could be seen through the front window at all hours, seated at their sewing machines, transforming furs into hats and slippers. In addition to the ferry, intermediate-size tourist boats stopped in Wrangell every few days, and local businesses would put out hand-painted signs and card tables stacked with knickknacks. Having come from Ketchikan, it was like visiting a yard sale after a trip to Macy's on Black Friday.

Alaskans are a diverse bunch, but I feel safe making two generalizations about them. First, they are unusually welcoming people. Anyone who listens to public radio in New York City will eventually hear some version of the pointless debate over whether someone is or isn't a "real" New Yorker. If you move to Alaska and like it enough to stay awhile, you're an Alaskan. Maybe because life can be harsher up north than it is elsewhere, people are more likely to give you the benefit of the doubt. Whenever I approached someone in Alaska during my travels asking if they'd have time to talk, that person would usually politely answer my questions and then invite me over for coffee or dinner or to sleep in their spare bedroom for a few nights. It was clear within about thirty seconds of my entering his fur emporium that Mike and I could not be further apart politically. He kept railing against the "Soviet state of Washington," where he'd lived previously, and hated Obamacare so much that in spite of a long, deep scar on his neck that made clear his familiarity with hospitals, he'd dropped his medical insurance. But he also told me to borrow his truck if I needed to drive anywhere. (He left the keys in the ignition. Anyone stupid enough to steal a vehicle on Wrangell Island wouldn't get very far.) A lot of the Wrangell Extended Stay's clientele are men traveling solo, laborers in the seafood business or itinerant health care workers who move around between Alaska's small towns. Lydia, sensing correctly that I was a little lonely, strongly suggested I come out with them on their boat to check their crab pots.

The other observation I feel safe in making is that Alaskans see themselves as an extremely self-reliant people. They like to chop and burn their own wood so much that in winter, the smoke in places like Fairbanks can cause worse air quality than Beijing's. Mike liked to go out alone trapping for a week at a time. Above all, Alaskans take advantage of what Muir called the territory's "foodful, kindly wilderness" by hunting, fishing, and gathering. "Never before in all my travels, north or south, had I found so lavish an abundance of berries as here," Muir wrote of his first trip to Wrangell, and it's still true. In early summer, bushes heavy with wild berries poked through fences and threatened to encroach on the roads.

As we motored out of the marina toward open water, Mike sat behind the wheel, and Lydia and I stood in the back. Lydia told a story that encapsulated how living in Wrangell was different from living in the Lower 48. After they'd purchased the Extended Stay, they needed to move a safe upstairs. Four local men were recruited and completed the job. When Lydia asked how much she owed them, they seemed confused. "They wouldn't take any money," she said. "They said it was just the sort of thing you do for your neighbors."

"I sometimes feel bad for kids who grow up on Wrangell Island," Mike said. "They go to Seattle and they've never seen a stoplight. But then I think about kids like that" — he pointed at two boys in a small boat with an outboard motor. "Ten and twelve years old, not allowed to leave the marina, and they pulled in a king salmon the other day." Wrangell's annual salmon derby was under way, and some eleven-year-old had landed a twenty-two pounder.

We continued on toward Etolin Island to check on some crab pots. Lydia said that they liked to use halibut heads as bait; she sometimes baked cookies for the guys down at the cannery, in exchange for some choice ones. We stopped at a buoy marking the spot of the first pot and reeled it up with a mechanized winch. It was the size of a laundry basket and filled with huge Dungeness crabs, at least a dozen. At the bottom, the halibut head had been picked as clean as a Georgia O'Keeffe cow's skull. Lydia pulled the crabs out one by one and measured them against a wooden stick to make sure they were big enough to keep. After an hour on the water, we had two massive plastic tubs of shellfish, most of which would be cleaned, frozen, and shipped off to Lydia's daughter in Washington.

"I always tell Lydia, 'If the world ends, I'll make sure you don't go hungry,' " Mike said. " 'You might not get a lot of variety in your diet, but you'll eat.' "

There was zero variety in my lunch, which consisted of nothing but boiled Dungeness crab and butter, consumed at the Matneys' dining room table. I wasn't hungry again for twenty-four hours.

Chapter Thirteen:
The Morning of Creation

The Stikine River

Wrangell owes its existence to the nearby Stikine River, which flows from the mountains of British Columbia and ends a few miles north of town. The Stikine Tlingit who inhabited Wrangell Island for centuries used the river to fish and to trade with peoples from the interior. Petroglyph Beach, just outside Wrangell, has rock carvings that may indicate habitation in the area going back eight thousand years. The Russians built a fort here that they later leased to Britain's Hudson's Bay Company. After the United States took over in 1867, Wrangell was the base of operations for a minor gold rush that sent panners and miners up the Stikine to Canada's Cassiar District. By the time the *Elder* sailed through, the gold bugs had moved on to Juneau and the Klondike.

Not long after arriving in Wrangell in 1879, Muir joined Hall Young and his fellow missionaries for a steamer trip up the Stikine. It would be Muir's first major encounter with Alaska's glaciers. For a decade, the uncredentialed alpine scholar-gypsy had been carrying on a battle with California's state geologist, Josiah Whitney, over the formation of Yosemite Valley. Whitney, for whom California's tallest peak had been named, believed that the floor of the valley had collapsed in a single catastrophic event. Muir, who had discovered glaciers still at work in the heights of the Sierras, insisted that the valley had been scraped out by a much more deliberate process. Muir's glacial hypothesis combined cutting-edge science with spirituality, historian Stephen Fox explains, as it "suggested a cosmic plan" showing that God was working from a divine blueprint. Whitney wasn't buying any of it. He referred to Muir as "that shepherd."

Muir was struck by the beauty of the Grand Canyon of the Stikine and — taking up a theme he would return to again and again — its similarities to his beloved Northern California. "The majestic cliffs and mountains forming the cañon-walls display endless variety of form and sculpture, and are wonderfully adorned and enlivened with glaciers and waterfalls, while throughout almost its whole extent the floor is a flowery landscape garden like Yosemite," he wrote.

It was the glaciers that impressed him most — their size, their number, the variety in their personalities. Alaska's rivers of ice were unlike anything Muir had seen in the Sierras. Some loomed like hulking monoliths, others curved gracefully through the evergreens. Standing before the face of the Big Stickeen Glacier — now Canada's Great he marveled at "the sunbeams streaming through the ice pinnacles along its terminal wall" and "the broad, sparkling crystal prairie" extending into the distance.

A few weeks later, some of the Wrangell missionaries chartered a steamship to go up the coast in hopes of meeting with a clan of Tlingit. Muir saw a chance to explore the ice firsthand. At one stop, he and Young managed to climb "a mile or two," through a "maze of shallow caves and crevasses," into what seemed to be a glacier's beating heart. The missionaries, overwhelmed by the grandeur of one ice-filled fjord, peppered Muir with questions about the glaciers' physical properties. How deep was the ice? How had it formed? How old was it? Muir jotted scientific observations in his notebook as he was struck by "the peculiar awe one experiences in entering these mansions of the icy north . . . the natural effect of appreciating the manifestations of the presence of God."

The earth was being sculpted according to God's plans. In the Sierras, God's glacial work was nearly complete. In Alaska, it was "still the morning of creation."

Eager, like Muir, to see my first Alaskan glacier, I booked a jet-boat trip up the Stikine as far as the Canadian border. My guide was Eric Yancey. Also along for the ride were a father and son from Texas who'd come to Wrangell to kill a black bear. (Thus disproving Kenny the tattooed fisherman's theory about local wildlife population control.) They didn't talk much, perhaps because their mouths were occupied chewing tobacco and drooling into Coke cans.

Eric had started running jet-boat charters while working the swing shift at the local sawmill. "In the 1990s, the logging business sort of sputtered out," he said; this was the same downturn that had killed Ketchikan's timber industry. FOR SALE signs went up on homes and businesses all over town. "A *lot* of people left, maybe eight hundred," which would be about a quarter of the population. "You could get money from the government for job retraining, but by that time I'd started this business."

Eric was what might qualify as an Alaskan moderate in terms of the environment: a believer in what he called "the right mix" of wilderness and resources. Unlike most people I met in Wrangell, he knew a lot about John Muir and couldn't understand why the town didn't do more to promote its history with him. "If this were Juneau, they'd make a *huge* deal out of the Muir connection," he said, pointing to a rocky piece of shore. "There's a great photo of him standing in that exact spot right there." Eric had what he admitted was "a classic 'not in my backyard'" attitude about exploiting Alaska's natural resources. "I'm a resources guy. I'm in favor of mining and logging," he said with a smile. "I just prefer they don't do it on this river."

The day had threatened to be an ugly one, but the area wildlife seemed to be enjoying the sun while it lasted. We idled at the end of one island where thirty or more bald eagles were loitering, and saw a group of harbor seals lounging on a sandbar. We stopped at a small wooded island to pick up some kayakers who were going fishing up the river. The Texans, who were going fishing the next day, nodded and spit in unison to show their approval.

We crossed the shallow, braided waters of the Stikine's delta and began to see signs of the wilderness that had attracted Muir. Snow dusted the tops of mountains on each side of the river, and waterfalls poured down from the heights. A moose and two calves slipped and slid as they climbed a muddy riverbank. We dropped the kayakers at the Canadian border, demarcated by a wide gap cut in the spruce forest. "Legally, you're not supposed to cross without permission," Eric said, reading everyone's mind and ostentatiously turning away. "But I don't suppose they're watching too closely today." Anyone who wanted to relieve himself or violate international law had five minutes to do so privately.

Safely back inside the United States of America, we entered a deep canyon. The gray rock walls were like elephant hides, striated in some places, scoured in others, evidence of long-ago ice grinding. Ten thousand years ago, when people may have been migrating across the Bering Land Bridge, the glacier in this canyon had been a mile deep. "Those sharp mountaintops you see are the only peaks that were above the ice," Eric said. "Anything rounded was under the ice." Muir noted that the views

along the Stikine changed with "bewildering rapidity" and, in one early travel dispatch, called the Stikine "a Yosemite one
hundred miles long." This section in particular could have been an Ansel Adams slide
show. I asked Eric about the hundred or so
glaciers that had so captivated Muir, and he
agreed that they were in steady retreat.
Some were gone. Several hanging glaciers,
isolated ones that cling to mountainsides at
higher elevations, have disappeared in the
past twenty years. He suggested we pay a
visit to Chief Shakes Glacier, which was a
tidewater glacier, meaning one long enough
to flow from the mountains into the sea.

We followed an inlet through a narrow
canyon that widened into a lake. The water
was clogged with icebergs of various sizes,
some of which glowed blue like berry
Slurpees. "I've seen bergs half the size of
downtown Wrangell in here," Eric said,
maneuvering the jet boat around obstacles.
"Sometimes it's so full of ice chunks, you
can't get through unless you really work at
it." At the far end of the lake was the frozen
wall of Chief Shakes Glacier, which wound
backward like a wide dirt path into the
mountains.

Muir hadn't seen any of this in 1879,
because it didn't exist. What was now

Shakes Lake had been ice. "Actually, the glacier was out this far the first time I was out here in '92," Eric said. "It's receded a mile and a half in that time."

We cruised toward the glacier's majestic face, the jet boat's metal hull clanging against blocks of ice. Up close, the sixty-foot-high ice wall looked haggard and unhealthy, the molars of a beast with a fondness for candy and an aversion to flossing. Chunks of ice were calving off frequently enough that we maintained a safe distance. "I don't know where you fall on this subject," Eric said after a block the size of a mobile home plunged into the water, "but I think the weather's just getting warmer. Ice melts, the air gets warmer, more ice melts; and it creates a self-fulfilling cycle. I'm sure humans haven't helped, but are we really gonna give up our big vehicles and flying around the world on vacations?"

When he put it that way, sacrificing comfort seemed almost unpatriotic. I departed Wrangell the next day on the MV *Columbia,* the largest and probably nicest ferry in the Alaska fleet. Edward Harriman himself would have appreciated my accommodations: a four-person room with a shower.

CHAPTER FOURTEEN: WARNING SIGNS

Treadwell Mine

After their brief stop in seedy Wrangell, the Harriman Expedition happily departed for Juneau, two hundred miles to the north. John Burroughs observed how the scenery grew more extreme as they advanced up the coast. Devil's Thumb, a dramatic spike of dark granite that rises like a mile-high smokestack, stood in the distance behind Patterson Glacier, the first serious ice seen from the *Elder.* Muir, eager as always to assert his knowledge of glaciology, shared the story of his twenty-mile hike to find its source. When Burroughs became overwhelmed by "the vast panorama of the encircling mountains," he lowered his eyes to water level, where the views were more in tune with his pastoral sensibilities. A row of seven eagles, "like Indian chiefs," regarded the *Elder* with indifference, he wrote. "Many whales are seen blowing, their glistening backs emerging from the water, turning slowly like the periphery of a huge wheel."

Listed among the expedition's experts in the natural sciences was one specialist with a decidedly commercial bent, the mining engineer Walter Devereux. He ran a consultancy in New York City but had made his fortune from silver and coal in Colorado. The expedition had arranged to tour Juneau's massive Treadwell Mine complex, so, before arriving, Devereux gave a presentation on the *Elder*'s upper deck. Technological breakthroughs, he explained, were now allowing mining companies to extract tiny flecks of gold from quartz deposits. Though overshadowed by the Klondike Gold Rush, in the Canadian Yukon — the effects of which the expedition would shortly witness firsthand — Juneau's advanced methods had made it possible to process thousands of tons of gold-bearing ore each day, making the Treadwell the world's largest gold mine for a time. In less than twenty years, mining had transformed Juneau from a tiny Tlingit fishing village to a city of two thousand. In 1906 it would become Alaska's new territorial capital.

In his diary, artist Frederick Dellenbaugh described stepping from his stateroom in the morning to soak in the future capital's picturesque placement at the foot of Mount Juneau. Then, as now, Juneau from afar resembled an alpine hamlet in a model railroad set. His placid thoughts were shattered by a dynamite blast so loud that he assumed it had come from the *Elder*'s cannon.

The noise of detonations was nothing compared with the din of Juneau's battery of ore stampers. Three hundred steel hammers, each weighing a thousand pounds, pulverized ton upon ton of hard quartz chunks ninety-eight times a minute, twenty-four hours a day. Burroughs wrote that, next to the stamping mill's roar, Niagara Falls was but "a soft hum"; the very air was "torn to tatters" by the unnatural clamor.

From across the Gastineau Channel, the Treadwell Mine had been a loud curiosity. Up close, it was apocalyptic. A wide, deep hole a quarter of a mile long had been gouged out of the earth. The surrounding forests of Douglas Island had been reduced to stumps. As the deafening thrum of the stamping machines continued ceaselessly in the background, Dellenbaugh stood on the edge of the massive hole and watched the miners "looking like pygmies . . . working to get out more gold," for two or three dollars a day. One mining company employee lamented to Dellenbaugh that the hills surrounding Juneau were likely rich in ore, "but the timber is so dense that prospecting is extremely difficult."

The owners of the Treadwell Mine could proudly claim to have taken out gold with a greater value than the price paid for Alaska just thirty years earlier. Aside from wages, very little of that profit remained in the territory. The possibility that Alaska might also be absorbing nonfinancial costs had not yet occurred to anyone. Powdered ore was processed with mercury, cyanide, arsenic, and other chemicals, with the worthless leftover tailings dumped into Gastineau Channel. In the Juneau chapter of her *Appletons' Guide-Book to Alaska and the Northwest Coast,* first published in 1893, travel author Eliza Scidmore mentions in passing that "the heavy plume of smoke from the Treadwell's chlorination works has killed vegetation for a mile up and down the island's edge."

CHAPTER FIFTEEN: BLACK GOLD

Juneau

Perhaps due to its overabundance of real estate, zoning laws and urban planning aren't high priorities in Alaska. Nestled in one of the most spectacular natural settings of any city in America, downtown Juneau is like an aging Hollywood star who still looks gorgeous in panoramic shots but suffers under the scrutiny of close-up. The state capitol building, at the corner of Fourth and Main, might be mistaken for an elementary school anywhere else and looks out onto a district courthouse that could pass for the world's largest Arby's. Usually, the Alaska State Legislature meets only three to four months per calendar year, ending in April or May. When I arrived in June, legislators were deep into an emergency overtime session with no end in sight.

The financial problem Alaska's government faced was a doozy. In part because of

131

its size and varied topography and climate, Alaska spends almost three times the national average per capita on its citizens. The state once had the highest taxes in the United States. That burden quickly vanished when Prudhoe Bay crude began flowing though the Trans-Alaska Pipeline System in 1977. Much as New York City's mood rises and falls to the rhythm of Wall Street's movements, Alaska's fortunes fluctuated for the next thirty-five years based on the price of crude. Starting in mid-2014, that figure began to fall precipitously, from nearly a hundred dollars a barrel to below thirty in less than eighteen months. Most of the United States celebrated as fuel prices tumbled. Alaska was suddenly looking at a deficit of four billion dollars in a 5.4-billion-dollar budget. Legislators had argued among themselves and with the governor for months about possible savings, but the most significant cut everyone had agreed on was chopping fifty million dollars from the state university system.

Alaska's economy differs from those of other states not merely by degree. It has more in common with Venezuela's than California's. While fishing, mining, tourism, and other sectors of the economy account for a large percentage of Alaska's jobs, the generous state budget relies on oil industry taxes for 90 percent of its revenues. Because of that, Alaskans now pay far and away the lowest average across-the-board individual taxes (i.e., state income tax, sales taxes, and property taxes) of any state in the nation. In 2015, Alaskans paid 524 dollars per person. The next-lowest state, New Hampshire, paid nearly three times that amount. Vermont residents paid the most: more than four thousand dollars per person.

But Alaska not only doesn't tax its citizens much — it pays a lump sum to every man, woman, and child in the state each year simply for living there. The funds come from revenues earned by the Alaska Permanent Fund, a gigantic pile of money collected from oil companies and carefully invested since the pipeline opened. Over the past twenty years, the annual payout per person (called the Permanent Fund Dividend, or PFD) has averaged well over a thousand dollars and twice has exceeded two thousand dollars. The annual announcement of the dividend amount is major news in Alaska, a Powerball jackpot drawing in which everyone wins. About a month before the money's dispersal, electronics stores and car dealers around Anchorage start posting signs that read SPEND

YOUR DIVIDEND HERE. Libertarian Alaskans love to complain about government interference, but they love free money, too. (The head of one rural religious compound became a hero to property rights advocates when he fought the federal government over the right to bulldoze a road through a national park while collecting PFD checks for himself, his wife, and fifteen children.) When I arrived in Juneau, state legislators up for reelection were proclaiming the sacredness of PFD checks at a volume not heard in town since the ore-stamping machines shut down.

Not surprisingly, the oil industry is not shy about throwing its weight around in the capital. As I walked up and down the steep hills and wooden staircases of Juneau's downtown, I couldn't help but notice a surprising number of good restaurants for a city of thirty-three thousand people. The abundance of fine dining options makes more sense when you consider the quantity of lobbyists in town. It was no coincidence that the ten-digit deficit in Alaska's state budget included five hundred million dollars in largely ineffectual tax credits for oil exploration. Sometimes the appeal on behalf of clients was more direct than a nice dinner. Just a couple of floors up from my room at the downtown Baranof Hotel, lobbyists for an oil services company had been recorded dispensing cash to lawmakers like an ATM. One state representative with his hand out was caught boasting that he "had to cheat, steal, beg, borrow, and lie" to help defeat a bill opposed by the oil industry. Another pleaded guilty to withdrawing a prospective piece of oil tax legislation for the grand sum of four thousand dollars. An environmental activist who joined me for a couple of cocktails bemoaned the difficulty of fighting Big Oil in Alaska. "What kills me isn't just that these people prostituted themselves; it's that they did it for *so little money,*" he said.

In their book about the Harriman Expedition, *Looking Far North,* historians William Goetzmann and Kay Sloan write that the experts aboard the *Elder* faced the "two Alaskas" problem, which was an environmental twist on Freud's Madonna–whore complex: "the dual vision of Alaska as a wilderness to be preserved and a frontier to be exploited." Modern Juneau was a good example of the two Alaskas. On one end of town, there is the Mendenhall Glacier, which is staggeringly beautiful, as impressive as anything in Yellowstone or Yosemite and, if you're already in Juneau, remarkably accessible. I visited by catching a two-dollar public bus and then walking about a mile.

At the other end of Juneau, you have a small city founded on gold money and lubricated by petroleum dollars. I did visit one nice new building downtown, the Alaska State Library, Archives and Museum. Its construction had been funded by money from the last oil price spike, in 2008. It was Celebration week in Juneau, when Tsimshian, Haida, and Tlingit from throughout Southeast Alaska converge on the capital for several days of events and socializing. I recognized one dancer from Metlakatla by his conical hat and animal-skin singlet; he must've recognized me, too, because he looked at me as if I'd been following him. Celebration had siphoned off most of the museumgoers, and I had the huge state history hall almost to myself. The exhibits were excellent, and much of the space was devoted to the outsize role of oil in Alaska history.

The very quotable governor Wally Hickel put Alaska politicians' buy-now-pay-later attitude toward resource development into practical terms when he famously said, "You can't just let nature run wild." After the largest oil field ever found in North America was located in one of the world's least-friendly environments in 1968, Hickel dispatched a team of bulldozers to blaze a 550-mile dirt road through the pristine wilderness of what would soon be Gates of the Arctic National Park. When the spring thaw came, the path known informally as the Hickel Highway flooded, creating a muddy ditch that was soon obsolete.

Before settling on a pipeline, various other modes of getting Alaska's oil to market were considered, including flying it out on jumbo jets. In August and September of 1969, the thousand-foot-long supertanker SS *Manhattan,* retrofitted as a sort of mega-icebreaker, attempted to make a trial run via the Northwest Passage and nearly got trapped in the polar ice. The verdict was that commercial sea traffic through the Arctic wasn't feasible. Less than half a century and more than ten billion barrels of burned Prudhoe Bay crude later, the Arctic ice had melted so much due to climate change that adventurous tourists were now able to transit the route that Norwegian explorer Roald Amundsen had pioneered between 1903 and 1906. As I walked around the new state museum in Juneau, the luxury *Crystal Serenity* was preparing to become the largest cruise ship to cross the Northwest Passage, departing from Anchorage in August and sailing through the once impassable Arctic en route to New York City. Nine hundred tickets, starting at twenty thousand dollars and rising to more than a hundred thousand, had sold out almost immediately.

Chapter Sixteen:
The Budget Crisis

Anchorage

Juneau may be the political capital of Alaska, but Anchorage is its power center. Almost half the state's population lives within its metropolitan area, and all of its oil businesses are headquartered there. People in other parts of Alaska tend to describe Anchorage in terms that make it sound like a cross between Dubai and Gomorrah; a favorite joke is that the best thing about Anchorage is that it's just thirty minutes from Alaska. Even more than Juneau, its big buildings can be dated to spikes in oil prices (future scholars of early-eighties Brutalism Lite architecture will find much to study), and the city bears more than a passing resemblance to its midsize peers like Wichita. Actually, because Anchorage is tucked between the Chugach Mountains and Cook Inlet, it looks like Wichita dropped on top of Chamonix if the

Alps were fifteen miles from the Mediterranean. When the weather was clear, I could see Denali from my hotel room. "It might be a sorry town," John McPhee wrote of Anchorage in the 1970s, "but it has the greatest out-of-town any town ever had."

When I'd visited Anchorage in the spring, I met with Scott Goldsmith, an emeritus professor of economics at the University of Alaska at Anchorage (UAA). Now semiretired, he was wearing a very un-Alaska suit and tie for a board meeting later in the day at the university's Institute of Social and Economic Research. Anchorage has matured into a much more livable town than it was when McPhee was here, and its downtown is filled with nice cafés. (For a taste of contemporary dystopian horrors, one must head an hour north to Sarah Palin country and the sprawl of Wasilla.) Goldsmith had agreed to meet for a cup of coffee because I wanted to ask him about a paper he'd written, "The Path to a Fiscal Solution: Use Earnings from All Our Assets." In it, Goldsmith explained that the long-term situation in Alaska was potentially even more dire than the per-barrel price drops and budget deficit indicated. Alaskans had been conditioned to expect excellent state services and annual PFD checks during a period when

140

the oil floating those checks was slowly running out. Production from the North Slope oil fields had peaked at around two million barrels per day in 1988 and had since declined to six hundred thousand per day.

The Permanent Fund was set up by Governor Jay Hammond shortly after oil started flowing through the Alaska Pipeline in the 1970s. "One part of the idea was 'We need to put some of this money aside for when the oil's gone,' " Goldsmith said. "The second part was 'We need to put some of this money aside, otherwise we're going to piss it all away.' "

That seemed like extraordinary foresight for a politician. Goldsmith and I had both grown up in Illinois, where stealing from taxpayers is considered a fringe benefit of holding public office.

"Right, it's incredible. And then, shortly after the creation of the fund, Hammond pushed the idea of the Permanent Fund dividend." This was the source of the magic checks that came dancing into Alaskan mailboxes each autumn. "Since its creation, the only thing the Permanent Fund has spent any money on has been the dividend, and so it's been able to accumulate more than fifty billion dollars," Goldsmith said. "That money is invested all over the world and throws off, after inflation, like two and a half billion a year." Typically about half that amount is distributed in PFD checks.

Goldsmith compared Alaska, with its dependence on a single resource, to the tiny Pacific island of Nauru. A century ago, someone discovered that beneath Nauru's lush tropical rainforests lay immense deposits of guano, bird shit deposited over centuries as a by-product of avian digestion. Guano is an excellent source of phosphate, which was a much-desired ingredient in fertilizer. (It supplanted an earlier bountiful fertilizer source that had run out: bone meal manufactured from the thousands of tons of buffalo skeletons left behind on the Great Plains.) Throughout the twentieth century, a series of colonial rulers and native leaders strip-mined the mineral as quickly as they could. For a time, Nauru's per capita GDP was second only to Saudi Arabia's. Today its phosphate reserves are exhausted, the country is bankrupt, and its once green forests are a lifeless, pitted wasteland.

A lot of people in Alaska seemed to be hoping that the solution to the present crisis would be the same as it had been with previous ones. A coup in the Middle East or a strike in Nigeria would cause prices to spike, evening news shows in the rest of the

United States would start interviewing angry motorists for segments titled "Pain at the Pump," and everything in Alaska would return to normal. Goldsmith said those days were gone for good.

"In order to balance the budget now, as oil production continues to decline, the price has got to go back up to 115, 120 bucks," he said. As we sat there, the price of oil was about forty-two dollars. Nobody wanted to cut services, and even if every state employee were fired, it still wouldn't cover the deficit.

"Reminds me of the old Winston Churchill line that everybody wants a pound worth of services for ninety-five pence worth of taxes," I said.

Goldsmith shook his head in disagreement. "Everybody wants a pound worth of services for *no* taxes."

Alaska isn't an entirely tax-free zone. The oil companies pay royalties and a production tax, and some municipalities levy sales and property taxes. Cruise ship passengers pay a per-head tax that is supposed to cover infrastructure costs related to tourism. I wondered if taxing other iconic Alaskan industries might help.

"I used to do analyses looking at how much you'd have to tax every salmon commercially caught in order to equal the taxes of the oil industry," Goldsmith said. "It'd be something like ten bucks a salmon. Or how much would you have to tax each tourist in order to generate as much. It'd be like a thousand dollars per tourist."

There was a woolly mammoth in the room that almost no Alaskan politician wanted to acknowledge. The same fossil fuels that pay for everything are the primary contributor to the changing climate that is already hitting Alaska harder than any place else in the United States. Strictly from an economic point of view, rising temperatures are likely to cause billions of dollars in damage. Alaska had just recorded its warmest spring on record. For the second consecutive year, the city of Anchorage needed to import a trainload of snow from Fairbanks for the start of the Iditarod sled dog race. Highways and building foundations constructed on permafrost were now buckling throughout the state as the ground thawed. Coastal erosion was threatening to dump villages into the rising sea; Natives who hunted on sea ice were increasingly cut off from traditional food sources that are a large part of their diet. Alaska has a state task force assigned to deal with moving coastal settlements to safer ground, an extremely expensive process. The cost of each relocation is estimated in the hundreds of millions of dollars.

I asked Goldsmith if there was any economic silver lining to climate change — lower heating bills, perhaps? "Well, a longer agricultural growing season, that's one," he said after a few seconds. For a hundred years, the U.S. Department of Agriculture has been trying to figure out how to grow crops in Alaska, an idea that's not as crazy as it sounds. The soil in the Matanuska-Susitna Valley, north of Anchorage, is fertile and deep. Farmers in the region are known for raising beach-ball-size cabbages that thrive in its twenty hours of summer daylight. During the Great Depression, the federal government had transplanted two hundred farm families here from the Midwest, though most eventually moved back south. They may have departed too soon. During that hundred-year span, rising temperatures have greatly extended Alaska's growing season; in Fairbanks, researchers found that the season had increased from 85 to 123 days between 1906 and 2002. Alaskans had recently voted to legalize marijuana, and there was some talk that the Mat-Su's reputation as the state's "pot cultivation capital" (per the Anchorage newspaper) might create more jobs.

Most attempts to diversify the Alaska economy have failed miserably. A fifty-million-dollar investment by the state development agency in an Anchorage seafood-processing plant flamed out, and the building is now occupied by, among other things, an extremely large nondenominational church. An appetite for megaprojects with the potential to strike it rich, usually tied to exploiting the state's natural wealth, seems to be encoded in Alaska's DNA. "You have all these schemes to develop the Alaskan infrastructure to make it easier to get access to minerals," Goldsmith said. "It's not just the Bridge to Nowhere; it's the Road to Nowhere, or the Railroad to Nowhere. People say, 'If only we had extended this railroad, or built a road to western Alaska, where there is one viable operating mine.' Supposedly, the next boom after oil is coal. Because we have incredible reserves of coal up on the North Slope. But, A, how the hell are you going to get it out, and, B, who wants it? Other than that, it's a great idea."

Goldsmith told me the state had a full slate of dubious megaprojects that it was studying, ranging in size from a highway connecting Juneau to Skagway (and the rest of North America) to an eight-hundred-mile natural gas pipeline that would cost at least forty-five billion dollars. These seem unambitious compared with some Alaska projects that never came to fruition. In the early 1950s, the U.S. Army Corps of Engineers proposed building a dam on the Yukon River that would have produced many times the electricity used by the entire state and created a freshwater reservoir bigger than Lake Erie. Project Chariot was a late-1950s plan to gouge out a deepwater port 250 miles north of Nome by detonating five nuclear devices. Though strongly supported by hydrogen-bomb mastermind Edward Teller and approved by Alaska's new state legislature, Project Chariot was scrapped when the local Inupiat people objected. Their case was buttressed by the fact that no such port was actually needed.

My personal favorite megaproject is the Bering Strait crossing. This one could be traced back to the Harriman Expedition. In the years after Harriman's death, in 1909, a story circulated that part of his motivation to visit Alaska had been to explore the possibility of building a round-the-world railroad. This trans-global line would include a tunnel beneath the Bering Strait. Considering that the longest railroad tunnel at the time was less than three miles long, and the

Bering Strait is more than fifty miles wide at its narrowest point, the tale doesn't quite hold up to scrutiny. Over the years, the idea has resurfaced in various guises, including one supported by the Reverend Sun Myung Moon, to foster world peace. One Anchorage businessman was still promoting the tunnel as a potential boon to the world economy.

Aside from tourism, there were a few non-oil sectors of the economy that were growing, Goldsmith said. One was air cargo, with companies like FedEx and UPS taking advantage of Anchorage's central location between Asia, Europe, and North America to refuel planes and change crews. Another was senior citizens. Residents who in the past came up to make money and then departed now stick around because of the low taxes. "We're not exactly Florida, but our senior population has experienced the fastest rate of growth of any state for the last couple decades," he said.

There was another possible solution to Alaska's budget problems being discussed, which was to drill for more oil. Alaska's D.C. delegation — all pro-development Republicans — has been pushing for years to allow oil companies to develop petroleum reserves in the Arctic National Wildlife

Refuge (ANWR), the largest protected wilderness in the United States. This enormous swath of land stretching north from the Brooks Range to the Beaufort Sea is one of the last intact landscapes of its size in the world. The area was initially preserved under President Dwight Eisenhower in 1960, and is home to so many animal species that it is often called "America's Serengeti."

One phrase heard constantly from Alaska politicians is "federal overreach." The term refers to the belief, widely held in Alaska, that necessary development is strangled by the U.S. government's ownership of 61 percent of Alaska's land (including national parks, national forests, and millions of acres overseen by the Bureau of Land Management) and the regulations Washington imposes. Republicans up for election everywhere agitate about limiting the size of government, but Alaska's officials have a special gift for making it sound as if the state's citizenry were living under some sort of martial law imposed by the Environmental Protection Agency. When President Obama proposed that a slice of ANWR's nineteen million acres that had been designated for potential oil and gas development — and, beneath it, an estimated ten billion barrels of oil — be set aside permanently, Senator Murkowski called the idea "a stunning attack on our sovereignty."

The same officials who rail against federal overreach do not often mention that Alaska receives more money per capita from Washington than any other state — about $2.50 for every dollar it pays in taxes. Federal spending accounts for about one-third of all jobs in Alaska, about the same as from the oil industry.

"Everybody understands that the primary job of the congressional delegation is to get federal money," UAA history professor Stephen Haycox told me. "Because Alaska is such a conservative place, you've got this bizarre disconnect between tenaciously clinging to this self-identification as rugged individuals — people who say to themselves, 'I came here to be free of government regulation' — and the current and historical reality, which is dependence on the federal budget. It's like living in a floodplain. People are just in total denial about it."

CHAPTER SEVENTEEN:
CHILKAT COUNTRY

Haines

A few years ago, Norwegian television created a strangely popular series of hypnotic, hours-long videos composed solely of point-of-view footage shot during train or ferry trips. The action, for lack of a better word, consists almost entirely of trees, water, and rocks slipping past. Once you give yourself over to a meditative mind state, the appearance of something like a bridge or a bird can be thrilling. The journey up Lynn Canal from Juneau is the real-time version of these POV videos.

Lynn Canal is the longest and deepest fjord in North America. This is the Inside Passage of cruise commercials, a colonnade of jagged snowcapped mountains and, farther north, glaciers. The waters are smooth and quiet. The only interruptions come from the occasional whale or, more frequently, ship. The Harriman Expedition departed Juneau for Skagway, in the northernmost reaches of the passage. I was making a pit stop in the town that might be considered Skagway's fraternal twin, Haines.

Haines and Skagway are just twenty miles apart. They are the only two real Inside Passage towns connected to Alaska's highway system; the third, far to the south, is Hyder (pop. 87), which is so isolated its residents use a British Columbia area code and the local bar accepts Canadian dollars. It's possible to drive between Haines and Skagway via the Canadian Yukon, but it'll take you eight hours, assuming there's no hassle at the two border crossings. A couple of Alaskans told me that Canadian border patrol agents are suspicious of Americans who don't declare weapons. "They're always like, 'Come on, everyone in Alaska carries a gun,' " one Alaskan told me. He was thinking of purchasing a firearm to avoid searches.

Ketchikan and Juneau are two of the holy trinity of cruise ship stops in the Inside Passage. Skagway is the third, and certainly the most proudly touristy. Haines was the free-spirited half of the pair, and a rare creature in these parts: a town that had stood up to the cruise ship industry and survived when punished for its impudence. When one major company pleaded guilty to dumping "toxic effluent" in Lynn Canal in 1998, Haines introduced its own per-passenger tax. The cruise lines quickly erased Haines from their itineraries. "Ships enter our lives, small cities on the move, consuming beauty, belching waste," Haines historian Daniel Lee Henry has written. "At the very least, we expect them to behave." Almost twenty years later, the town sees an average of only one or two big ships a week. Haines has decided to be itself, and it seems to be doing just fine.

Haines is also a place that can claim John Muir as a founding father of sorts. By the time of Muir's first Alaska voyage, in 1879, word of Sheldon Jackson's missionary schools had spread north to the notoriously hostile Chilkat Tlingit tribe. Its chiefs inquired about obtaining a teacher for their people. Hall Young was excited by the missionary possibilities to be found up Lynn Canal. Muir had heard stories from prospectors about extraordinary glaciers at the top of the Inside Passage that might exceed those he'd already seen near Wrangell. With Young's help, he was able to arrange "a good canoe and crew" in Wrangell, loaded with provisions and blankets.

The crew was made up of four Tlingit. Their leader was Toyatte, a Stikine chief and experienced seaman who owned the thirty-six-foot red cedar canoe they traveled in. His second was Kadachan, whose status as the son of a rival tribe's chief made him an excellent go-between in a region where a warm reception could not be guaranteed. As the crew prepared to depart Wrangell, both Toyatte's wife and Kadachan's mother expressed deep wariness about an excursion into unfriendly territory; the latter warned Young that "if anything happens to my son, I will take your baby as mine in payment." Filling out the four-man crew were two younger men: another Stikine Tlingit named John, who acted as interpreter, and Sitka Charley, who had traveled widely. Muir later recalled that when Charley noticed his interest in glaciers, he told him that as a boy, "he had gone with his father to hunt seals in a large bay full of ice, and that though it was long since he had been there, he thought he could find his way to it."

I'd first come into contact with Dave Nanney through the website for his Chilkat Eagle Bed and Breakfast, in Haines. Its home page was designed in a palette of neon yellows and pinks that appeared not to have been updated since the GeoCities era. (Nanney later told me that he did professional Web design.) Nanney was also the founder of the Haines John Muir Association. The online reviews for his B & B weren't great, but most of the reviewers agreed that Dave was a very nice guy who knew a lot about Haines. Also, he charged seventy dollars for a room — far and away the biggest lodging bargain I'd found in Alaska — and Dave drove the five miles out to the ferry terminal to pick up his customers at no extra charge.

"You want the full John Muir tour?" Nanney asked hopefully from the driver's side window when he pulled up to the dock. His hair and mustache were silver, and his outfit was eclectic: a frayed visor adorned with flames, black sweatpants, and a fleece vest embroidered with a Tlingit bird pattern. He wore fingerless gloves and a timepiece on each wrist — one smartwatch and one analog. When he opened the back of his SUV, he had to move some kites to make room for my bag. "You never know when you'll get the sudden urge to fly a kite," he said.

Dave had moved to Haines after a couple of years in the military and studying computers at Stanford in the 1960s. "The guys

I was at Stanford with spent all their time talking about how someday we'd have computers at home and everyone would be connected," he said as we drove through the few blocks of downtown. With a population of twenty-five hundred, Haines wasn't very big — "Sometimes people drive off the ferry and go straight through town, looking for Haines, and then have to turn around" — but it had all the hallmarks of a picture-postcard Alaskan town: a library and bookstore that towns ten times larger would envy, a pedestrian-friendly layout (I never did find an explanation as to why Inside Passage towns had been laid out with such fine sidewalks, which predated cruise ships), an excellent coffee shop with picnic tables outside where dogs lounged in the shade under their owners' feet, a brewpub, and at least one oddball tourist attraction (a museum devoted entirely to hammers). The town was also surrounded by some of the most beautiful scenery in Alaska: snowy peaks on three sides standing over the serene waters of Lynn Canal, all of it likely to be visible, because a row of tall mountains blocks most of the rain that soaks other Inside Passage cities. It was a Tuesday just before the start of summer, and half the cars in town had mountain bikes and kayaks lashed to their roofs. A trio I sat next to at the Bamboo Room restaurant had sun-burned faces and white raccoon circles around their eyes. They'd just finished a photo shoot for a snowboarding catalog.

"All over Alaska, people dream of moving to Haines, and I can't blame them," Nanney said as we drove up Route 7 toward the airport.

Nanney's interest in Muir had been kindled when he got involved in community planning and began to explore possible things to market about Haines other than its natural beauty and abundance of eagles. "The Chilkat ran this region, and they knew all about the coming of the Americans," he said. "Muir came right up this canal in 1879 and landed right around here." What had been the village of Yendustucky, site of one of the most important cultural exchanges in Alaska history, is today covered by the tarmac of an airport runway.

Nanney knew the story of Muir's time in Haines almost verbatim from the account in *Travels in Alaska*. The Chilkat, ensconced in the natural citadel of the northern Lynn Canal, were "the most influential" of all Tlingit tribes, Muir wrote, and the most feared. "Whenever on our journey I spoke of the interesting characteristics of other tribes we had visited, my crew would invariably say, 'Oh, yes, these are pretty good Indians, but wait till you have seen the Chilkats.' " As his crew approached the Chilkat Peninsula, Toyatte and his men asked to stop and "prepare themselves to meet their great rivals," Muir wrote. From boxes that had remained unopened for weeks during their journey, his Stikine companions removed new hats and boots, clean white shirts and neckties. Muir was startled by the sartorial transformation and attempted to spiff up his own shabby attire with an eagle feather in his cap. Several miles from the Chilkat village, the canoe was spotted by an observer who shouted, "Who are you? What are your names? What do you want? What have you come for?" Their replies were shouted to another messenger a quarter mile away, "and by this living telephone the news was delivered to the chief as he sat by his fireside." As the canoe neared the village, a volley of musket balls was fired over their heads as both a welcome and a warning.

The moment the canoe touched the shore, a team of forty or fifty men charged forward and lifted the craft and its occupants out of the water and carried them to the door of Chief Daanawaak. Muir's team was feted with a sumptuous meal heavy on seal grease, a delicacy. ("Mon, mon!" Muir said to Young after yet another such course had been laid before them. "I'm fashed we'll be floppin' about i' the sea, whiles wi' flippers an' forked tails.") After the meal, Young made his appeal: It was time to leave old ways behind and embrace the teachings of the Lord, through whom one may find everlasting life. Amen. When Young had finished, the Chilkat requested that the Ice Chief, as they called Muir, speak as well. Muir reluctantly gave a speech that he would repeat over the next three days, praising the natural bounty of their land, sharing his belief that it was fed by the grinding of glaciers, and "dwelling principally on the brotherhood of all races of people, assuring them that God loved them and that some of their white brethren were beginning to know them and become interested in their welfare."

The Chilkat liked what they heard from Young. They loved what they heard from Muir. The Ice Chief and the Preacher Chief (as Young was called) spoke five times, not only to the Chilkat but to their neighbors the Chilkoot. Spectators crowded around doorways and poked their heads through the smoke hole of the roof of Daanawaak's house. Young heard the sound of tearing coming from the building's walls and realized that "they were prying off the planks in order that those outside might hear." Following Muir's last talk, an old shaman rose slowly and said to Muir, "It has always seemed to me while trying to speak to traders and those seeking gold-mines that it was like speaking to a person across a broad stream that was running fast over stones and making so loud a noise that scarce a single word could be heard. But now, for the first time, the Indian and the white man are on the same side of the river, eye to eye, heart to heart."

After four days, the Chilkat agreed to consider accepting a missionary and teacher. Their overwhelming preference was Muir. They even put together an enviable compensation package, according to Muir: The chief "promised that if I would come to them they would always do as I directed, follow my counsels, give me as many wives as I liked, build a church and school, and pick all the stones out of the paths and make them smooth for my feet." It was the second generous offer he had received. Early in their visit, Muir had been disturbed by the cries of a newborn. The child's mother had died, and he was starving to death. Muir fetched the cans of condensed milk he and Young had brought to serve with their coffee and mixed some with warm water. This he fed the boy through the night as he walked the baby to soothe him. In appreciation, Daanawaak told Muir he could take the boy with him, but he declined the offer. Seven years later, Young returned to find the boy alive.

Before his visitors departed, Chief Daanawaak escorted Young down to the harbor while Muir went off to climb a mountain. The chief apparently motioned with his arm to indicate a spot where the Presbyterians could build a mission and school. Young interpreted the motion as indicating hundreds of acres — land claimed by the church, which now constitutes the center of Haines.

"The natives didn't know surveys and deeds," Nanney said as we drove back through town. "In their minds, they were granting the *use* of the property. They were incredibly surprised to learn they'd given all this away. The whole downtown had been surveyed and sold off for lots."

Nanney's B & B was a little cluttered, and certainly the interior indicated that whoever had decorated lost interest in the late eighties. I had a brief moment of panic when I saw that amid the VHS tapes and inexpensive jewelry for sale, Nanney had assembled a large number of instruments, including a one-man-band arrangement that allowed him to play flute and keyboards simultaneously. "Do you like to jam?" he asked. "We've had some great jam sessions here."

I was the evening's only guest. At day's end, Dave invited me to help myself to anything in the kitchen for breakfast and showed me where the extra blankets were stored. "I heat with wood," he said, indicating a large black cast-iron stove, "but I don't think we'll need it tonight."

When I woke the next morning, the temperature outside was forty-eight degrees. Judging from my visible breath, it wasn't much warmer inside. I came downstairs to find Dave zonked out on the couch, oblivious to the laugh track of *The Bob Newhart Show* blaring from the TV, his fingerless gloves pulling the blanket up to his chin.

Haines has long been rumored to be the model for the oddball Alaskan town in the early-nineties dramedy *Northern Exposure,* which, for those of you too young to remember, was the quirkiest show on TV outside of *Twin Peaks.* I didn't give the comparison much thought until I walked downtown for a cup of coffee. The local station KHNS was playing quietly on the stereo. The DJ played a Moody Blues song, followed by the local weather and an announcement about a change of location for the weekly vinyasa class, followed by a long fiddle instrumental, followed by an interview with one of the local museum's curators about its Tlingit art collection. My favorite part was the listener personals.

"Tyler lost his wallet, has searched the house high and low, and, yes, even in the couch. It's brown leather, so if you find it, please call him at 766-XXXX, because he's running really low on cat food. . . . Maureen is driving to Whitehorse this weekend and has room for one more in her car; call her at 766-XXXX. . . . Amy, Sylvester is trying to reach you and you probably know why, so please call him at 766-XXXX.

"And now, a little something from the Jerry Garcia Band."

CHAPTER EIGHTEEN: KLONDIKE FEVER

Skagway

When I left Dave Nanney at the Chilkat Eagle Bed and Breakfast to catch the forty-five-minute ferry ride to Skagway, he had a worried mother-hen look on his face. "Just remember, Skagway was totally about the almighty dollar when the Harriman Expedition got there back in 1899, and it's still all about the almighty dollar now," he said.

In 1899, Skagway was a magnet drawing a personality type never in scarce supply in Alaska: those who dream of getting rich quickly. In contrast to the orderly if oppressive corporate Treadwell Mine at Juneau, Skagway was a free-for-all. Muir had visited the new port city in 1897, on his sixth trip to Alaska, and described the scene as "a nest of ants taken into a strange country and stirred up by a stick."

Muir had arrived in August and was witnessing the start of the Klondike Gold

Rush. Word of a major strike in the Canadian Yukon the previous year had circulated south during the winter, and the arrival in San Francisco and Seattle of two ships carrying gold in the summer of 1897 inspired subtle headlines like these from the July 17 *Seattle Post-Intelligencer:*

GOLD! GOLD! GOLD! GOLD!
Sixty-Eight Rich Men on the
Steamer Portland

STACKS OF YELLOW METAL!
Some Have $5000, Many Have More,
and a Few Bring Out $100,000 Each

THE STEAMER CARRIES $700,000
Special Tug Chartered by the
Post-Intelligencer to Get the News

I had smiled at Nanney's concerns about Skagway — after all, the town's population was less than half that of sleepy Haines, so how bad could it be? But as the ferry pulled up to the dock, I immediately grasped his point. Skagway is wedged tightly between two rows of mountains. At its compact waterfront were four massive white cruise ships, parked like felled skyscrapers. Downtown Skagway was an Old West theme park, with false-front buildings and people dressed as gold rush characters posing on the street for photographs. The main thoroughfare was lined with shops catering to cruise ship passengers and could serve as the setting for a climactic movie shoot-out between rival turquoise-jewelry dealers. Because much of the town is part of the Klondike Gold Rush National Historical Park, there were also a lot of NPS rangers on hand. I joined the fringes of a tour group being led through downtown by a perky ranger named Sandra.

"What's the biggest reason people have always come to Alaska?" she asked the crowd.

"Scenery?" someone suggested.

"Yes, but the Grand Canyon has scenery, too."

"Wildlife?"

"Not exactly. A lot of places have wildlife." Several seconds of uncomfortable silence followed. "What about *money*?" Ranger Sandra finally asked, her eyes flashing wide as she held up a wad of fake bills. "Ten thousand people just arrived here today because Skagway is famous for *gold*. A lot of young people come here every summer hoping to make a lot of *money* by selling things to people like you, who paid a lot of *money* to get here." She waved her bills over her head. "Money! Money! Money!"

Ranger Sandra reached into her ample portfolio of visual aids and pulled out a large photograph that is one of the most famous images in Alaskan history. A single-file line of would-be prospectors, each laden down like a pack animal, inches its way up the steep, snowy Chilkoot Pass. To cross into the Canadian Yukon, where all the gold was, the Mounties guarding the border required each miner to have a year's worth of food and gear — about two thousand pounds of stuff. Multiple trips were needed to haul everything up, and that was just the start of the odyssey. Once prospectors reached the headwaters of the Yukon River, a 550-mile water journey lay ahead.

"The Panic of 1893 had set off a nation-wide depression," Ranger Sandra continued. The Panic of 1893 was one of the worst economic crises in U.S. history, driving unemployment in some urban areas above 25 percent. "It certainly didn't hurt that newspapers in Seattle and Chicago and New York were making a lot of *money* printing advertisements that promised anyone could get rich if they came to Alaska!" Some of the greatest fortunes made during the Klondike Gold Rush were amassed by those who "mined the miners" — the suppliers and hoteliers and steamship owners.

More than a hundred thousand sufferers of Klondike fever made their way north in an almost unbelievably short span of time. At the start of the summer of 1897, the port town of Dyea, a neighbor of and competitor to Skagway, had a single building. A year later, Dyea had four thousand residents, 150 businesses, and two newspapers. By the end of 1899 it was a ghost town again, and it remains so today.

The gold rush was already waning when the *Elder* arrived in 1899, but an excited mob on the dock greeted the steamship: "Hotel runners flourish their cards and call out the names of their various hostelries," John Burroughs wrote. "Women and girls, some of them in bicycle suits, push to the front and gaze intently at the strangers." (Burroughs may have been overreacting; a bicycle suit is about as revealing as a pair of mechanic's overalls.) Boys swarmed the *Elder*'s deck the moment the boat touched the pier, only to be "swept ashore again" by the crew. The two-year-old town was littered with fresh tree stumps, Burroughs wrote, "but the people already speak of the 'early times,' three years ago."

Getting to Skagway was relatively simple

if one could afford passage north from San Francisco or Seattle. It was at the back end of town, where the mountains began, that things became difficult. "Of all the routes into the Klondike, the Skagway Trail across the White Pass, more than any other, brought out the worst in men," writes historian Pierre Berton. The path into the mountains looked deceptively easy, a gentle incline through what one Harriman team member called Skagway's "suburbs." Within a few miles the trail became a steep, twisting ascent on a muddy path. Horses that arrived in Skagway having never borne a load suffered the most. "They died at the rocks, they were poisoned at the summit, and they starved at the lakes," wrote Jack London, who made the White Pass journey in late 1897. "They fell off the trail, what there was of it, and they went through it; in the river they drowned under their loads or were smashed to pieces against the boulders." Before long the White Pass route was nicknamed the Dead Horse Trail.

A new engineering marvel promised to put an end to the suffering. Edward Harriman probably didn't think much about building a railroad to Siberia, but the man who had spent his previous summer tinkering with grades and curves on the Union

Pacific took a keen interest in Skagway's new White Pass and Yukon Route Railroad. Twenty-one miles of track had been grafted onto the inhospitable trail with phenomenal speed. Two thousand laborers were laying down a mile or more of rail per week. The railroad had not yet been completed when the *Elder* arrived, but Harriman had arranged for a ride as far as the summit of White Pass. Any passengers who looked back toward town could have taken in breathtaking views of the Lynn Canal fjord.

The scenery immediately outside the windows was a mixture of the sublime and the terrible. The train rolled through a morgue of animal carcasses — packhorses that had dropped dead during the previous two winters and had not decomposed in the high-altitude chill. The artist Frederick Dellenbaugh recoiled from two animals whose legs stuck straight up like a dead beetle's. Team members admired the engineering feat as the train crossed trestles hundreds of feet high and followed a path gouged into the face of the inhospitable mountain. Burroughs brooded on the "cataclysmal" scenery and felt as if "I were seeing for the first time the real granite ribs of the earth." As if to prove he could find a familiar face anywhere, partway up the mountain Hart

Merriam spotted a group of scientists making the slog up the trail and shouted, "There are some of my boys!" A trio of colleagues from the U.S. Biological Survey were heading to the Alaskan bush to study life under the frugal field conditions familiar to scientists. The train backed up and the wildlife biologists enjoyed a strange and welcome ride to the top.

At the end of the line was a bleak, rocky expanse covered in mosses and lichens, and a desolate cluster of canvas huts known as White Pass City. A tattered American flag flapping in the cold rain marked the disputed boundary between the United States and Canada. Inside one of the huts, railroad officials had prepared a sumptuous meal for their esteemed visitors. Harriman asked Edward Curtis to photograph the assembled guests, but the poor midday light made the task impossible. The return trip down to Skagway was halted momentarily when someone noticed that Harriman was missing — the railroad man had wandered off to have a look around.

What the builders of the White Pass line did not know at the time was that the party in Skagway was closer to its end than its beginning. Gold fever in the Klondike was breaking; by 1900 Nome would be Alaska's new destination for fortune seekers. William Dall, the dean of Alaska experts, declared in *The Nation* that Skagway was Alaska's "town of the future," but for reasons other than gold. His prediction about the White Pass railroad was premature but prescient: "It will not be long before a ride to the summit will form a part of every well-conducted tourist trip."

Seven A.M. is rush hour at Skagway's cruise ship dock, when the white giants moor and disgorge their thousands of passengers for a day of gold rush fun. I lingered in my comfortable hotel bed and watched the smiling Anchorage newsreaders rattle off the day's top stories. The state had just broken another record for warmest spring. Towns as far away as Nome, which receives just a tiny fraction of the tourists Skagway sees, were eagerly preparing for the August maiden cruise of the *Crystal Serenity* through the Northwest Passage. Oil prices had climbed above fifty dollars, their highest level in almost a year, but not nearly enough to solve the ongoing budget crisis in Juneau. Police were investigating an illegal moose shooting near Denali. Bristol Palin had gotten married again.

With its corseted waitresses and fake streetcars, modern Skagway may have felt like a Gay Nineties amusement park, but unlike at Disney World, it wasn't hard to get a peek at the machinery that made it function. Just a block off the main drag at 8:55 in the morning, one could see twentysomethings with wet hair hustling to work from their dormitory-like lodgings, juggling jumbo coffees and smartphones. Two brothers from Mumbai whom I met at the gym said they'd come for the summer on H-1B work visas. Their airfares would be reimbursed only if they completed their contracts. The Skagway library was empty on the inside but bustling outside as cruise ship workers on break for the afternoon used the free Wi-Fi to make Skype calls home in a half-dozen languages.

The train ride up the White Pass route was fun, if ridiculously overpriced — an adult day pass to Universal Studios Hollywood is cheaper. When we returned to town, the day's cruise ships had already boarded for departure, and Skagway had emptied. The view down vacant Main Street toward the mountains was rather pretty.

Chapter Nineteen:
Russian America

Peril Strait

The *Elder* departed Skagway for Glacier Bay, from which it continued on to Sitka. Some people I wanted to meet near Glacier Bay were out of town for the week, so I headed to Sitka first. Since the southbound Marine Highway ferry wasn't due back in Skagway for several days, I flew out on one of Alaska's many small subregional carriers. Shortly after eight, I checked out of my hotel and walked five minutes to the airport. I rummaged through the collection of paperbacks that accumulates at every small transportation hub in Alaska. I waited for the pilot to come by, glance down at his clipboard, and ask for me by name. I climbed onto the wing of the four-seater after the other passenger, who was carrying a Jack Russell terrier, and squeezed into the copilot's seat. I had a nice chat with the pilot about his days flying for the navy in

Iraq while I took in the mountains and glaciers of Lynn Canal in reverse. By nine thirty I was sitting down to breakfast in Juneau, awaiting the twice-a-week ferry to Sitka.

The quickest water route from Juneau to Sitka, which lies about ninety miles southwest, is a crooked course via Peril Strait. Its treacherous channels are just a few hundred feet across between islands in some places. In 2004, the Alaska marine ferry MV *Le-Conte* grounded on a reef while making the run and nearly sank. The Harriman Expedition navigated Peril Strait at night, which is both impressive and a pity, because it is an exceptionally beautiful stretch of non-glaciated waterway in the Tongass National Forest. The proximity to the shoreline enhances the colors of everything — the whiteness of the snow on the peaks, the blue of the water, the green of the spruce trees, which were now near enough to see the eagles' nests in their branches.

The MV *Fairweather* was a catamaran and seemed to float like a hovercraft. I must have zoned out staring at trees in the observation lounge, because I started when I heard the words "Do you mind if I sit here?" spoken about six inches away from my ear. A fellow with a kind face and torn jeans had sat down next to me. His hair was short, with a tiny braid in the back like a taproot. He appeared to be riding out a skull-cracking hangover. He was headed to Sitka hoping to find work.

"I'm gonna go down to the harbor, look for my friend who's got a boat," he said. "I'll find something. And if not, there's always the cannery. They'll hire *anybody.*"

When I was in college, stories circulated every year about adventurous friends of friends who'd gone off to Alaska for the summer to work in a salmon cannery and returned with an ungodly pile of money. From what I could tell, the stories were probably true. Alaska is a very welcoming place for anyone who's willing to bust ass. Every town I'd seen on the Alaska coast had a fish-processing plant, but most of the labor force was now coming from the Philippines or Central America. College kids had moved on to mining the tourism riches of Skagway and Ketchikan.

My seatmate pulled out a small spray bottle and spritzed his palms with citrusy-smelling liquid. "This is herbal stuff; my girlfriend from Australia sent it to me," he said, rubbing his hands like a surgeon scrubbing for an operation. "That's how I came up here in the first place, in '91. Running away from a crazy lady in Oregon. It's hard to have a relationship working on the boats. Once you leave town you gotta follow the fish, and if you catch some, you stop wherever's closest to sell 'em. I might not get back to Sitka for two weeks.

"A lot of salmon have bites from other animals; you know, you can't sell those. The good ones, you fillet 'em, cut out the gills. Use a spoon on the back of your knife to pull out the blood vessels, rinse, pack 'em in ice, head to tail, like this." He stacked his hands in front of him. "Cover that with ice, make another layer. We might pick up four thousand pounds of ice when we're in harbor. Gotta hose everything down first."

"After that, can you still stand the taste of salmon?" I asked.

"Oh, yeah. I love salmon. Baked, smoked, barbecued. It's all good."

He scanned the room. Sitka is the sort of town that frequently turns up on "Best Places to Live" lists. It has historic architecture and a classical music festival and a very good French restaurant. The *Fairweather* passengers were more upscale than what I'd seen on other ferries, with more L.L.Bean hiking boots in view than XtraTufs. "They used to have bars on these boats," my new friend said. "I'd pull out my guitar and start playing and people would send over drinks. I'd get all tore up. One time I started playing 'Your Cheatin' Heart' by Hank Williams, and about three notes in, some dude from Metlakatla starts playing along at the piano! Man, I miss those bars. This boat don't even have a shower."

Peril Strait has a lot of twists and turns. My seatmate knew them all and announced each a minute in advance, a little kid who couldn't help spoiling the plot of a favorite movie. "I'm gonna step outside and have a look down," he finally said. "Water might be fifty feet deep, but you can see straight to the bottom it's so clear. Well, I'll be talking to you my brother."

The *Fairweather* squeezed between islands and snaked through a series of tight channels. The bank was now close enough that I could discern the personalities of individual spruce trees, the variation in their isosceles heights like those of people in a crowd. Some had crooked spines or missing limbs. A brown patch of dead trees sheltered shorter, younger trees within it. One passenger standing in the aisle pointed his camera toward the port side, and I turned to see porpoises turning cartwheels in the water.

"Yeah, this is the best part of the trip right

here," said a scratchy voice. A familiar scent, perhaps 90 percent Australian herbal spray and 10 percent metabolized ethyl alcohol, wafted from behind me. My friend with the taproot walked to the picture window at the front of the boat and pressed his nose against the glass. I wondered again how the *Elder* had ever managed this journey at night.

The deckhands gathered on the bow to perform their arrival rituals with the ropes. We made one final turn and were greeted by the bulk of Mount Edgecumbe, lurking over Sitka Sound.

In 1899, Sitka was the capital of the District of Alaska, home to a small population of cultured Americans. "People actually live in Sitka from choice, and seem to find life sweet," wrote John Burroughs, who was growing a little weary of Alaska's charming settlements but never tired of encountering people who'd read his books. "We met teachers from New England and people who keep in touch with current literature." The town's most striking buildings were left over from before the 1867 purchase, a time when Sitka had been the nexus of Russian economic and political activity in North America. The Harriman team toured the onion-domed Russian Orthodox church, filled with religious icons decorated in silver leaf. They showed more Byzantine Christian influence than Roman.

Following the church tour, Harriman hosted several of Sitka's most prominent citizens for champagne and a lavish dinner aboard the *Elder*. Among the guests was the district governor, John Brady. Brady had been a street urchin wandering downtown Manhattan when Theodore Roosevelt Sr., father of the future president, spotted him and funded his foster care with a family in Indiana. Brady eventually graduated from Yale and became an ordained Presbyterian minister and a protégé of Sheldon Jackson. As with Muir, it was Jackson who had directed Brady to Alaska. Even today, people in Alaska say that their state is like a very large small town, in that any person is rarely separated from any other by more than two or three degrees. (I found this to be largely true.) For whites in 1899, Alaska must have seemed like an extremely small town.

What was evident to many expeditioners as they toured the capital was that Sitka's prime had long since passed. During its heyday as a Russian port, it "was regarded as the most civilized town on the North

American Pacific coast," according to one historian. Buildings constructed by the Americans following the handover were shabby in comparison with the solid Russian ones. The spectacular three-story Russian governor's residence overlooking the harbor, known as Baranov's Castle, was in the years after 1867 "looted of every belonging, wantonly stripped, and debased," according to guidebook author Eliza Scidmore. It burned to the ground in 1894.

With its quaint downtown, farmers' market, and Pacific-facing view, Sitka is probably Haines's top competitor for cutest town in Alaska. To get a sense of what life had been like during the Russian era, when it was still known as "the Paris of the Pacific," I called local historian Harvey Brandt. We met in front of the Russian Bishop's House, one of the two best-known buildings remaining from Sitka's pre-American period, along with St. Michael's Cathedral. (The cathedral burned down in 1966 and was rebuilt using the original plans. Then as now, one of the more striking things about the building was its placement in the middle of Lincoln Street, the city's main avenue. Traffic divides around the church like a stream flowing around a rock.) In his crewneck sweater and ball cap,

Harvey looked a lot like Paul Newman during his doting-grandfather years. He had worked at the Bishop's House as a park ranger decades ago, and he retained a proprietary feeling about the building and grounds. "Here, smell this," he said, reaching down to pluck one of the decorative plants in the well-manicured front yard and holding it under my nose. "It's sweet cicely, used to make licorice. All this was a garden when the bishop was here." Harvey was a big fan of the bishop.

"Seventy percent of this building is original," Harvey said as we walked behind what had been the main residence. "When I arrived here in 1967, this was decrepit! Saint Michael's Cathedral was started immediately after this building was completed and dedicated. Probably the same crew. Finns." (Harvey was also a great admirer of Finns.) The chief manager of the Russian-American Company, a commercial arm of the government that oversaw its affairs in Alaska, was a Helsinki native who imported a team of Finnish master carpenters in the 1840s. The Bishop's House was owned until 1969 by the Russian Orthodox Church, headquartered in Moscow, which must have been a little strange during the Cuban Missile Crisis.

"How long are you in town?" Harvey asked. "I suppose you'll need access to the Park Service library. They've got the best collection of materials on the Russian era here outside of Juneau. I know that because I put it together."

We entered an NPS building next to the Bishop's House, surprising the young ranger on duty, a tall fellow with auburn dreadlocks who had almost gotten to his feet when Harvey started to grill him. "What happened to the organizational system I set up here? How late are you open? This man has come all the way from New York City to use this library." Sixty seconds earlier, I hadn't known of the library's existence.

"I, uh, don't know. I'm kind of new here. I could call . . ."

Harvey was already taking books from a shelf, flipping through them and handing them to me. "You'll want to look at this. And this. And especially this, by George Emmons. He lived right down the street here." Emmons was a friend of Hart Merriam's who had conducted extensive ethnological research among the Tlingit. While the *Elder* was in port, he gave Merriam and Grinnell a tour of the Tlingit village, where Merriam purchased a brown bear's skull. "We need a map," Harvey said. He turned to the ranger, who was mumbling nervously into the phone. "I assume you have copies of the 1845 map?"

"Um, I don't think so," the ranger said. "But your friend can use the library from two thirty to four thirty."

"It'll have to do," Harvey said, disappointed. We walked around to the front door of the Bishop's House and went inside. "I hope they'll let us see the attic," he said, eyeing a gate blocking the stairs. "Maybe we'll just go up later."

We walked through some rooms until we reached an enormous diorama of Sitka in 1845. This was, according to one nineteenth-century travel guide, the "golden age" of Sitka. Harvey had helped to design the miniature city, using old paintings as well as maps. Most of the tiny structures had been painted yellow with red roofs, bringing to mind William Dall's description of Sitka just before the sale: "The warm colors of the buildings, above which rose the pale green spire and bulbous domes of the Greek church, seen against steep, snow-tipped mountains densely clothed with somber forests of spruce, produced a picturesque effect unique among American settlements."

A four-way power struggle was under way

in the Pacific Northwest during the first half of the nineteenth century. Russia attempted to solidify its North American holdings by establishing a colony in Spain's territory of Alta California, less than a hundred miles north of the Spanish mission at San Francisco. The hope was to use what eventually became known as Fort Ross as a base of operations for fur gathering and agriculture. Neither venture quite panned out. The difficulties of administering a territory that ran from Sonoma County to the Aleutians eventually forced Russia to sign treaties opening the area to trade with the United States and Britain's Hudson's Bay Company. Spain's presence in North America ended with Mexico's independence, in 1821. Fort Ross was abandoned and sold in 1841 to John Sutter, who just a few years later would discover gold at his famous mill in the Sacramento Valley. By the mid-1840s, Russia was signaling to the United States that Alaska might be for sale, relatively cheap.

One outcome of this geopolitical jockeying is Alaska's strange border, which looks like it was made by someone who started cutting a straight line with a jigsaw and then suffered an epileptic seizure. The cause was a territorial dispute between the Hudson's

Bay Company and the Russian-American Company over whether Russia or Britain possessed trading rights in specific places along the Pacific coast. In 1825, a treaty fixed an international border at latitude fifty-four degrees forty minutes north — now the southernmost point of the Alaska panhandle. A much less specific line of demarcation was drawn parallel to the irregular coast by connecting the dots of mountain summits near the Pacific. Everything west of that imaginary crooked line was Russian. That vaguely defined boundary was still uncertain when the Harriman team saw the flags waving over White Pass City, where Canadian officials extracted duties from miners on land claimed by the United States. The dispute remained unresolved until an international tribunal established the international border in its current location in 1903. Canadian frustration with Britain's weak negotiating on its behalf — frustration that was completely justified, incidentally — accelerated the movement toward independence from the British Crown.

Harvey pushed through a door marked EMPLOYEE EXIT ONLY, which opened onto a stairwell. He looked in both directions, then picked up what looked like a miniature bearskin rug. "You ever see a sea otter pelt? Feel this. A hundred thousand hairs per square centimeter!" The fur had the softness of cashmere and the silky density of Vaseline.

One of the house's largest rooms had been converted into a gallery of major figures in Alaska and Sitka history. The first face we saw was a portrait labeled as Vitus Bering.

"That's not actually Bering; that's his uncle," Harvey said, scowling at the chubby face. In 1991, a team of archaeologists had ventured to the treeless island where Bering died of scurvy to dig up the explorer's grave. Forensic analysis of his remains showed that he was built more like a middleweight boxer than the oil-on-canvas fatso staring back at us. "Bering didn't discover Alaska, either. That's just stupid," Harvey said. "The Tlingit had long since established themselves here. There's an old story that the Tlingit were already here when Mount Edgecumbe was smoking." Edgecumbe, the dormant volcano that looms over Sitka, last erupted between 2500 and 2000 B.C.E. "That would mean they were here at least four thousand to forty-five hundred years ago."

By far the most gallery space had been dedicated to the namesake holy man for whom the Russian Bishop's House was built. "Now *this* guy, Bishop Innocent, was a genius!" Harvey said, gazing admiringly at his portrait. "He grew up penniless in Siberia, but by the time he spent the winter of 1823 here in Sitka, he'd become a good writer, a good scientist, and a very good priest. He was gifted with languages!"

Of all the extraordinary characters who have come through Alaska during its recorded history, one could argue that Bishop Innocent is the most fascinating. After stopping in Sitka, when he was still known as Father Ivan Veniaminov, he moved on in 1824 to Unalaska, a town in the Aleutian Islands. To the surprise of the Aleuts who'd lived under decades of abuse from Russian fur traders, Veniaminov set to constructing his own house and church and taught the local residents basic building skills as they were completed. He was a huge man, often described as "Paul Bunyan in a cassock," with a nimble mind. He built his own clocks and furniture, including a desk with an ingenious secret compartment that was still on display at his old home. Veniaminov quickly learned to speak the Aleut language, Unangan, then helped devise its first alphabet so that textbooks could be written and scriptures translated into the local tongue.

If the Aleuts were skeptical of Veniamenov's intentions, the Tlingit who greeted him upon his 1834 promotion to serve in Sitka were downright hostile. Only thirty years before, the Russians had laid siege to the town and built a heavily fortified stockade. When Veniaminov arrived, Harvey said, "the Russians had their cannons trained on the Tlingit village just outside the walls." Once again, Veniaminov showed unprecedented respect for the local culture and seems to have made a breakthrough after the inoculations he promoted spared lives during a deadly smallpox epidemic. "The Tlingits thought, 'Hmm, we *will* read this guy's Bible,' " Harvey said. In 1840, Veniaminov was named Bishop Innocent and put in charge of a diocese that stretched from Siberia to California.

What impressed me most about Bishop Innocent was his sea voyages. In the Aleutians he paddled from island to island in a *baidarka,* or Aleut kayak. While traveling, he took detailed scientific notes; one paddler I met later in Unalaska said that Innocent's journals were still useful for locating sources of drinking water. In 1836, he sailed to Fort Ross, the southernmost outpost of his enormous parish. Upon returning to Sitka, he built two small pipe organs that he donated to Catholic missions he had visited in California. After his promotion to bishop in Sitka, the historian Walter R. Borneman writes, "Between 1842 and 1852 he made three major visitations of some 15,000 miles each to newly created parishes in Alaska and Kamchatka."

While I was catching up on Bishop Innocent's achievements, Harvey's attention had been caught by a door with a sign that read MUSEUM STAFF ONLY, which he opened without hesitation.

"Because the Russians had trading agreements, like the one with the Hudson's Bay Company, you could get almost anything here, even a great bottle of wine," he shouted. I tiptoed in behind him. We were in somebody's office. "They moved my filing cabinet," he said, sounding displeased as he pulled a box off a shelf.

"You sure we're supposed to be in here, Harvey?" I said, looking over my shoulder.

"Oh, it's fine. I *made* this collection." He opened a large box, inside of which was a large brown square object imprinted with something. It looked like a giant Chunky bar. "You ever see a tea brick? You know how a samovar works, right?" He reached up for a giant serving urn and I imagined the smell of 180-year-old tea wafting through the building and wondered if the police would be called. Did I know any lawyers in Alaska? But Harvey had changed his mind and was already walking toward the front door, pausing for a second to look intently up the stairs to the attic. I never did find out why he wanted to go up there.

The end of Russian America came swiftly. In 1854, a conflict with Turkey over Russia's expansionism into the Black Sea region erupted into the Crimean War, which brought Britain and France in as allies on the Turkish side. Russia suffered a humiliating and costly defeat. Its Alaskan territory was expensive to maintain, and returns from furs had dropped. Wary of sea power Britain strengthening its position across the Bering Strait, Russia made clear to the United States that someone — anyone other than the British — would soon be purchasing Alaska.

Serious discussions between the two parties were delayed until 1865 because of the American Civil War. The process wasn't helped when the United States' primary negotiator, Secretary of State William Seward, was attacked and brutally stabbed, along with five other members of his household (plus one who was pistol-whipped), as part of the same assassination plot in which John Wilkes Booth shot and killed Abraham

Lincoln. None of the victims at Seward's house died. According to Harvey, the would-be assassin's blade may have been thwarted by a neck brace. "If Seward hadn't been run over by a carriage he wouldn't have been covered in casts," Harvey said. "That accident saved his life."

Contrary to the myth of Seward's Folly, the opportunity to purchase a massive piece of land rumored to be rich in resources for two cents an acre was popular from the start. The U.S. Senate approved the deal by a vote of 37 to 2. Seward is credited with choosing the name Alaska — "mainland" in Aleut — for the entire territory. The transfer of Alaska from Russia to the United States took place on October 18, 1867, in front of Baranov's Castle.

Harvey and I walked up to Castle Hill, the spot where the signing had taken place and the Stars and Stripes were first raised over American Alaska. There was a nice view of the harbor and an old Russian cannon that kids liked to climb on, but not much else was left from the golden age. Under our feet, though, was a giant midden heap attesting to Sitka's onetime role as the most cosmopolitan city on the West Coast. In the late 1990s, archaeologists had found thousands of artifacts including coconuts from Hawaii, Japanese coins, British buttons manufactured in Haiti, bits of French armaments, and tobacco pipes from the Ottoman Empire. "I suppose Sitka was a cultural stop when Harriman came in 1899, but they were really living on the reputation of the Russian era," Harvey said.

Baranov's Castle may have been gone by the time the *Elder* arrived, but its passengers were given a reception at Governor Brady's residence. Frederick Dellenbaugh noted the strangeness of donning formal clothing in the middle of an expedition and running the "gauntlet" of a receiving line made up of Sitka's elite. Harriman had asked Brady to invite the local Tlingit chief and several members of his tribe. He surprised them with a graphophone, with which he recorded the natives talking and singing. To their amazement, Harriman then played their voices back to them. Governor Brady volunteered to make what was presumably the first recorded speech by a politician in Alaska history.

As the *Elder* prepared to depart the next day, Harriman was showing off his machine to a group in front of Brady's home when an all-Native brass band marched up the street. The steamship left the dock to the sounds of Sitka rain and "The Stars and Stripes Forever."

CHAPTER TWENTY:
BEAR ESSENTIALS

Sitka

Harvey suggested that, rather than rush back for the last few minutes the NPS library was open, I should visit Sitka's public one. He thought they might have some old news clippings about the Harriman visit. They didn't, but they did have something just as good: original hardbound copies of the first two volumes of the *Harriman Alaska Series,* published in 1901. Harriman had paid to have Edward Curtis's gelatin silver prints reproduced as photogravures, giving them a rich, almost tactile texture. The most inviting of them was identified as *Footpath Along Indian River, Sitka.* I walked the mile from St. Michael's down to the end of the main waterfront road, which terminated at the Sitka National Historical Park. This was a large collection of totem poles with a nice visitor center where you could pick up maps and escape from the rain, which had begun to fall again. I inquired at the information desk about hiking the Indian River Trail the next day.

"Oh my God, that is my favorite trail — it is *so* gorgeous," said the young ranger on duty, who appeared to be about fifteen. The sinuous path cut through a rainforest of spruce and hemlock to reach a waterfall. "Just one thing — there was a bear spotted yesterday, so you'll really need to bring bear spray." She held up a small can that looked like a miniature fire extinguisher and contained weaponized chili pepper extract. "It's fifty dollars for the can, and I'm sorry you're not allowed to take it on an airplane," she said.

As it happened, I was planning to depart Sitka by air, because the ferry couldn't get me to my next destination for a week. There have been many occasions in my life, often after the consumption of hard liquor, when I have spent fifty dollars on goods and services less useful for my long-term health than bear spray. You need only watch and read the Alaska news for a few weeks in the spring and summer to understand that unpleasant human-ursine interactions are common enough to deserve their own news category: SPORTS — WEATHER — ENTERTAINMENT — MAULINGS. Dealing with

196

bears in Alaska was something you were just supposed to pick up by osmosis before getting yourself in trouble, like proper subway etiquette in New York City.

According to the various sources of information I had been collecting from the Park Service, the best strategy was to avoid bears altogether. This applies to both black bears and brown bears. (Grizzly bears are a variety of brown bear that lives inland.) Bears do not like to be surprised, so hikers are advised to make noise by clapping or attaching to their clothing the sorts of bells usually associated with sleigh rides and court jesters. Mother bears with cubs are especially ill-disposed toward unexpected visitors. ("Defensive encounters usually occur suddenly and at close distances," said one NPS brochure. In other words: "Oops. Hey! *Aaaaaaah!*") Bears are curious and may want to check you out; should you encounter one that is stationary, back away slowly. Though if the bear follows you, another brochure warned, "STAND YOUR GROUND." Never run from a bear, because it can move at thirty-five miles per hour and will happily chase you down like other prey animals. I was advised to keep in mind that "bears often make bluff charges, sometimes coming within 10 feet of their adversary, without making contact. Continue waving your arms and talking to the bear." This is the moment one is supposed to whip out the bear spray.

And if the bear isn't dissuaded by your flailing and oratory and aerosol Tabasco sauce and decides to attack you? A brown bear will typically stop attacking once it no longer feels threatened. We did say this was a brown bear, right? Because if it's a black bear, "DO NOT PLAY DEAD," one of the more dramatic brochures advised. "Most black bear attacks are predatory." (Fun fact: Black bears often have blond, brown, or cinnamon-colored fur. The easiest way to tell a black bear from a brown bear is that the latter has a distinctive shoulder hump. I guess if you're attacked, you should calmly reach around the bear's neck and feel for the hump.) You are *also* supposed to fight back ("vigorously!") against a brown bear "if the attack is prolonged and the brown bear begins to feed on you." What I really needed was a checklist for determining the moment a bear ceases her defensive attack and commences tearing into your flesh with the intent to swallow and digest you. Ideally it would be laminated.

I mentioned some of this at breakfast the next morning at the Sitka B & B at which I was staying. Everyone had strong opinions. A couple from Anchorage told how they'd moved from down south unaware of bear danger but quickly got brought up to speed.

"My first day at work, I met a coworker with one arm," the woman said. "You can't exactly introduce yourself and say, 'Nice to meet you — how did you lose your arm?' So I asked someone else and she told me, 'Oh, that? Bear attack.' Like she'd been in a fender bender."

"I won't show you the picture my buddy sent me of *his* coworker, but his face is ripped off," her husband said, spreading jam on a slice of toast. "They sewed it back on, but only one eye works. You probably saw they just found a guy in Anchorage, near dead. They thought he was a stabbing victim. The hospital up there has a doctor who's like the world's leading expert on bear attack injuries. He took one look at the guy in the ER and said, 'This wasn't a stabbing — this guy was mauled.' "

Ann, our grandmotherly host, came in from the kitchen with a pot of fresh coffee. "One time I was out hunting and I saw a grizzly knock down a tree and jump on it until it splintered," she said. "I thought, Well, I guess I'm going to hunt somewhere else today." There was a brief debate over whether it was preferable to bring a .38 or a .44 for protection when in bear country. The .44 was the majority choice.

"What about bear spray?" I asked. "Or wearing those bells to warn the bear you're coming?"

"Ha!" Ann laughed. "The spray is just as likely to hit you in the face as the bear. And they say those bells are effective mostly as a way to call the bear to dinner." Someone told a joke that I was to hear several times during my time in Alaska. When in the backcountry, you can tell if animals are nearby and active by watching for bear poop, but you need to be able to differentiate between black bear scat and brown bear scat. Black bear droppings contain twigs, berry seeds, and fish bones and smell like the forest. Brown bear droppings contain twigs, berry seeds, fish bones, and bells and smell like pepper spray.

"And it's no use bringing a dog, because if the dog sees a grizzly, it'll turn tail and lead the bear right back to you," Ann said. "I like the old saying: Bring a gun and someone slower than you."

It rained hard for the remainder of my time in Sitka. I took the fifty dollars I'd saved down to the slightly seedy Pioneer Bar, where on a Sunday afternoon not long ago, one patron pulled a gun on another in the men's room following an argument. Almost every flat surface had an ashtray on it — smoking in bars is against the law even in Alaska, but I didn't get the sense anyone in the P-Bar minded, or at least didn't care enough to pull a gun in the bathroom. Through the faint Marlboro haze I noticed photos all over the walls of what looked like Roman centurions standing with their shields. A closer inspection revealed that they were fishermen posing with hundred-pound halibut the size of surfboards.

"Do bears eat halibut?" I asked the man to my right.

"Brown bears? No, no," he said. "But polar bears, yeah, sure."

CHAPTER TWENTY-ONE:
THE ICE MOUNTAIN

Glacier Bay

Metlakatla, Wrangell, Juneau, Skagway . . .
For a boatload of outdoorsmen who'd given
their summers over to Harriman, the early
stops on the *Elder* provided frustratingly
few opportunities to explore the Alaskan
wilderness. Glacier Bay marked the beginning of the adventurous part of the expedition. The decision to budget five days there
was a testament to the area's spectacular
beauty and potential for scientific exploration. More than that, it was a tribute to John
Muir's role in making that splendor known
to the world. When Muir first paddled into
Glacier Bay in 1879, Alaska was still a
frozen mystery to virtually all Americans.
By the summer of 1899, a voyage through
the Alexander Archipelago was popular with
tourists and scientists alike; they often traveled on the same steamer. Many of them
came to see Muir Glacier, the spectacular

river of ice named for its scientific discoverer. Muir Glacier was the obvious first stop for the *Elder,* and its growing popularity did not go unnoticed. "A curious feature is a number of sections of boardwalk laid over the top of the moraine" — the accumulation of rocks and sediment bulldozed by a glacier's leading edge — "probably by some steam boat company that brought tourists," Frederick Dellenbaugh wrote in his journal.

Among the many curious features of John Muir's first voyage to Glacier Bay, in the fall of 1879, was its timing. October is not a great month to embark on a trip to the supermarket in Southeast Alaska, let alone an eight-hundred-mile paddle in a canoe open to the elements. "I would never dream of doing fieldwork in October in coastal Alaska," said glaciologist Martin Truffer, who has, among other things, camped out in Antarctica. October is the soggiest month in a very wet area — Ketchikan averages more than twenty inches of precipitation during those thirty-one days — and the temperatures at the northern end of the Inside Passage regularly fall below freezing. One legacy of a boyhood spent chiseling through sandstone was that Muir was blessed with an adventurer's immunity to discomfort. Hart Merriam recalled hiking deep into the Sierras during snow season with Muir, who brought along neither blankets nor bedding. An unfortunate side effect of Muir's spartan ethic was an almost autistic tendency to ignore the suffering of his travel companions. Once he heard reports from miners who'd ventured into Chilkat country, in the far north reaches of the Inside Passage, that extraordinary glaciers could be found there, Alaska's rainy season became a mere inconvenience. "Though this wilderness was new to me, I was familiar with storms and enjoyed them," Muir wrote. "I determined, therefore, to go ahead as far north as possible, to see and learn what I could."

Glacier Bay was the backup plan. Muir had originally intended to explore the northernmost reaches of Lynn Canal (which stretches from Juneau up to Haines and Skagway) with his Tlingit team from Wrangell. When he heard reports of drinking and fighting among the fearsome Chilkat — Kadachan's father had been shot in the melee — he turned his attention to "a large bay full of ice" that Sitka Charley recalled having seen while hunting seals as a boy. None of the others in the boat had ever seen treeless country of the sort Charley described, but Muir pushed his team on to the mouth of Glacier Bay. "Here we made a cold camp on a desolate snow-covered beach in stormy sleet and darkness," he wrote. In the morning they would "go in search of the wonderful 'ice-mountains' that Sitka Charley had been telling us about."

Muir's recollection of Charley's description clearly echoes the "solid mountains of ice" described by George Vancouver, whose 1794 chart Muir was using. A foggy morning revealed nothing. "Vancouver's chart, hitherto a faithful guide, here failed us altogether," Muir wrote. They had moved beyond the realm of terra incognita. According to the Englishman's exacting cartography, the bay in which they were camped didn't exist.

A trace of smoke appeared across the water, which led the six men to the camp of some Huna Tlingit seal hunters. The Huna were skeptical toward white men who arrived in so isolated a spot so late in the season yet professed not to be looking for gold. The hunters asked, perhaps tongue in cheek, if Young's missionary work included plans to "preach to the seals and gulls . . . and to the ice mountains." Soon, though, they not only confirmed Charley's report but augmented it. Muir recorded that they called the place Sit-a-da-kay or "Ice Bay."

(A more accurate translation of the Tlingit name, Sit' Eeti Gheiyi, would be "The Bay in the Place of the Glacier.") His interest was piqued by the information that "the ice mountain they knew best was at the head of the bay." Sitka Charley begged off acting as navigator; from what he'd already seen, the landscape he visited as a boy had changed drastically. Muir agreed to hire one of the Huna hunters as a guide.

Glacier Bay is shaped roughly like a leafless elm tree, with a wide trunk that branches into several fjords and inlets to the north. At the tip of most branches, where the salt water ends, a glacier begins — or rather, since glaciers are dynamic, this is the point where a slow-moving river of ice collides with the sea. As Muir and his team paddled northwest into the barren wilderness in a driving rain, they spotted their first enormous glacier. Muir was awed by the power of its calving ice and spellbound by the visible effects of its force. "All the rocks are freshly glaciated, even below the sea-level," he wrote, "nor have the waves as yet worn off the surface polish, much less the heavy scratches and grooves and lines of glacial contour."

Eager to reach the great ice mountain waiting at the head of the bay, Muir insisted that the team push on. The Huna guide overruled his client, reporting that the distance was too far and that "landing there was dangerous even in daylight." The next day was a Sunday. Young wished to observe the Sabbath, and the others wished to avoid traveling through another storm. Muir, impatient, climbed the slope above their camp alone, fording muddy torrents of rain and meltwater and "wallowing in snow up to my shoulders." Muir was a gifted climber who in Young's opinion seemed to "slide" up mountain faces as if he had a "negative gravity machine strapped on his back." Muir scrambled fifteen hundred feet up to a ridge and waited for the view to clear.

At length the clouds lifted a little, and beneath their gray fringes I saw the berg-filled expanse of the bay, and the feet of the mountains that stand about it, and the imposing fronts of five huge glaciers, the nearest being immediately beneath me. This was my first general view of Glacier Bay, a solitude of ice and snow and new-born rocks, dim, dreary, mysterious.

Muir returned to camp wet, cold, and ecstatic. His awaiting companions were wet, cold, and mutinous. It was now late October, and parts of the bay had begun to freeze over. Toyatte feared that Muir was leading them into a "skookum-house," or jail, of ice. The Huna guide, unaccustomed to Muir's personality quirks, questioned the sanity of a man who climbed ice mountains in a storm. The five Tlingit sat around a small fire, "telling sad old stories of crushed canoes, drowned Indians, and hunters frozen in snowstorms." Muir understood that, having at last found himself "in the midst of so grand a congregation of glaciers," his chance to see them up close might be slipping away. The off-the-cuff pep talk he gave around their little fire that night was surely one of his masterpieces.

"For ten years I had wandered alone among mountains and storms, and good luck always followed me," Muir told them. "With me, therefore, they need fear nothing." *Have faith in God,* Muir told them, *and in me, and everything will be okay.* When he finished, Toyatte told him "that even if the canoe was broken he would not greatly care, because on the way to the other world he would have good companions."

The heavy rain and snow continued the next day as the team continued north. Shortly before reaching the day's camp, they stopped at what is now called the Hugh

Miller Glacier to examine what Muir described as the "imposing army of jagged spires and pyramids, and flat-topped towers and battlements" lurking behind its imposing face. Its range of colors began at pale indigo and intensified in cracks to "the most startling, chilling almost vitriol blue." The ice seemed to rise up from the water like a staircase, then flattened into a white prairie that sloped gently upward to infinity.

The wind accelerated, pushing the canoe deeper into the bay. "We were driven wildly up the fjord," Muir wrote, "as if the storm-wind were saying, 'Go, then, if you will, into my icy chamber, but you shall stay in until I am ready to let you out.'" Floating bergs observed through the curtain of sleet crowded against the massive ice wall that had discharged them, a signal that the ice mountain was near. The team landed on a rocky strip of land near the wall.

While camp was being set up for the night, Muir again climbed into a storm hoping for a better view of his surroundings. As he ascended, the weather calmed, the clouds "slowly lifting their white skirts," to reveal "the highest of all the white mountains, and greatest of the glaciers I had yet seen." This many-tentacled ice beast had as its body "a gently undulating plain" that filled the fjord for a relatively smooth fifteen to twenty miles. This mass was fed from above by frozen streams that flowed down from the ring of tall surrounding peaks, "mountains which were as white as the snow-covered ice in which they were half, or more than half, submerged." The glaciers Muir knew from the Sierra Nevada, having nearly completed their work, were almost exhausted. This massive blanket of ice was "covering the hills and dales of a country that is not yet ready to be brought into the light of day."

Muir spent a jubilant day exploring his discovery. The next morning dawned clear and cold, the sun hidden beyond the cliffs of the fjord as the team made preparations to return home. As the sun emerged above the peaks to the east, "we were startled by the sudden appearance of a red light burning with a strange unearthly splendor on the topmost peak of the Fairweather Mountains," Muir wrote. "Instead of vanishing as suddenly as it had appeared, it spread and spread until the whole range down to the level of the glaciers was filled with the celestial fire." The crimson intensified until the peaks above seemed to glow like molten iron. Slowly, the blazing light descended, catching every peak and glacier "until all the mighty host stood transfigured, hushed, and thoughtful, as if awaiting the coming of the Lord."

The moment obviously stuck with Muir, who spent several hundred words describing it in his final book, written more than thirty years later. Hall Young recalled the explorer's immediate reaction being more succinct: "We have met with God!"

Chapter Twenty-Two:
Hunting with Harriman

Howling Valley

Edward Harriman had not forgotten about his bear. As the *Elder* entered Glacier Bay, Captain Peter Doran struggled to find anchorage in the eighty fathoms of water just two miles off Muir Glacier's face. A photo taken by Hart Merriam shows a slurry of densely packed bergs bobbing in waters that have the consistency of a poorly blended daiquiri. Muir knew this country well; during an extended visit in 1890, he had constructed a small cabin at the foot of the glacier. With bear hunting once again on the agenda, Muir conveniently recalled once having wandered into a gap that he nicknamed Howling Valley because of the hundreds of wolves that could be heard caterwauling there. It was only about eighteen miles away on foot. "It's so easy to get at; that's the beauty of it," Muir declared, ticking off the varieties of big game whose tracks he'd seen there: bears, wolves, caribou, mountain goats. "When ye're there, all ye have to do is hunt." With the summer solstice fast approaching, hours of daylight remained after dinner. Harriman immediately dispatched seven packers with camping gear, then followed closely behind with five other hunters, including Grinnell and Merriam. All of them carried Winchester rifles.

There is something irresistible about watching the face of a calving tidewater glacier, the anticipation of beautiful violence. Gazing at Muir Glacier, Frederick Dellenbaugh was mesmerized by "the way the great masses seem to hesitate a moment or two in the air" before plunging into the water below. The wonders of Glacier Bay seem to have left even Burroughs, known for his ability to effortlessly churn out reams of prose, momentarily stymied; he recounted that "we were in the midst of strange scenes, hard to render in words." All night, as the passengers slept aboard the *Elder,* they were intermittently awakened by the cracks and roars of calving ice and rocked by the waves that followed.

Muir had yet to resolve his feelings toward Harriman after two weeks in his company. He was suspicious of his fortune and contemptuous of his desire to shoot a bear. Muir never carried a gun on his adventures and, though he ate meat, he disapproved strongly of killing for sport. Near the end of the 1879 trip, when everyone was hungry, Hall Young asked Toyatte why he and his men hadn't shot any ducks. "Because the duck's friend would not let us," the chief replied. "When we want to shoot, Mr. Muir always shakes the canoe." Twenty years later, his feelings had only deepened. He described the shooting of a deer by one local in Sitka like a double homicide: The man had "murdered a mother deer and threw her over the ridgepole of his shanty, then caught her pitiful baby fawn and tied it beneath her dead mother."

Harriman was proving to be more difficult to pigeonhole than the trigger-happy hunters Muir despised. As the *Elder* departed Juneau, Harriman spotted a skinny stray dog that had wandered onto the ship. When he learned that the pooch had come aboard following one of the crew, Harriman sought out the sailor and informed him firmly that he was responsible for keeping his friend well fed until he could be taken back to Juneau on their return south. "As long as this dog is on board, he is our guest," Harriman said.

As the doting father of two daughters back in California, Muir also admired Harriman's hands-on parenting. Here was a man who could be seen racing his young sons around the deck of the *Elder* and took joy in marching alongside the youngest, three-year-old Roland, as he pulled a toy canoe on a string. The Harriman daughters were curious and eager to get their feet dirty (once they'd lifted their long skirts) and assist with scientific work. As their father tramped off into the mountains in pursuit of bear, Muir led Mary and Cornelia Harriman, their cousin Elizabeth Averell, and friend Dorothea Draper — a group he had dubbed "the Big Four" — on a three-mile hike across the glacier named for him.

Muir seems to have left out a few important details from his account of Howling Valley's big-game potential, such as how his trek there had ended with him snow-blind, stumbling into a pool of meltwater over his head and shivering naked through the night in his sleeping bag. Harriman's bear-hunting party walked up and down over the slippery glacier until 11:00 P.M., slept lightly, and started again at 4:00 A.M. The second day, "we trudged slowly over ice in a drenching rain," Merriam recorded in his journal. This was a prelude to a long march through knee-deep wet snow. The experienced scout Yellowstone Kelly,* who'd spent the prior summer in Alaska, took stock of conditions and dropped out. Urged on by Harriman, team members roped themselves together to forge ahead across several snow-filled crevasses. When they finally gazed down into Howling Valley, Merriam wrote, "we not only saw no signs of life, but not a single track." The hunt was abandoned.

One bit of drama remained near the end of the party's twenty-four-mile slog back to camp. As they arrived, a sequence of icebergs began cracking from the face of Muir Glacier, the salvo escalating until most of the ice wall seemed to be crashing into the sea. Merriam watched in wonder as the tremendous splash birthed a wave a hundred feet high — "one of the most impressive things I ever saw." His excitement turned to fear when he realized that the

* Luther "Yellowstone" Kelly was famous throughout the Old West as a hunter, trapper, explorer, and army scout. He'd fought in the Civil War, survived a Sioux warrior's arrow, and befriended Theodore Roosevelt. By the end of 1899 he was back in the army, fighting a rebellion in the Philippines. A fictionalized version of his life was released as the film *Yellowstone Kelly* in 1959.

photographers Curtis and Inverarity were rowing a small canvas canoe directly in the path of the giant wave. The two were experienced with small craft in rough seas, and they paddled furiously into the face of the oncoming wave. As their fellow expeditioners held their breath, the two men rode up and over to safety.

All the Howling Valley hunters returned in bad shape, but Merriam seems to have suffered the most, crippled by an arthritic knee and a bruised foot that would lay him up in bed the next day. Muir was among those who went out to assist him back to camp. His sympathy may have been motivated by guilt. John Burroughs observed later that "there might not be any bears in Howling Valley after all — Muir's imagination may have done all the howling."

To men who had never before witnessed the power of glaciers, the entire land around Glacier Bay seemed to be in transition. "We saw the world-shaping forces at work," Burroughs wrote of the debris that glaciers had unearthed. The smooth and rounded rocks deposited by the glacier's retreat "had evidently passed as it were through the gizzard of the huge monster," leaving behind the mineralogical raw ingredients for future forests. Accustomed to the eastern landscape, shaped by glaciers thousands of years ago, Burroughs marveled at the opportunity to scramble "over plains they had built yesterday." A group of bird specialists spent three days collecting specimens on Gustavus Peninsula, a long, flat stretch of land formed from glacial deposits that appeared to be "not much over a century old." (William Dall named the new peninsula after the king of Sweden in 1878.) The spot was now wooded enough to host more than forty species of birds.

Perhaps most striking was the shrinkage of the glaciers themselves. Muir Glacier had lost four miles of ice in the twenty years since its namesake had first laid eyes on it. At the head of the bay, the Grand Pacific Glacier had retreated far enough onto land that its ice had separated into three individual glaciers.

CHAPTER TWENTY-THREE: TRANSITIONS

Gustavus

The official website for Gustavus advises visitors that, while it is possible to rent a car or call a taxi to meet one's transportation needs, "most guests just prefer to borrow a bike to get around town . . . or put out your thumb." Things are a little more informal and spread out in the northern half of the Inside Passage, including the ferry schedule. Sitka-to-Gustavus ran only once a week and took twenty-seven hours on two boats, but I could fly the same route any day I wanted. The flight from Sitka to Juneau took five minutes. The one from Juneau to Gustavus lasted twelve.

The tiny airport parking lot doubled as the informal baggage claim. A guy from Alaska Airlines carried out everyone's belongings by hand, much of it fishing gear. The mood among the few dozen people gathered felt more like a block party than an arrivals area. Neighbors stood chatting in small groups, trading funny stories and bits of gossip and asking about mundane details related to family members. I happily would have hitchhiked into town, except there really isn't a "town" part of Gustavus in the same way there is in Juneau or Skagway. Also, Kim Heacox had come to pick me up.

Heacox was easy to recognize — slight build, glasses, collar-length hair. We'd met a couple of months earlier in Anchorage, a city where he'd once lived but which he said now sometimes overwhelmed him with its crush of traffic and people. He was one of Alaska's best-known writers, an acclaimed photographer, an expert on John Muir, a former park ranger, and a serious national parks enthusiast. (I'd first heard his soft voice waxing poetically about the great outdoors in a Ken Burns documentary.) He'd channeled his passions into several books, including one that argued convincingly that Muir's six visits to Glacier Bay were the cornerstone of the American conservation movement.

Due to the town's proximity to Glacier Bay, Gustavus is growing. Not so much in ways the Chamber of Commerce might promote, though the population did see a bump from 429 to 434 between 2000 and 2015. It's the size of the landmass on which Gustavus sits, rather, that is increasing. Just as climate change has brought more rain to Southeast Alaska (because a warming ocean sends more moisture into the atmosphere through evaporation), the melting of billions of tons of ice in Glacier Bay is causing land that was depressed under the massive weight of glaciers to rise as much as two inches per year. This process is called isostatic rebound. One waterfront property owner in Gustavus unexpectedly found himself with so much bonus acreage that he built a rudimentary nine-hole golf course on land that had been underwater during the Harriman Expedition.

Heacox drove us out to the tidal flats near the town's ferry dock and pointed at the acres of new land that had emerged since he first visited Glacier Bay, in 1979. "Look at that," he said. "This is a land that is in the process of creation. This is land being *born,* man. That still amazes me."

Heacox had been another of those young men who wander the West as a circuitous route to Alaska. A geology professor had planted the seed with a talk about a bay near Juneau where ice was withdrawing, revealing nature's secret recipe for transforming rock into soil, grassland into forest. Down in the deserts of the Four Corners area, he searched for his hero, Edward Abbey, the radical environmentalist and author of *The Monkey Wrench Gang,* a novel about eco-saboteurs who gleefully break the law to preserve threatened wilderness. Instead of Abbey, Heacox found a nine-fingered blues guitarist who told him, "Alaska: There's nothing like it. It makes all these other parks down here look like *boutique wildernesses.*"

Kim had met his wife, Melanie, while they were both wearing "the old green and gray" as seasonal park rangers at Glacier Bay National Park. Ninety percent of visitors to Glacier Bay arrive on cruise ships that never stop in Gustavus, and couldn't even if they wanted to, because the dock can't accommodate them. Instead, the Park Service dispatches rangers who climb aboard the various *Princess Somethings* and *Whatever of the Seas* that sail through and give lectures to guests.

As we followed the dirt road that led to his house, Kim told me that he and Melanie had Frank Lloyd Wright's philosophy of organic architecture in mind when designing a place to live; the winding driveway alone took him a year to map in order to avoid chopping down big trees. Its seamless integration of two connected buildings with the surrounding woods did remind me of Wright's Taliesin. I didn't, however, remember seeing cans of bear spray strategically placed on the front porch at Wright's home. (The Heacoxes purchased the land on which they'd built their house from the estate of a photographer friend who'd been killed by a brown bear.) The scene's Enchanted Forest effect was magnified when we arrived to find Melanie outside in a colorful headscarf, watering the flowers in her hummingbird garden.

Melanie was finishing up her annual stint training the interpretive rangers who explained Glacier Bay to visitors. Like many gifted teachers, she combined infectious enthusiasm with rigorous organizational discipline; the Heacox home was filled with to-do lists, encouraging messages written on Post-its, and neat stacks of reading material to be devoured. She was preparing to spend a day on a cruise ship offering support to her last interpretive trainee for the season, who would be giving her first solo presentation before a crowd. "I'll step off that ship, file the payroll paperwork I've got filled out, press SEND on the thank-you e-mails I have queued up on my computer, and I'll be done for the year!" Melanie said. When she finished watering the flowers, she took five minutes to show me how to set up a tent, a skill that had eluded me for three decades.

The Heacox home phone number was a good one for a contestant to have on hand if the subject of John Muir or Glacier Bay came up on *Who Wants to Be a Millionaire*. I'd asked them to help me find locations that Muir had visited. Melanie had picked Russell Island, the spot where Muir had climbed a small mountain to catch his first glimpse of the vast Grand Pacific Glacier. "They put up the tents on October 27, 1879 — I just looked that up the other day," she said. "You'll be camping where John Muir camped! Of course, the island was half under ice at that time."

The years 1879 and 1899 appear frequently on maps of Glacier Bay, marking the positions of glaciers as witnessed by Muir during his first visit and his last with the *Elder* team twenty years later. Most of these were now in what Melanie called "catastrophic retreat." Unlike the glaciers that covered much of the American Midwest twenty thousand years ago and created the Bering Land Bridge, Glacier Bay's ice is the product of a rather recent phenomenon, the

Little Ice Age. This period of unusually cool temperatures lasted roughly from 1300 to 1850 and is known primarily for its effects in Europe. The River Thames frequently froze over solid enough that London winter carnivals were held atop its ice. In 1644, the French alpine village of Les Bois summoned the bishop of Geneva to combat an ice river that was advancing at a rate of "over a musket shot every day."

Similar effects were felt in Alaska. The graphics on the detailed NPS Glacier Bay map that Melanie unfolded for me on her kitchen table told an incredible story. In 1680, Glacier Bay — today more than ten miles wide in some parts and more than a thousand feet deep — does not exist. Its upper two-thirds are covered by ice, and its lower third is a green valley bisected by a stream. By 1750, at the peak of the Little Ice Age's effects in Glacier Bay, the ice has marched all the way down to the mouth of today's bay and beyond, extending into Icy Strait. According to Tlingit oral history, Kim told me, the ice had advanced "as fast as a limping dog could run." (Similar, more scientific, observations were also recorded in 1950 for the Muldrow Glacier, on Denali, which surged more than a thousand feet in a single day.)

When Vancouver arrived, in 1794, the ice had retreated a few miles back inside the mouth of the bay. In 1879, Muir found Vancouver's charts no longer accurate, because the glacier had pulled back another forty miles, leaving behind the thousand-foot-deep bay it had gouged out of the valley. Today the ice is sixty-five miles back from where it was 250 years ago. A visitor who stops at the pile of rocks that remain from Muir's cabin at the foot of his namesake glacier now has to travel thirty miles up an inlet to see the remnants of the ice that once discharged bergs so large they threatened to capsize Harriman Expedition canoes.

Melanie compared the conditions necessary to maintain a healthy glacier to balancing a checkbook. If the amount of snow that falls during the winter and gets compacted into glacial ice is greater than the ice that calves off or melts during the summer, everything is okay. There is no deficit, and sometimes there is a surplus. Glaciers are finicky beasts, though. When snowfall declines or temperatures rise too high to maintain that equilibrium, they retreat. Usually. In Glacier Bay, the Johns Hopkins Glacier retreated catastrophically for the first three decades of the twentieth century, then reversed course and began growing. It extends farther now than it did in 1929.

Ten years ago, Melanie said, rangers in Glacier Bay would often find themselves cornered by climate change deniers. Now visitors were uncertain what to think. The effects of climate change were becoming harder to ignore, but half of the country's politicians (and most of Alaska's) were insisting it didn't exist. Not everyone was conflicted. When I accompanied Kim down to the boat dock at Bartlett Cove to watch him give a short presentation about Glacier Bay to the passengers of a high-end eco-tour boat visiting the bay, one red-faced guest was screaming to the expedition leader that climate change was a liberal conspiracy in which scientists were being paid off. After the tirade ended, I asked the trip leader how he'd responded. "I told him that if I had a lump on my neck and went to a hundred doctors, if ninety-five of them told me to get it removed and five told me to treat it with herbs and roots, I'd get it removed," he said.

The next morning Kim made fruit smoothies with vanilla ice cream and we discussed the Harriman Expedition's legacy. His take was that the real value of the trip wasn't in the research conducted but in the "cross-pollination of ideas."

"These guys spent two months together," Kim said. "You can't measure the importance of something like the growing friendship between George Bird Grinnell and John Muir."

Muir's self-identification as "author and student of glaciers" in the *Elder*'s logbook may have been Scottish modesty, or it may have been a realistic acknowledgment of how his status had changed since his first visit to Alaska. While few equaled his expertise in glaciology, it was his writing on behalf of safeguarding wilderness that had catapulted him to national fame. No person played a more important role in that development than Robert Underwood Johnson, the associate editor of the prestigious *Century Magazine*. There is no record of Muir and Grinnell's having communicated with each other prior to the Harriman Expedition, but they definitely shared ideas with Johnson as the intermediary.

Johnson traveled to California from New York City in 1889 looking to assign stories. Among his goals was to get work out of Muir, who spent most of the 1880s running the fruit farm he had taken over when he had married Louie Strentzel in 1880. "I am degenerating into a machine for making money," he lamented to Hall Young during a visit from the minister. Johnson's timing was excellent. Muir was eager to start writing again and had a general subject in mind: the horrible state of affairs in Yosemite Valley. Amid one of the most iconic landscapes in America, virtually unregulated entrepreneurs were raising livestock ("hoofed locusts" was Muir's term for the wildflower-munching sheep), operating sawmills, and luring tourists to seedy hostels. "Perhaps we may yet hear of an appropriation to whitewash the face of El Capitan or correct the curves of the Domes," Muir wrote. Johnson joined Muir on a camping trip to the valley and was struck by its beauty and its abuse. "Obviously the thing to do is make Yosemite National Park around the Valley on the plan of Yellowstone," Johnson told Muir.

Johnson likely had in mind a conservation strategy pioneered by Grinnell. Yellowstone had been named America's first national park in 1872, but more as a cabinet of wild curiosities for tourists to gawk at than as a nature sanctuary. Almost no federal funds had been set aside for its care. Poachers killed Yellowstone's trophy animals with impunity, including some of the last remaining buffalo; tourists carved their names into rocks; residents of towns outside the park's boundaries treated its forests as a ready source of firewood. The greatest threats to Yellowstone were the railroads and developers who wanted to maximize the park's commercial potential. Grinnell was the first major figure to combine publicity and politics in the name of defending public wilderness, using the pulpit of *Forest and Stream* and his connections in Washington to convince congressmen that Yellowstone belonged to all of the American people. The formation of the Boone and Crockett Club with Theodore Roosevelt was the logical next step, creating the first organization with "the explicit purpose of affecting national legislation on the environment," as historian Michael Punke writes.

With much pleading and cajoling, Muir produced two articles he had promised Johnson for *The Century,* which appeared in the magazine's August and September 1890 issues. His message was explicit: Yosemite was one of America's natural crown jewels and deserved to be protected. Johnson, meanwhile, lobbied legislators in Washington. On October 1, 1890, Congress named Yosemite America's newest national park. In a somewhat awkward arrangement, the state of California maintained ownership of

Yosemite Valley, which, along with the Mariposa Big Tree Grove, had been granted to the state for safekeeping by President Abraham Lincoln in 1864.

Not long after, Johnson inquired of Grinnell whether the Boone and Crockett Club might be interested in establishing "a Yosemite and Yellowstone defense association." Both Grinnell and Muir agreed it was a good idea, but Grinnell's fellow Boone and Crockett members disagreed.* Muir instead joined forces with a group of Bay Area professors who had discussed a similar plan to preserve land in California. On June 4, 1892, twenty-seven men met in San Francisco to form the Sierra Club. Muir was chosen as president, a title he would hold until his death.

When they set foot on the *Elder,* Muir and Grinnell were leaders of a crusade that had not yet found its way. In the years following the Harriman Expedition, the two branches of American conservation — the spiritual children of Henry Thoreau and the practi-

* Natural historian Paul Brooks points out that a probable dilemma was skirted by the B and C's reluctance: Would Muir have been required to hunt three big-game animals to satisfy the membership requirements?

cal sportsmen of the Boone and Crockett Club — would rub together to ignite the modern environmental movement. When he died, in 1938, the *New York Times* obituary called Grinnell "the father of American conservation." Environmental history has since largely overlooked the practical Grinnell's contributions, though. The mystical Muir is the figurehead who has appeared on postage stamps and coins.

"He came along at the exact right time," Kim said of Muir's prominence. "He's got a catchy name and a great image. Thin, long beard, hat, walking stick. He knew his Bible front to back, so he could use spiritual language that caught a lot of people. He could come up with these catchy little phrases, beautiful one- or two-sentence summations of the value of nature. 'Climb the mountains and get their glad tidings. Nature's peace will flow into you as sunshine flows into trees.' Or, 'When we try to pick out anything by itself, we find it hitched to everything else in the Universe.' That is ecology before there was the science of ecology."

By 1899, Muir had also become a major irritant to businessmen who made their fortunes from exploiting natural resources. "The outcries we hear against forest reservations come mostly from thieves who are wealthy and steal timber by wholesale," he wrote shortly before receiving Harriman's invitation. Muir's ability to mix dreaminess with feistiness reminded me a little of Kim. He loved to wander off in the woods and to walk around the house shirtless, strumming Beatles tunes on his guitar, but as president of the Friends of Glacier Bay, he had fought successfully to phase out commercial fishing in the park, much to the annoyance of some neighbors and powerful political foes, such as Senator Frank Murkowski. (Murkowski later became governor and appointed his daughter Lisa to his vacant Senate seat, an unpopular move that helped open the door for a little-known candidate named Sarah Palin to take his new job.) As Alaska's ecology mutated in unpredictable ways and its economy suffered from the collapse of oil prices, the state's two senators and its lone congressman, Don Young, had committed to a clear path for the future: to push for new oil drilling in places like ANWR.

"Alaska isn't the last frontier when it comes to climate change," Kim said. "It's the first frontier." Having just completed the warmest spring on record, the state was well on its way to its hottest year ever.

"When someone like Don Young wants to drill for oil in the Arctic National Wildlife Refuge, that's the exact wrong thing to do. It's morally bankrupt. That's the equivalent of saying in 1859, 'Bring over more slaves.' "

It occurred to me, as I rode one of Kim's rusty old mountain bikes a mile up the two-lane road, over the Salmon River, past purple fields of lupine in which a moose ambled gawkily like a preschooler trying on her mother's high heels, that one of the nicest things about Gustavus is that while it feels about a million miles from the rest of America, it's a hard place to get lost. A game of Chutes and Ladders promises more potential twists than the roadways of Gustavus. Once I'd hung a left out of Kim's driveway, even the wildest of wrong turns could dead-end only at the ferry dock, the airport, or the national park headquarters. The closest thing to a business district was the intersection where the coffee shop and café sat kitty corner from a refurbished 1930s gas station. A couple of times I pedaled straight toward the mountains to the one-room library, where I could check e-mail. Gustavus has been wired for electricity only since the 1980s, and I got the sense that if the power went out for a few weeks, people would carry on just fine; some might not even notice. At the tiny post office, people conducted epistolary correspondences through messages scribbled on notices taped to the wall. To an Outsider, each was a short story that raised more questions than it answered.

Does anyone know how Alice is doing now? I haven't seen her since she moved away.

I saw her recently in Florida and she looked a lot better, considering.

I didn't even need to wear a bike helmet, since the only safety risk was losing one's balance when waving back at the drivers who passed every few minutes. Kim and Melanie insisted that the interminable October rains kept the population down, but I wondered if the indoor time enforced by that gray weather came with a productivity bonus. Three of the first five people I met in town had written novels, including one homeschooled twelve-year-old neighbor who could field-dress a black-tailed deer and whose expertise on edible spruce tips was widely sought.

When I first contacted him, Kim had

insisted that in order to understand the excitement Muir had experienced on his trips to Glacier Bay, I really needed to do so from the vantage point of a kayak. "You might want to get out on the water alone; it could really be a life-changing experience," he said. Since I'd never paddled a kayak, or even a canoe, it seemed more likely to be a ending experience. Kim said he knew someone who'd keep me from drowning.

My second day in town, David Cannamore picked me up in a borrowed van belonging to the kayak rental company he worked for. David was twenty-seven, a former prep basketball star who'd grown up outside Anchorage. He was six foot four and blond and had a scruffy beard; when he walked, he had the tall man's habit of ducking slightly, as if he'd banged his head on one too many doorframes. He was a man given to epiphanies. He knew he wanted to marry his wife, Brittney, the moment he'd laid eyes on her. ("She took a little longer to come around," he recalled.) On a kayak trip he'd taken with his dad the summer after he graduated from high school, he'd spotted an orca and knew instantly that his basketball career was doomed.

"You know how people say, 'I didn't realize it at the time, but it was a moment that changed my life'? Not me. I knew at that moment I wanted to work with orcas. Something had changed chemically." He and Brittney now spent their winters as caretakers at a remote marine biology institute on the British Columbia coast, where they tracked whales all day and night, got a lot of reading done, and looked forward to weekly baths heated by firewood.

Gustavus wasn't a place where you ran in to the store to grab milk while someone waited in the car with the engine running. At each of our three stops, the shopkeeper inquired about how the kayak business was shaping up for summer, how David and Brittney were doing on their search for a piece of property in town, and how Brittney's side business making and selling botanical lotions and sprays was doing. At two of those stops we lingered long enough that Brittney herself showed up. Pickings were a little slim at Toshco, a market that resold stuff that the owner purchased at the Costco in Juneau, because the ferry was a day behind schedule. We had better luck at the natural foods market (where David sometimes worked part-time) and at Pep's Packing, a shop that sold large plastic packages of smoked wild salmon that cost less per pound than some of the lunch meats at

Toshco and tasted better than any sashimi I could recall having eaten.

Before venturing into Glacier Bay, I attended a mandatory orientation at the Bartlett Cove ranger station. Perhaps because it was relatively early in the season, I was the only attendee and received what amounted to a private tutorial in a dark room filled with folding chairs. I watched a video that for several minutes expressed what makes Glacier Bay special: whales, sea lions, puffins, icebergs, tall mountains, solitude.

The second part of the video was devoted to bears. The theme was "what not to do" and was broken down into easily digestible chunks. I learned the signs of bear activity that I should watch for: fresh footprints, large-diameter droppings, and claw marks on trees. I learned the three primary types of bear encounters.

1. Passing bear: Stay out of its way and it will likely miss or ignore you.
2. Defensive bear: Talk calmly to the animal, get away when you can.
3. Curious bear: Group together and yell to intimidate the animal and prevent it from getting too close.

Above all, I was told, do not let the bear

near any food, because once it gets a taste of human grub it will never go away. Even if you run away from your sandwich or bag of Funyuns screaming in terror, the bear is likely to start making Pavlovian connections between shrieking humans and easy sources of nourishment. Once a bear makes that cognitive leap, it will pester any humans it comes into contact with long after you have returned to civilization, aggressively if necessary. Therefore, any food needed to be kept in bear-proof screw-top canisters.

The video ended and the ranger handed me my official pin to signify I was ready for Glacier Bay. She asked if I had any questions.

"Will a bear bother you if you're asleep in your tent?"

"They leave you alone as long as you don't have any food," she said, smiling.

CHAPTER TWENTY-FOUR: THE FULL MUIR

Glacier Bay

The morning that David and I departed for Glacier Bay, I got up at around five and tiptoed toward the Heacox kitchen. Melanie had already gone to support her last interpretive ranger's solo debut. Before leaving, she had laid out a full breakfast, along with a note on formal stationery thanking me for coming to visit and a plastic bag of brownies with instructions to eat them if we got hungry. At six fifteen, David and Brittney arrived in the Econoline and we drove down to the dock at Bartlett Cove. We loaded our kayak and packs and bear canisters stuffed with food onto the daily tour boat that makes the 130-mile run up and down Glacier Bay.

Considering it costs about the same as a trip on the White Pass and Yukon Route Railroad, the Glacier Bay "day boat" (as everyone calls it) may offer the best bang for your buck in all of Southeast Alaska. You get a full day of sightseeing in one of the world's most beautiful places, a soda and sandwich for lunch, free coffee, and narration from one of Melanie's well-drilled park rangers. Ours was named Kaylin. She sat in a booth with David and me as the day boat cruised into the bay and told us about her plan to return to Iowa at summer's end to attend nursing school. Then she excused herself, walked to the front of the room, and grabbed a microphone.

David and I went out to the stern to observe some cute wildlife, mostly backstroking sea otters and birds. When Kaylin announced over the PA system, "There are puffins at two o'clock," a woman with a howitzer-size camera rushed over from the opposite side of the observation deck and elbowed her way past us to the railing. Mostly, everyone wanted to see whales.

"There was a week out here last year when you could almost walk across the whales," David said. "You almost don't want to paddle nearby, because when a whale goes down you don't know where it's going to surface. It could be a quarter mile away."

We slowed as we approached South Marble Island, a small lump of limestone amid fertile waters that made it irresistible to the

241

thousands of birds that nest in the island's slopes and crevices. A chorus of belching sounds began to fill the air, followed by a powerful stench. "It's not a full sea lion experience until you smell them," David said. Sea lions crowded all over the island's lower rocks, like ants on a dropped lollipop, waddling awkwardly and shoving one another into the water. The instant they submerged, they began to swim with the grace of dolphins. As the other passengers snapped photos of a cormorant swallowing a fish that wriggled its way down the bird's long neck, David tapped me on the shoulder and said, "Look behind you." To the south, six whales were spouting, their spray like depth charges in the still water.

"Off to the right you can see Muir Point," Kaylin said over the PA. "There's a pile of rocks there that was once a cabin built by John Muir." She ran through some of the highlights of Muir's visits to Glacier Bay: the skepticism about his Yosemite glacier theory, Fort Wrangell, Hall Young, the four Tlingit guides, Vancouver's charts. A passenger asked why we couldn't visit the Muir Glacier, and Kaylin explained that it had pulled back so far that it no longer reached the water. We'd gone about twenty miles since Bartlett Cove and still hadn't covered half the distance that the glacier had retreated between 1794 and 1879.

The further we followed Muir's path, the younger the landscape became. With each mile, trees shrank in size until they vanished altogether. Mountain goats loitered on scarred rocky faces decorated with patches of green. We eventually reached the head of the bay. The ice had retreated northward more than ten additional miles since 1899. For half an hour we idled in front of two adjacent glaciers. The one on the left was the Margerie Glacier, which had stepped into the Muir Glacier's starring role as the bay's berg-discharging crowd-pleaser. Every ten minutes or so, a sound like a shotgun blast rang out and a chunk of ice would calve off its blue face, making a roar and a splash.

The glacier to the Margerie's right, the Grand Pacific Glacier, looked sad by comparison. This was the primary remnant of the ice mountain that had so fired Muir's imagination, the mighty glacier that had once filled and carved Glacier Bay. From the observation deck of the day boat it looked pathetic, like a pile of dirty snow left to melt in the corner of a mall parking lot.

I'd been enjoying the ride so much that I almost forgot our ultimate plan, until David stepped away for a few minutes and returned wearing waterproof pants and knee-high rubber boots. "It's about that time," he said, and I went off to change. The day boat pulled into a cove and the captain slowly idled toward the rocky shore, taking us so close that with a running start we could've leaped to dry land. (Well, one of us could have.) A deckhand dropped an aluminum ladder from the bow, David and I climbed down, and with help from the boat's crew we unloaded our gear, bucket brigade style: packs, tents, bear cans, and finally the kayak. The whole process took less than five minutes. Our fellow passengers with whom we'd been chatting all day crowded to the edge of the top deck and watched us. The boat backed away. A little girl waved. And then we were alone in the wilderness.

I wasn't quite sure where we were geographically, but a quick glance at the map oriented me in history. We were at the Scidmore Cut, named for the early Glacier Bay travel enthusiast Eliza Scidmore. The Scidmore Cut connected the mainland to the Gilbert Peninsula, named for the Harriman Expedition's *other* glaciologist, G. K. Gilbert. Across the water stood Mount Merriam.

David gave me some basic paddling instructions, pantomimed how to step into our two-person kayak without tipping it over, and demonstrated how to put on a waterproof apron called a spray skirt. "When I'm leading groups, I can pretty much tell it's going to be a long day when I use the term 'spray skirt' and the guys moan," he said. "Sometimes I say 'spray kilt' instead, to skip the aggravation."

And then, before the strangeness of being abandoned in a giant stone tureen of chilled soup could sink in, we were in the water and paddling. The vastness of the space made us feel as if we'd entered another dimension, like Gulliver in Brobdingnag. Row after row of towering dark rock with white caps extended in all directions. The lower hillsides beneath the peaks were a velvety green. The water was blue and clear, except where glacial grinding was doing its work, the rock dust creating pools of what looked like chocolate milk. Since I had no idea what the scale of anything was, I had no idea how fast we were moving. (The answer, I later learned, was "not very fast.") The motion was rhythmic and satisfying. When I got tired, I floated while David continued paddling. The kayak would slow down a little. When David took one of his occasional breaks, we slowed almost to a stop. Sometimes we talked, sometimes we put our paddles down to eat a mouthful of trail mix, but mostly we were quiet. As we approached our final turn, the reflection of the sun shimmered on the water's glassy surface like millions of fireflies.

We had paddled for four hours into a relatively strong wind, finally entering into the mouth of Reid Inlet, a two-mile-long cove with a neon-blue glacier anchoring one end. The air chilled and a breeze rose up as we reached the spit of land on which we would be camping. "Every glacier makes its own weather," David said. The spot was cartoonishly idyllic: a curved, secluded beach with a waterfall that hummed in the background, a rhythm track supporting the massive glacier creaking through its growing pains.

David pulled out the tide chart that he kept in his pocket and checked every so often. The tides in Glacier Bay can rise or fall twenty-five feet, and do so twice each day. We emptied the kayak and carried it up past the fringe of dried seaweed that demarcated the high-water mark. Just beyond that, the bare sand stopped and tall vegetation sprang up suddenly. "Bears like to walk along the tree line," David said, pacing the strip. "If you look just inside and outside the line, it often looks just like a manicured path from all the traffic." He found a few old tracks and some ancient-looking scat, which meant we were probably safe. We pitched our tents on a bed of tiny yellow flowers that crunched under our boots.

Geologically speaking, this spot was brand-new. When the Harriman team sailed past here in 1899, Reid Inlet had been filled with ice. The alchemical process that was taking place around us is called primary succession, nature's way of turning stone into forests. The flowers were dryas, plant gentrifiers that enriched the new soil with nitrogen. Low, dense thickets of willow, alder, and cottonwood would follow. Once a layer of decaying biomass had been laid down over several decades, giant spruce and hemlock trees would colonize the land.

The idea of Glacier Bay National Park as "a world unaltered by humans," as the orientation video described it, makes sense when you're sitting on virgin soil in front of a glacier. Half a million visitors come through on cruise ships each year, and many more would if they could: The National Park Service limits entry to only two large ships each day, in addition to some smaller tourist vessels. Only a tiny fraction of that number spend the night — 568 backcountry campers in 2015, in an area the size of Connecticut. (Yosemite, less than a quarter of Glacier Bay's size, hosted more than two hundred thousand backcountry campers in the same period.) Maintaining the same environment for future generations is a primary goal of the NPS.

David is a staunch environmentalist, but he thinks the Park Service might be overdoing the pristine-wilderness angle. "The definition of 'wilderness' isn't what this place looked like before the first white man got here — there were people living here for thousands of years," he said. It was also a little silly to pretend that giant cruise ships weren't coming through every day. Their presence didn't bother David nearly as much as I expected it to. "I think anyone who wants to visit this place — young, old, in a wheelchair — should be able to," he said. "If people never see the parks, they don't care about them."

David prepared a pot of lentils over the camp stove and talked about the clever eating habits of some of the animals we'd seen during our parade. Sea otters will find a sharp rock they like and keep it tucked under one forefoot as they dive for shellfish. "Starfish — people think they're cute, but they're brutal killers," he said, holding up a mollusk shell with a hole punched in it. The starfish forces its way into a bivalve's shell, pushing its stomach into the prey's space and digesting the creature in its own home. I'd never given much thought to ravens until coming to Alaska, where they are prominent in Native culture. (All Tlingit traditionally belong to one of two moieties, or clans — Eagle or Raven. A person is supposed to marry someone in the opposite moiety.) David said the respect for ravens was well deserved. "I've seen ravens in Gustavus drop clams and mussels on the road, wait for someone to drive over them to crack the shell, then swoop down and eat them," he said. "A raven will not only remember if someone has been kind or unkind to them; they'll tell their friends, too."

As for the most famously omnivorous member of Alaska's animal community, David disagreed with the idea that guns are the best insurance policy. "Statistically, you're better off with bear spray than a firearm, which tends to turn people into Dirty Harry," he said. "Bears are kind of like cats. They're curious. They either take one look at you and decide they want to hang out with you or they just skulk off. I've never had a bad experience with bears. I've only pulled my bear spray once and never fired it."

David was one of Gustavus's citizens who'd written a novel in his spare time. (Like most first-time fiction writers, he'd drawn heavily on his autobiography. Unlike most *male* fiction writers, he'd made his protagonist a woman.) He asked a few questions about what it was like to make a living from writing. Did I enjoy it? Did I jump out of bed in the morning eager to get to work?

"Working as a guide, I meet so many people who just don't seem to be happy," he said. "I guess I don't understand someone who has a job only to make money." He'd asked a friend who's an alpine guide, which certainly sounds like the sort of dream job you're supposed to get after realizing you're not cut out to be a tax lawyer, how much she liked guiding. "She said, 'You enjoy it when you summit, and especially when you get back down.' I love *everything* about kayaking: the beginning, middle, and end. I'm not getting rich here, but I *love* kayaking, and I get to do it every day." When his parents wanted to give David a special gift after graduating from college, they'd purchased him a handmade kayak.

David had recently lost his temper in Seattle, sitting in traffic, thinking about the colossal waste of time. "I realized there might be people out there driving an hour *each way,*" he said. I told him I knew several people who drove twice that daily in New York. He was mortified, but supposed that it was necessary due to NYC's high cost of living. "You'd probably pay two thousand dollars a month for an apartment like they have on TV, right?" He was not comforted when I told him that amount might rent you a nice parking space in Manhattan.

David rinsed out the dishes and confiscated my toothpaste for the bear canister, and we went off to sleep. As I was lying in my tent, the Reid Glacier calved a goodnight salvo of thunderclaps. All night it discharged chunks into the water. In one of nature's finest lodgings, I'd managed to book a room next to the ice machine.

In the morning, the winds had died down and swarms of biting midges and brown flies had converged on camp. I pulled out my mesh bug net and secured my ball cap over it. This, I soon learned, was the exact wrong strategy, since it compressed the net against my forehead, giving the insects a handy place to rest their legs as they bit my face ad libitum. For the next three weeks I wore a line of red dots across my forehead like a doll's hairline as a scarlet letter, broadcasting my ignorance to veteran Alaskans.

The Park Service may promote a "leave no trace" philosophy to Glacier Bay visitors today, but there was a time when even homesteading was possible here. After breakfast, David and I paddled across the cove to what remained of the summer cabin that Muz and Joe Ibach had built around 1939 to trap furs and prospect for gold. When Kim Heacox paddled through here in 1979, the Ibach cabin had contained enough elements of a preserved twentieth-century archaeological site to mount a production of *Death of a Salesman:* dishes, cutlery, books, playing cards, a table and chair, an old copy of *Life* magazine. Today all that remained was a pile of planks, three spruce trees planted by Muz, and some of the detritus of long and lonely Alaska days: a fifty-five-gallon drum, a red can of heating oil (advertising "2 cents off" on the label), one leather shoe. A bear had gathered moss in a pile for a bed and left behind plenty of evidence that it had been subsisting on a diet of mollusks. "That's got to hurt passing through," David said, wincing as he toed the sharp-edged shells with his rubber boot.

We walked through a patch of tall rye grass that looked like wheat. David said that some early Alaska homesteaders had noticed the similarity and used it to make flour. Only later did they learn that the grain was infested with a fungus called ergot, which when consumed can have an unpleasant and powerful hallucinogenic effect. "Imagine what a long and strange winter that must've been," he said. While studying the alkaloids produced by ergot in the late 1930s, the Swiss chemist Albert Hoffman first synthesized lysergic acid diethylamide, better known as LSD.

We kayaked leisurely across the bay toward Russell Island. One of us who was not a particularly skilled swimmer tried not to fixate on the water being just a few degrees above freezing and almost a quarter mile deep. A pair of bald eagles perched at the water's edge on Russell's south end eyeballed us, a two-on-two staring contest rigged in their favor. Muir had come to this very spot in 1879. Back then, the thousand-foot-high island had been half-embedded in ice, marking "the head of the bay" and the furthest reach of the glacier that in Vancouver's time had stretched all the way to Gustavus. "A short time ago," Muir wrote of the rock, "it was at least two thousand feet beneath the surface of the over-sweeping ice; and under present climatic conditions it will soon take its place as a glacier-polished island in the middle of the fjord." And so it had.

From the seat of our kayak, Russell Island didn't look like a particularly easy climb even without ice, but Muir in his usual way had managed to scramble to the top for a better view of the Grand Pacific Glacier, the greatest he'd ever seen. Looking north from this spot must have been like sitting in a cathedral of ice.

We spent much of the day paddling a circle around the island, landing at the rocky beach on the north end. The stones ranged from tiny M&M-size scree to massive, sharp-edged hunks of granite the size of large appliances — multi-ton reminders of the pushing power of the ice river that had once plowed through here.

Once again we unloaded the kayak, carried it up past the seaweed line, and set up camp. Nature had thoughtfully left behind one flat rock on which to set up the stove, next to another that made an ideal dining table. The weather was probably a little too perfect. With no wind, the midges had returned, so thick that we put on our mosquito nets. We lay down on the stone beach and took in the view. "Wow," David said.

Our campsite was centered, like the bubble on a carpenter's level, between two rows of snowcapped peaks. The mountains on each side of Glacier Bay converged toward the horizon to frame the Grand Pacific Glacier. What had looked dirty and stunted up close now shone blindingly white in the midafternoon sun. The glacier swirled up deep into Canada. I could finally understand how its ice might be capable of filling this entire bay.

I awoke around four to the *pop-pop-pop* of bloodthirsty bugs hurling themselves against the liner of my tent. This being mid-June in Alaska, sunrise was at 3:51 A.M., so even though some time would pass before the sun cleared the peaks to the east, the day had already broken when I pulled on my knee-high boots and my fine-mesh bug net and walked down to the beach, looking like a pig farmer turned bank robber on a lost episode of *Kojak.* I sat on a rock pushed there by a glacier and stared down the fjord. The ravenous midges had been joined by swarms of Alaska's state bird, the mosquito, and both swirled around my head like commas and periods in the sort of bad punctuation nightmare a grammarian might have after eating hallucinogenic rye grass.

The air was chilly, part morning temperatures and part glacial cross-breezes. Chunks of ice glided slowly past in the water. A high ceiling of cloud obscured the tops of the highest peaks. The day's first strong sunlight flashed like rosy lightning into the shadows of the fjord, and I thought of Muir's reaction to the same phenomenon from a nearby vantage point: "We stood hushed and awe-stricken, gazing at the holy vision, and had we seen the heavens open and God made manifest, our attention could not have been more tremendously strained."

I sat down, wrapped my arms around myself, and tried to absorb nature's magnificence. The water was like spilled paint. A pair of harbor seals poked their bowling-ball faces above its surface before diving and leaving concentric rings behind. All down the beach, seaweed-covered rocks glowed brown and gold in the rising morning sun.

And then, in the corner of my eye, one of the rocks started moving.

I stood up suddenly and kicked a loose stone down the beach. The noise caught the attention of the moving object, which on further review was a brown bear, perhaps 150 yards away. I tried to gauge its size, but what the hell did I know — this was the first bear I'd ever seen outside of a zoo. The details of the bear safety video I'd been required to watch at the ranger station two nights earlier were suddenly proving to be elusive. The bear and I stared at each other for a moment before it jogged off toward the thick wall of saplings that grew just behind the beach, stopping a few feet short.

A second bear emerged from the brush. A pair of bears likely meant cubs. Cubs meant their mother would soon follow. The first rule of bear encounters finally popped into my head: *Never, ever, ever get between a mother bear and her cubs. Ever.* In the canon of grisly deaths from grizzly attacks, accident reports involving angry moms were those most likely to employ nouns like "sinew" in conjunction with verbs like "tearing" and "chewing."

As quickly and casually as a man can while walking backward in borrowed boots on slippery rocks, I retreated toward our tents as the bears watched.

I knew that David was expecting to sleep for at least a couple more hours, so it was with perhaps a shade more politeness than was merited under the circumstances that I leaned over his tent and spoke through the nylon. "Uh, David, I really hate to disturb you, but I think there may be two bears down here on the beach."

"I'll definitely get up for that," David said groggily.

David was someone who didn't function at peak speed until he'd had his morning coffee. He stepped out of his tent with serious bedhead and wearing baggy pajama bottoms with little wolves on them, looking like a giant second grader who awakened at a slumber party bewildered to find himself not in his own home. He had the can of bear spray in hand as we walked down to the beach.

"These two look about four years old," he said as we approached the pair, who sniffed around the rocks near the waterline. "They were probably just recently separated from Mom. This island has no salmon, no blueberries, so there are no other big brown bears for them to worry about." We watched them for a couple of minutes. "Those are some skinny, scraggly bears," David said as he alternated tucking each of his sandaled feet behind the opposite calf to wipe off hungry mosquitoes. "Looks like the population of Russell Island today is two people, two bears, and two billion bugs."

I wondered how — and when — they'd gotten here. "Are bears good swimmers?" I asked.

"Oh, sure. Bears swim. Moose swim. Deer

swim. Wolves swim. If they think there's something better to be found on another island, they'll just go."

David hopped up on a rock, clapped his hands, and shouted "Hey, bears!" a few times, in a tone that sounded as though he was trying to be encouraging. The pair walked back into the woods. David scratched his head and turned to look down the fjord. "Wow, look at this view, how the green light on the mountains turns the water emerald green. My favorite moment of the day." He lifted his bug net for a moment to take in the colors of the Cinema-Scope panorama. "Actually, this might be my favorite spot I've ever woken up in in the park. And you got to see two bears! How about that?"

David set to work at the camp stove making breakfast, unscrewing the food canisters to take out the coffee and cereal. I'd assumed that if I ever saw a bear, I'd evacuate my bowels like an antelope that spots a lion on the savanna before fleeing, but in the event, I'd been more intrigued than terrified. David said that was pretty normal. "The park biologist here calls it bear-anoia. Beforehand, you're all worried about gigantic teeth and claws, and then you actually see one and you go, 'Oh!' You clap your hands and it stands up and looks at you and runs away."

The bears walked out of the woods once more, this time a little bit closer. David stood, clapped, and shouted a few times, a little louder than before. "Mark, come stand next to me so we appear bigger," he said. "We want to look like a super-creature. See, there they go." Once again, the pair stopped and turned toward the woods.

"I think we'll just make coffee and skip the oatmeal today," David said, pouring hot water into a water bottle with coffee grounds as the bears slunk off into the alders. One of them paused to look back at us, seemingly less than enthused about returning to the brush, before galloping away.

"Facing down a bear is like facing down a drunk: You just have to bluff that you're tougher than he is," David said.

I sat on the beach waiting for the coffee to steep while David went to fetch his rubber boots. The bears appeared again, but this time they were behind us, only about thirty feet from our tents. "Mark, I think we'll take that coffee to go," David shouted from up the beach. "Would you bring the bear spray, please?"

I stood next to David, waving, clapping, and screaming, this time with some edge to it. "*Hey,* bears!" The bears had the high ground. The bolder of the two had taken a sudden interest in my tent. A memory from yesterday passed through my mind: I had left a Clif Bar wrapper in the bottom of my backpack, hadn't I? I was relieved when the bear left my tent and ambled in the direction of the kayak.

David, who had the sangfroid and the G-rated vocabulary of a man who works in the service industry, did not like this development at all. He started screaming so angrily that the vein stood out in his neck. "GET THE FUCK AWAY FROM MY KAYAK, YOU FUCKING BEAR!" The bear stood down as if taking offense and went back to sniffing outside the tents. "We have two days' extra food and redundant water sources," David explained. "But only one kayak." If a curious bear stepped onto the thin fiberglass shell, it would punch a hole. The possibility of being trapped on this sliver of beach with two bears and one can of spray did not appeal to me, either. I remember this vividly, because I underlined it in my notebook, which, when I pulled it out later, had dozens of midges smushed between the pages.

"Are you *taking notes*?" David asked, his arms waving like semaphore flags high over his head.

"This is my job, dude," I said, alternating scribbles with hand waves. "Gotta get this stuff down while it's still hot."

We shouted and waved, shoulder to shoulder, hoping the intruders would get the message. David unlocked the safety catch on the spray. The bolder bear was maybe thirty feet away, while the other hung back. The pair disappeared momentarily into the alders, but then returned right away.

"Guess they're calling our bluff," David said. "Mark, just throw all your stuff into your tent and drag it down to the beach. We'll load up quickly and get the heck out of here."

We collected the food canisters and stove, tossed packs and boots into our tents, and retreated like the British at Dunkirk, dive-bombed by no-see-ums and mosquitoes. My tent snagged on a rock. David snapped a pole. Just as we reached the water's edge with the last pieces of gear, a gigantic white cruise ship with a sunburst painted on its side glided into view. I imagined the passengers looking through binoculars, wondering why two guys were frantically throwing things into a kayak as they swatted the air in front of their faces.

I coincidentally met the pilot of that ship

a few days later, and he recalled seeing us from the bridge. "I thought, Man, look at that setup!" he said. "Those guys must be having the time of their lives."

We shoved off, paddled away from shore, and paused to look back. The bears had come down to the water's edge to hunt for mollusks. David poured very strong luke-warm coffee into mugs and we watched the brown brothers go about their business. "They're actually pretty cute from this far away," David said. "I guess they just wanted to get down to the beach the whole time. But it's a good reminder about Alaska. You can be in awe of the beauty, but you have to remember that things can go from 'Ooh, aah!' to 'Oh, shit!' in an instant."

For a third day, we'd been blessed with beautiful weather. We stripped down to T-shirts. A row of skyscraping mountains to the north came into view, still blanketed with snow. "Look at that — it's like eight or nine Matterhorns all smashed together," David said.

We spent our last night camped atop a patch of blooming strawberry plants behind a sandy beach. The only threat from wildlife was a long-legged oystercatcher who was convinced David wanted to raid her nest and made her displeasure known in car-alarm shrieks. In the morning we paddled slowly back to Scidmore Cut. The day boat glided to a stop, we hoisted our gear and kayak up the aluminum ladder, and the boat backed away from shore. The interpretive ranger announced our arrival, and everyone on board turned to look at us. We were dirty and smelly, and one of us had a strange ring of bug bites circling his forehead, but judging from the excited reception we got from the other passengers, you'd think we'd just been plucked out of an Apollo lunar module bobbing in the ocean.

One more nice thing about the Glacier Bay day boat: They sell beer. And if someone really wants to hear your story about your near-death run-in with two vicious brown bears, they might even buy you one.

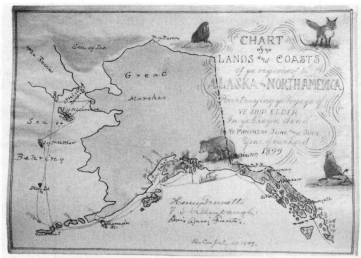

A souvenir map tracing the route of the 1899 Harriman Alaska Expedition, as rendered by several of its participants. *(Courtesy of Kay Sloan)*

1899, expedition patron Edward H. Harriman
s on the verge of becoming the most powerful
lroad baron in the country. *(Library of Congress)*

rriman outfitted the steamship *George W. Elder*
a luxury yacht and invited many of America's top
entists, artists, and writers to join him aboard for
: summer. *(Library of Congress)*

"The Two Johnnies," John Burroughs *(left)* and John Muir *(right)*. Burroughs was the most famous nature writer in the country, Muir the most influential. *(Library of Congress)*

George Bird Grinnell, "the father of American conservation." His polemical writings saved the buffalo from extinction and had a huge influence on Theodore Roosevelt's environmentalism. *(Library of Congress)*

Harriman tasked C. Hart Merriam, ch of the U.S. Division of Biological Surv with assembling an all-star team to ta to Alaska. *(Library of Congress)*

Inside Passage towns such as Ketchikan depend on the tourism brought by massive cruise ships, which disgorge thousands of passengers per day. *(Courtesy of the author)*

ıe no-frills ferries of the aska Marine Highway stem, such as the MV *nnicott*, are a lifeline to ıy towns with no road cess. *(Courtesy of Eli Duke, kimedia Commons)*

epy, blue-collar Wrangell has mellowed since the days John Muir declared it "a rough ıce," the wildest he'd ever seen. *(Courtesy of the author)*

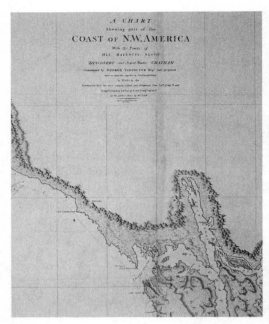

Charts assembled from British explorer George Vancouver's 1794 search for the Northwest Passage showed a frozen void in the spot where, in 18?? John Muir found Glacier Bay. *(National Archives, UK)*

Saint Michael's Cathedral recalls the fur-trading days when Sitka was the capital of Russian America and "the Paris of the Pacific." *(Courtesy of the author)*

During the Klondike Gold Rush, prospectors ascending the deadly Chilkoot Pass out of Skagway were required to bring two thousand pounds of provisions, enough for a year. *(Library of Congress)*

Kayaking guide David Cannamore in Glacier Bay. *(Courtesy of the author)*

n and Melanie Heacox at their ne in Gustavus. *(J. T. McLaughlin/ rtesy of Kim and Melanie Heacox)*

e view north from Russell Island. The glacier at the head of the bay has both advanced retreated over this spot since 1680. *(Courtesy of the author)*

Edward Harriman's desire to bag a trophy Kodiak bear, the largest variety of brown bear on earth, caused conflict with pacifist John Muir. *(Lisa Hupp/U.S. Fish and Wildlife Service)*

Harry and Brigid Dodge, with their dog, Lo on Kodiak Island. *(Courtesy of Harry and Brigid Do*

Photographs taken from the same vantage point in 1895 *(above)* and 2005 *(right)* show the catastrophic retreat of Muir Glacier, which has receded thirty miles since the 1800s. *(Courtesy of Bruce F. Molnia, USGS)*

ittier is known as "the weirdest town in Alaska," not least because of sparsely inhabited mer military buildings, such as Begich Towers. *(Courtesy of the author)*

e McDowell in the ash-covered
ley of Ten Thousand Smokes,
of the twentieth century's
gest volcanic explosion.
rtesy of the author)*

The author's alfresco accommodations aboard the *Tustumena* on the three-day voyage to the Aleutian Islands. *(Courtesy of the author)*

The return of the Harriman Expedition in 1899 was national news, though its full impact would not be felt for a few years. *(Courtesy of The New York Times)*

On their way back south, Harriman expeditioners chopped down several totem pole Cape Fox, a Tlingit village believed—erroneously—to have been abandoned. *(Librar Congress)*

Alaska's warming climate is altering its landscape. The town of Shishmaref has lost land and houses due to erosion from increasingly violent storms. *(Diana Haecker/Associated Press)*

CHAPTER TWENTY-FIVE:
SHAKEN AND STIRRED

Fairbanks

In 1899, as now, Glacier Bay and Sitka often marked the end of the line for visitors to Alaska. The Harriman Expedition had reached only the midpoint of its itinerary. Having completed "the usual Alaska excursion" up the Inside Passage, John Burroughs wrote, "we turned our faces for the first time toward the open ocean, our objective being Yakutat Bay."

If the weather cooperates along the coast stretching north between Gustavus and Yakutat (a big *if*), the sharp white teeth of the St. Elias mountain range come into view. The St. Elias chain is North America's Himalaya, where thirteen peaks top fifteen thousand feet and rise so rapidly from sea level that when the National Park Service hired a Seattle company to create a 3-D map of the region, its software was initially incapable of rendering such a sudden change in topography.

Because that moisture-trapping wall of rock captures the snow that condenses into glaciers, Yakutat Bay feels like a winter wonderland even on a rare seventy-degree sunny day. Eighteen-thousand-foot Mount St. Elias stands over the bay like a heap of sugar. From its base, the immense Malaspina Glacier spills out in the shape of a giant clam. Not surprisingly, it was Dall who named the glacier, after the eighteenth-century Spanish explorer Alejandro Malaspina, who'd sailed through searching for the Northwest Passage.

On a map, the notch of Yakutat Bay, just east of the 141st meridian, is where Alaska's panhandle attaches to its primary landmass. In 1899, it also marked the end of Tlingit territory. When a group of Natives paddled through the bay's ice-choked waters to approach the *Elder,* offering furs for sale, Harriman invited them aboard. He was so taken with one man, a gregarious fellow who wore a buccaneer hat and eye patch and who became known as Indian Jim, that he hired him as a guide to the bay's deepest recesses, whose waters had never before been navigated by a steamship. Burroughs, spooked by the severity of the glacier-scoured rock, felt as if he'd entered "a special playground of the early ice gods."

The Harriman team enjoyed a peaceful five days ensconced in the nook of Yakutat Bay, no one more so than Harriman himself. When he wasn't busy commandeering rowboats to drop off and retrieve scientists, entertaining Tlingit visitors with his graphophone, or advising local prospectors on their mineral discoveries, Harriman spent time spending: He purchased three canoes and the fur of a nearly extinct sea otter, the latter costing several hundred dollars because the Tlingit hunters drove a harder bargain than one of the toughest negotiators in the railroad business. When the scout Yellowstone Kelly reported having come close enough to a bear that he could smell the beast, Harriman rushed off with rifle at the ready. Once again, he returned to the *Elder* exhausted and empty-handed. Muir, who was already disgusted by the bloody Tlingit seal hunting that dominated the local economy, quietly rejoiced at his host's failure.

As the Harriman team enjoyed their idyll in Yakutat Bay, *The Atlantic Monthly* was preparing to publish the latest essay by Muir in its August 1899 issue. "Nature is ever at work building and pulling down, creating and destroying, keeping everything whirling and flowing, allowing no rest but in rhythmical motion, chasing everything in endless song out of one beautiful form into another," he wrote in the conclusion to "The Yosemite National Park," a spirited defense of national parks as both temples and classrooms. Having been awakened at two o'clock one morning in Yosemite Valley by the "wild thrilling motion and rumbling" of an earthquake, Muir runs out of his cabin "both glad and frightened, shouting, 'A noble earthquake!' feeling sure I was going to learn something."

Muir's essay resonated with me because I read it not long after David Cannamore and I played hide-and-seek with the brown bears on Russell Island. Some news had just come in with a rare Glacier Bay dateline. A pilot who had been flying over the park noticed that a rock face had collapsed above the Lamplugh Glacier, the face of which David and I could see from our island campsite. The mountains of Alaska's northern panhandle are still growing, the result of tectonic plates slowly smashing into each other. When glaciers retreat, these young mountains (millions of years old, but juveniles in geologic time) are susceptible to landslides. Colin Stark, a professor of marine geology and geophysics at Columbia University's Lamont-Doherty Earth Observatory, estimated to KHNS Radio that a hundred and fifty million metric tons of debris had been unleashed during the Lamplugh event, or the equivalent force of seventy million Toyota Highlanders tumbling down the slope. "The thing that really got me," he said, was that "if it just happened a bit further over, near the calving front, that would be a very bad thing." Stark pointed out that on Google Earth there's a tiny oval-shaped object in front of the glacier, one of Glacier Bay's daily cruise ships. Had a landslide occurred near the front of Lamplugh, any passing cruisers, as well as David and I and our bear friends, would have been directly in the path of a mega-tsunami. As the ice that holds rocks in place continues to melt, the frequency of such events is certain to increase.

Considering the prevailing trends in Alaska tourism in the summer of 1899, the well-publicized return of the Harriman Expedition would surely have catapulted Glacier Bay onto whatever sorts of "Where to Travel Next Year" round-ups existed at the turn of the century. The area was not federally protected until 1925, and the boardwalks laid down in front of Muir Glacier were likely harbingers of things to come at Alaska's top natural attraction.

Nature had other plans. On September 10, 1899, a magnitude 8.0 earthquake struck the northern panhandle, with its epicenter in Yakutat Bay.

Earthquakes in California, like the devastating 7.8 San Francisco quake of 1906, are taught in grade school history classes. Natural cataclysms that strike Alaska — like the Lamplugh slide — usually go unnoticed until later, because no one witnesses them. The 1899 Yakutat quake is an exception. A team of eight prospectors panning for gold near Yakutat Bay described a strong initial shock at around 9:00 A.M., followed by fifty-two tremors, one every few minutes. (How'd they arrive at such a precise figure? They'd strung together two hunting knives to make a rudimentary seismograph.) Then, at around 1:30 P.M., a final jolt, lasting between two and three minutes.

The force of the earthquake was powerful enough to lift part of the shoreline in Disenchantment Bay forty-seven feet, "the greatest recorded in historical time," according to one geologist who came to examine the site six years later and found himself looking up at barnacles that a few years prior had lived under the sea.

Muir Glacier, which to that point was drawing positive comparisons to Niagara

Falls as a tourist attraction, was shattered by the quake. Two scientists who visited Glacier Bay shortly after the September 10 earthquake estimated that the Muir had retreated two and a half to three miles from lost ice. Icebergs so clogged Muir Inlet that tour boats could no longer approach, and the next tour excursion didn't take place until 1907. "Formerly the Muir presented a perpendicular front at least two hundred feet high, from which huge bergs were detached at frequent intervals," lamented one Canadian geographer who visited, "something which once witnessed was not to be forgotten." Post-quake, the glacier's formerly imposing face was quiet, having flattened like a boxer's nose. Its body had split in two.

As the ground swayed and cracked beneath the feet of the Yakutat prospectors and rocks and water from a breached lake rained down upon their heads, one of them recalled, "We heard a terrible roar in the direction of the bay, and on looking that way we saw a tidal wave coming toward us which appeared about twenty feet high." Their boats were smashed to toothpicks, save one, a small craft that lodged itself in the upper branches of an alder. Once on the water, they could see that an ocean wave sixty feet high had crashed against the shore. For four days the prospectors subsisted largely on fish killed by the quake that were floating on the water's surface. When they arrived at Yakutat, they found the village intact and its population alive but shaken, camped out on a piece of high ground known thereafter as Shivering Hill.

Those of us who live Outside don't typically think of Alaska as tsunami territory, but the blue EVACUATION ROUTE signs posted in towns all along the coast make clear that the possibility is never far from the minds of Alaskans. The potential for havoc caused by a rockslide is illustrated by Lituya Bay, a quiet nook south of Yakutat where, a few decades ago, a few unfortunate boaters witnessed the highest wave ever recorded.

Lituya Bay is a fjord approximately seven miles long and two miles wide, with steep sides that rise up more than six thousand feet. "Lituya Bay has the form of a letter T," Harriman Expedition geologist G. K. Gilbert wrote after the *Elder* sailed past, noting the arms that branched off at the end of the fjord. (The northern arm of Lituya Bay's distinctive T shape was later named Gilbert Inlet in the geologist's honor.) This is one of the few natural harbors offering shelter between Glacier Bay and Yakutat. Experienced mariners know that its welcoming appearance is deceptive: A narrow entrance, just a few hundred yards wide, can be safely accessed only during the brief period every six hours when the tide is slack. The French explorer Jean-François de La Pérouse arrived in 1786 and lost twenty-one men in two boats while trying to survey the mouth of the bay. In their honor, La Pérouse erected a memorial on an island at the center of the bay, which he named Cenotaph Island.

Three fishing boats sought shelter in Lituya Bay on the evening of July 9, 1958. One of them, the thirty-eight-foot *Edrie,* was piloted by Howard Ulrich, who had brought along his son Howard Jr. The night was calm and the water smooth, though a storm front was apparently approaching. A team of Canadian climbers celebrating their country's first ascent of 15,300-foot Mount Fairweather were surprised when their seaplane pilot arrived a day early to collect them before the weather turned. They broke camp in a hurry and were airborne by 9:00 P.M. Two hours later their campsite had been scrubbed from the face of the earth.

One of Lituya Bay's defining characteristics is invisible. The Fairweather Fault, where two tectonic plates scrape past each other, runs through the crossbar of the T at the head of the bay. Such a formation is known as a strike-slip fault. Occasionally the energy built up by this slow friction is released suddenly, causing an earthquake. As happened on the Lamplugh Glacier in 2016, seismic activity can unleash huge amounts of debris. Because of Lituya Bay's long, narrow shape, these landslides can have the effect of dumping a load of gravel into a bathtub.

Shortly after falling asleep on July 9, Ulrich was awakened by the *Edrie* rocking violently. His watch said 10:17 P.M. He ran out to the deck and looked up in amazement at the snowcapped mountains that rise almost vertically from the water's edge. The peaks seemed to be writhing in pain. "Have you ever seen a fifteen-thousand-foot mountain twist and shake and dance?" Ulrich recalled afterwards. "I hadn't either, and I don't know that I want to see it again."

Ulrich's feet were glued to the deck from fear. After perhaps two minutes of watching the mountains swaying, he turned to look beyond Cenotaph Island at the moment thirty million cubic meters of debris fell free from the wall above Gilbert Inlet and plunged into the water. This sudden displacement created an enormous splash, a wall of water that surged more than seventeen hundred feet high against the opposite side of the inlet.

Water displaced by the avalanche bounced off the east side of the fjord, then gathered as a massive wave rolling toward the mouth of Lituya Bay and the *Edrie*. Ulrich threw a life jacket on Howard Jr., started the engine, and tried to raise the anchor. It wouldn't budge. With the wave almost upon them, he ran the chain to its full 240 feet. Just as Edward Curtis had with his canoe in Glacier Bay, Ulrich knew that his best chance was to ride *into* the oncoming water. "Perhaps, I thought, we can ride up and over the wave while the anchor holds us from being swept away," he recalled. Then his chain snapped.

Two other fishing boats were anchored in Lituya Bay at the time. The husband and wife aboard the *Sunmore* weighed anchor immediately and sped for the mouth of the bay, hoping to outrun danger. The wave caught them at the entrance and presumably dashed the boat and its passengers to pieces; an oil slick was the only trace of their final resting spot. The *Badger,* operated by William and Vivian Swanson, was still at anchor when the wave hit. The water carried their trawler across the low spit of land at the mouth of the bay, "riding stern first just below the crest of the wave, like a surfboard," according to the U.S. Geological Survey follow-up report. "Swanson looked down on the trees growing on the spit, and believes that he was about two boat lengths (more than 80 feet) above their tops." The *Badger* crashed down stern first. Ninety minutes later they were found by a fishing boat, freezing and in shock but alive.

Ulrich, certain that he and his son were about to die, grabbed his radio handset and yelled, "Mayday! Mayday! This is the *Edrie* in Lituya Bay! All hell has broken loose in here. I think we've had it. Good-bye!" Father and son rode nearly perpendicular up the face of the wave and reached the far side intact. Their ordeal wasn't over. The waters within the fjord were a roiling stew of tree trunks and icebergs, the larger of which rolled and smashed into one another as they tried to find equilibrium. Eddies and currents swirled all around. Ulrich struggled to keep control of the boat and somehow managed to slip through the mouth of the bay intact.

The next morning, USGS geologist Don Miller flew over Lituya Bay and tallied the carnage: Both arms of the bay's T and almost half of its main trunk were clogged with ice; logs and vegetation filled most of the rest and spilled out for miles into the Pacific. The front wall of Gilbert Inlet was still dripping water from its fresh scar, a third of a mile up, where the monster wave had peaked. Everything but the rock below that point had been obliterated.

If you were to take a map of the Pacific Ocean and trace a rough horseshoe-shaped line starting in New Zealand, jogging left through Indonesia, then up along the coast of Asia through the Philippines and Japan, across the Bering Strait, down along the Alaska coast, and finally hugging the coasts of North and South America through Chile, you would have outlined the Ring of Fire. This band of seismic activity accounts for 90 percent of the world's earthquakes and is home to most of the world's volcanoes. A rich mythology developed across cultures to explain this instability. In Japan, the Namazu was a giant catfish that occasionally escaped and shook the earth with its thrashing. The Tlingit people had several stories to explain the seismicity of Southeast Alaska. "Narratives set on this part of the coast indicate familiarity with earthquakes, giant waves, floods, and exceptional tides," writes Julie Cruikshank in her fascinating book *Do Glaciers Listen?* "They attribute these forces to the activities of Raven, who made the earth at the beginning of time." George Emmons, the American ethnologist who'd escorted Merriam and Grinnell to visit the Tlingit village in Sitka, recorded the story of Kah Lituya, "a monster of the deep who dwells in the ocean caverns near the entrance" of Lituya Bay. Resentful of anyone who entered his domain, he and his slaves would "grasp the surface water and shake it as if it were a sheet," engulfing the intruder.

Seismologists have advanced a long way from deep-sea monsters to explain the causes of earthquakes and tsunamis, but they're still somewhat hamstrung when it comes to determining when such events are going to occur. The Alaska Earthquake Center at the University of Alaska at Fairbanks was founded to monitor seismic activity and reduce "the impacts of earthquakes, tsunamis, and volcanic eruptions in Alaska" after the state was blindsided by the largest quake recorded in U.S. history, the 1964 Good Friday earthquake.

There's a black-and-white Super 8 film taken by two crewmen aboard the freighter *Chena,* which docked in Valdez on March

27, 1964. On the waterfront, longshoremen wait with hands in pockets for the unloading to begin, as children scamper with their dogs, waving at deckhands who toss oranges and candy. Then the earth ruptures. A chasm opens in the ocean. Somehow the cameraman keeps filming as the water is sucked out of the harbor, exposing the seafloor. A fifty-foot wave rolls in from the bay and crashes ashore, hurling the *Chena* into the center of town and pulling away much of the silty ground on which Valdez sits. The dock collapses, taking kids, dogs, and longshoremen into the sea. None of them survive. A visitor to Valdez today is actually seeing a different city, built four miles away from the original.

Mike West is Alaska's state seismologist, working out of UAF's Geophysical Institute, a funky complex of buildings with a huge parabolic dish on its roof. We met across the street at the campus's Museum of the North, which West described, accurately, as "easily the nicest building in Fairbanks." (Juneau is Florence compared to Fairbanks.) The museum was nice, with sort of a Frank Gehry–meets–Nanook vibe, but for someone like me, whose midwestern alma mater featured an experimental cornfield in the middle of its very flat campus, the view south of the Alaska Range was the real attraction.

"That whole range of mountains we're looking out at is being built by earthquakes," West said as we stared out the two-story windows. Just as the mountains along Alaska's Pacific coast were still growing, so were those of the interior, including Denali. It's this dynamic geology that makes Alaska's landscape unique. "Scenery is Alaska's thing, right? Mountains, glaciers, pristine rivers. It is not a stretch to trace all of those things back to the active geology. If there were no earthquakes, there would be no Denali."

West was funny and engaging by normal human standards; compared with most earth scientists I've met, he deserved his own late-night talk show. He had just returned on the red-eye from Washington, DC, where congressional staffers had been wringing their hands over a recent *New Yorker* article that warned of a future earthquake and tsunami that could destroy the Pacific Northwest. No one outside of the Alaska delegation had seemed too concerned that Alaska was more likely to see the next Big One. (Photos of post-quake downtown Anchorage, which has tripled in size since 1964, bear a strong resemblance to photos of San Francisco in 1906.) In times past, memories of natural disasters were often passed down orally in folktales. George Emmons had heard one in Sitka that he realized was an accurate account of La Pérouse's losing two boats in Lituya Bay a hundred years earlier. Among West's duties as state seismologist is reminding Alaskans that another disaster is coming and educating them to be prepared when it does. "One of the challenges that we face is history," West said. "Most of the population of Alaska was not living here in 1964."

Four out of five earthquakes in America occur in Alaska. I asked West why Alaska is so much more active than the rest of the country. "My colleagues hate when I distill it to this, but basically, all earthquakes in Alaska can be traced to three sources," he said. "Plate Tectonics 101: The northern part of the Pacific is one big tectonic plate. Alaska is part of North America. A rigid, solid continent, right? The Pacific Plate is impinging on Alaska." As the Pacific Plate meets the continent, it bends down beneath it, a process called subduction. This is why the deepest ocean trenches are often found close to land rather than in the middle of the ocean.

"These plates are closing in at the breakneck speed of two or three inches per year," West said. "What's two or three inches per year, right? But after ten years, you've got yourself maybe a couple feet. After a hundred years, you've got tens of feet. If you move the ground tens of feet in a matter of seconds, you've got a very, very significant event.

"Process number two: You're taking an entire tectonic plate and you're forcing it past another one." He rubbed one palm slowly against the other. "Once you get into the largest of the large earthquakes — magnitude eight and above — with few exceptions, you're talking about this motion." In Southeast Alaska, the Pacific Plate is scraping north against the North America Plate. "This is basically the northern cousin of the San Andreas Fault," West said.

"The third process is that Alaska's being slowly compacted north and south. As two giant landmasses collide, you have bending and flexing and mountains going up. A thousand years from now, those mountains are going to look roughly the same. The plates will not have moved much, but those few feet that they did move will manifest themselves through earthquakes."

Earthquakes and volcanoes are the most obvious demonstrations of Alaska's "active geology." Tsunamis are the deadliest. In the Good Friday earthquake, 119 of the 139 people who died were killed by tsunamis. Ground formed from the sediment that glacial action creates is unstable and can liquefy like Jell-O in seismic events; undersea landslides near the shore then displace huge amounts of water. In Hawaii, an advance warning system usually gives residents at least four hours before a tsunami arrives from across the ocean. In 1964, Alaska towns like Seward and Whittier were swamped by giant waves before the shaking had finished.

"Folks here have, if they're lucky, minutes," West said. "So we teach people in coastal Alaska towns that if the ground shakes for more than twenty seconds, get out. Just do it."

I had to ask: Wasn't there any way to foresee trouble coming? "This is a sore spot for all seismologists," West said. "We are not even going to utter the words 'earthquake prediction,' because that just causes problems." He borrowed my laptop and opened a map of Alaska covered in hundreds of dots of various sizes and colors, denoting their timing and intensity. "All those little earthquakes, they're tremendously important, actually, because a magnitude two earthquake — there's no damage, it doesn't knock buildings down, it doesn't kill people, but those little earthquakes are the clues to what we should expect in certain places. Any time we start to get several weeks of magnitude fours, magnitude fives, often out in the Aleutians, we always look at that very carefully and start to think, Are these fore-shocks to a magnitude eight that's coming?"

"Is it the kind of thing where it's like it happens every five hundred years?" I asked.

"Oh, no, no, no, no. We are in a dry spell," West said. The quake of 1964 had been preceded by one in 1946 that launched a tsunami that killed 159 people in Hilo, and a severe but less deadly one in 1938. "It has been fifty years since there's been a deadly tsunami in Alaska. Based on historic rec-ords, that is exceptionally long."

CHAPTER TWENTY-SIX:
END OF THE ROAD

Yakutat

As far as is known, there were no casualties in the 1899 Yakutat Bay earthquake, a fortunate result of extremely low population density. More than a century later, Yakutat still has a reputation as one of the most remote towns in Alaska. It sits on the least inhabited stretch of coast between Ketchikan and Anchorage and is backed by public wilderness for a hundred miles or more in all directions. If someone were really determined (and didn't mind fording rivers, scaling mountains, and dodging wolverines), he or she could walk from Yakutat to Nome, nine hundred miles away, and cross only two roads. Cell phone service didn't reach the town until 2012, and it's still pretty spotty. The ferry stops in Yakutat only once every two weeks, even in midsummer.

Melanie Heacox had suggested I visit Jim Capra, a ranger based in Yakutat, which is tucked between Glacier Bay National Park and the Wrangell–St. Elias National Park and Preserve. You could spend a lifetime exploring Elias, since the park is the second largest in the world — six times the size of Yellowstone and approximately equal in area to Switzerland, though with more impressive mountains. (The world's biggest national park is in northeastern Greenland, if you happen to be in the neighborhood.) The town of Yakutat is a little larger than Gustavus, population-wise (662 as of the last census), but more spread out. What had looked on my phone to be a short walk from my B & B to the Park Service office turned out to be several miles, so I stuck out my thumb and tried to hail a ride. Fifteen minutes went by and not one vehicle passed. I went back to the inn and borrowed one of the bicycles in the yard, which turned out to have a wonky chain that fell off every quarter mile or so.

The NPS offices were in an old airplane hangar, its door marked only by an arrowhead. I was a half hour late, and there was no cell signal to send a message, but people in rural Alaska are pretty laid-back about appointments. You'll turn up eventually, and if you don't, it's probably time to call search and rescue. I knocked, waited a few minutes, knocked again, walked over to the National Weather Service office to make sure I was knocking in the right place, and by the time I returned, Jim Capra was waiting in his uniform, smiling, with the door propped open.

Perhaps the most famous attraction near Yakutat is the Hubbard Glacier, renowned for two reasons. One: It is huge. The Hubbard's face is three hundred feet high and six miles wide, making it the largest tidewater glacier in North America. Two: Unlike most of the glaciers in Alaska, it is growing. This makes it very popular among those who believe climate change is a hoax.*

"The Hubbard has Mount St. Elias on one side and Mount Logan on the other," the second-and fourth-highest mountains in North America, Capra explained. We were sitting in a small office kitchen. Capra got up and drew his finger on a Forest Service map taped to one wall. "One theory is that

* See, for example, former governor Sarah Palin's response to a visit by President Barack Obama, during which he highlighted climate change's effects on Alaska. "Obama was up here looking at, say, the glaciers and pointing out a glacier that was receding. Well, there are other glaciers, though, that are growing up here."

because the accumulation zone is higher, it's less affected by climate change so far." Ned Rozell, at the UAF Geophysical Institute, has written that the Hubbard may also be located in the wettest spot on earth. No one can be certain, because no one has ever been able to install a precipitation gauge in the remote mountains outside of town. In 1986 and again in 2002, the Hubbard blocked the entrance to Russell Fjord — John Burroughs's "playground of the early ice gods" — causing the water level behind the ice dam to rise precipitously before bursting. One glaciologist estimates that the breach will seal again by 2025.

People who come to Alaska looking to escape from civilization are called end-of-the-roaders. During his 1879 excursion with Hall Young, Muir heard stories of a Harvard graduate "bearing an honored New England name" who had taken refuge among a remote Tlingit tribe. When they finally located what may have been the first end-of-the-roader ever recorded in Alaska, he was dressed only in a cheap blanket and mumbled monosyllabic answers to their questions.

Because of its total isolation, Yakutat is known for attracting the most extreme dropouts, people who've burned through every other place to live. "We're a little beyond the end of the road, so we get our share of them," Capra said. "They're usually not too scary." I asked if there were any hermits in the vast wilderness. "You occasionally see their tracks or hear accounts of people living out in the forest," he said. "Survivalists. One guy had fifty thousand rounds of ammo." A woman once hosted a meeting at her cabin just outside the park and multiple people showed up who not only were strangers to the host but whose existence had previously been unknown to anyone, including one another.

Capra talked a little bit about his own path to such an isolated spot, working two years as a ranger at Independence Hall, in Philadelphia ("I dealt with a lot of prostitutes and crack addicts — I'm told the neighborhood has gotten better"), and a stint in Arkansas. He'd grown up in Los Angeles and had family who worked in show business, but he wanted to get far away from Southern California and ended up here. "Yakutat is a different variety of isolation, surrounded by millions and millions of acres," he said. "Some people can't take the quiet."

Capra walked me out, took one look at the woeful chain on my bike, went back in, and returned with a wrench. "This won't solve the problem, but it should get you back to town," he said, bending metal and tightening a nut. I asked if by any chance he was related to the director of that epic of small-town American values, *It's a Wonderful Life.*

"Frank Capra was my grandfather," he said. He had fond memories of watching thirty-five-millimeter movies at his grandfather's ranch. Jim's dad had worked in TV news; other Capras had tried to ride Frank's coattails to Hollywood. "I just wanted to get away from the TV and movie business," he said.

Other than the glaciers, the one thing I knew about Yakutat was that it is Alaska's unlikely surf capital. Jim Capra, who'd grown up "as a punk surfer kid in L.A.," confirmed this and advised that if I wished to sample the local waves (which I did not), I should watch out for local hazards. "The sea lions here are bigger than the ones in California, and very curious," he said. Another surfer I'd met told me he'd ridden a Yakutat wave into shore only to find himself trapped between a brown bear and a storm cloud of mosquitoes.

The red-hot epicenter of this surf mania, I'd gathered from reading stories online, was Icy Waves Surf Shop. I rode back down Airport Road, passing people standing in the brush just off the shoulder picking salmonberries and tossing them into five-gallon buckets. I twice rode up and down the side road that, as far as I could remember, led to my destination, before I noticed that one of the houses had a back door plastered with surf stickers. One of them read ICY WAVES SURF SHOP: THE FAR NORTH SHORE. I took two steps toward the house, and a very unhappy guard dog rushed out to meet me, stopped short by his chain. The dog apparently doubled as a doorbell, because a head popped out, silenced the beast, and invited me to come around back.

Jack Endicott didn't look like a stereotypical surf kingpin, even an Alaskan one. He was tall and stocky, with a bushy white Santa Claus beard, and instead of board shorts was wearing Carhartt overalls and a baseball cap. The Icy Waves world headquarters turned out to be a room at the back of his house filled with all sorts of gear. Endicott sat next to the cash register, surrounded by photos of famous surfers. "You never know who's going to knock on the door," he said. Seven-time women's world surf champ Layne Beachley showed up on her own one time.

Endicott wasn't one of those guys who heard "Surfin' U.S.A." and drove west dreaming of woody wagons and longboards. "I came to Alaska to become a fisherman and trapper," he said. A job became available in Yakutat working as a meteorologist for the National Weather Service. "All the Gulf of Alaska storms come in — that's what makes the breaks," he said. If conditions are right, swells can reach twenty feet. I noticed that Endicott rented wetsuits for reasonable rates, a necessity in a place where water temperatures rarely reach sixty degrees even in summer.

The obvious question was how Endicott had gotten into the surf business at all. "We have seven children, and we'd go to Hawaii once in a while," he said. "The kids would say, 'The waves at home are as good as the ones here.'"

The local paper did a story, which got picked up by a Juneau daily, which was seen by a reporter at the AP, whose subsequent story caught the eye of someone at CBS News. Pretty soon surfing Yakutat became a bragging-rights thing. "People who come here say, 'I can go to Hawaii or Indonesia, but no one comes to Yakutat.'

"We're the most isolated community in

the United States," he said. "That's the good *and* the bad."

My amazing luck with Yakutat's notorious weather was holding, so I wandered over to Cannon Beach. The beach got its name from a group of large World War II guns, still in place where they once guarded the coast from Japanese invasion. The barrels had been sawed off and filled with asphalt because one too many local revelers had dumped gunpowder down a neck and fired his own projectile out to sea. STRIKE! BOWLING BALL SINKS CRUISE SHIP was a headline no one needed to see.

Walking on the beach was like stepping onto another planet. If ever a picturesque seashore on a warm, sunny June day could be said to be spooky, Cannon Beach might be the one. Dark sand stretched off for miles in both directions, littered with deadwood. School was out and tourism season had begun. With the aid of binoculars, I spotted eight people in an hour. Sea traffic consisted of one cruise ship in the distance and a girl kicking back and forth in the shallows on an inflatable raft. Jack Endicott had predicted decent wave conditions, but there wasn't a surfer in sight. To the north, snow-capped Mount St. Elias rose symmetrically from sea level like the Great Pyramid over the desert. "It is the most superb mountain I have ever seen, Mont Blanc and all the others are pygmies compared to it," artist Frederick Dellenbaugh wrote in his diary, and I had to agree.

Like Gustavus, Yakutat had no real downtown, just a loose cluster of buildings that made up the town center. A visitor could buy food at Mallott's General Store and alcohol at the Glass Door Bar, but if that same visitor wanted to sit down and consume food and alcoholic beverages together, he had to ride his lame bike all the way back out to the fishing lodge at the airport. Jim Capra had advised against stopping in for a drink at the Glass Door. "Every time I set foot in there, one of two things happens," he told me. "Somebody lines up six shots on the bar, hoping to play 'Get the Ranger Drunk,' or somebody starts an argument that they hope turns into a fight." I didn't need to know what sort of temptation a visitor from New York might present.

The only other establishment was Fat Grandma's, a large purple building that billed itself as a gift shop and bistro but was more of a gift shop and coffee shop that sold a daily hot lunch on paper plates and also offered indoor tanning. Three walls were occupied by thousands of used books, which the proprietor, Candy Hills, told me were free for the taking when she rang up my coffee. I asked if she knew anyone interesting in town whom I could speak with. She said she'd think about it.

A few minutes later, as I sat sipping my coffee and wondering whether a slightly dog-eared first edition of *Humboldt's Gift* was worth the space in my backpack, a disheveled man pulled out the chair next to me and sat down. He had a wispy beard and wore a dirty, untucked denim shirt. "Candy says you want to talk to the most interesting person in Yakutat," he said, pointing a thumb at his chest. "That's me. I've been in Yakutat sixty-six years, since there were no lights or heat."

His name was Roy. His father's father had come to Yakutat after a disagreement elsewhere. "I'm pure-blood Tlingit — Eagle. Vietnam vet. Marines. Went to school in Oregon, traveled in California. Yakutat is the most beautiful country in the whole world. Rich in its own way, in food. In my father's day, if someone brought in a seal, everyone shared. They took care of widows. But the green dollar bill came in and changed everything."

Roy had lived a bumpy life. "I got married, got divorced. I regret some things I've done. One time a white guy started a fight and I lost my cool. He never knew he was out. In 1976, they said I was shouting at cops in Angoon" — a small town northeast of Sitka. "They lied about me in court. They sentenced me to three years and I pleaded to parole.

"My father's Tlingit nickname translates as 'womanizer.' He had six different lots down in the village. Traded one for a leather jacket and a quart of whiskey. He died in Juneau, an eighteen-wheeler ran him over. My brother was killed in Seattle, beaten unconscious by three men. My little brother Walter wrapped himself around a telephone pole in Kodiak. My little sister was killed execution style. Killed her dog, too." He paused. "Mom died of old age.

"I'm homeless. Put in an application for a home with the military. My sisters are coming up, maybe on the ferry." The *Kennicott*, my old friend from the Bellingham-to-Ketchikan run, was due to make its every-two-weeks stop that evening. "It might be the next one. I don't have a phone. If you put me in your book, send me a copy, okay?" He took my pen and wrote a P.O. box address in my notebook.

When the *Elder* departed Yakutat Bay, Frederick Dellenbaugh noted the solitude into which they were sailing. "Not a sign of a sail is visible anywhere on the wide waters," he wrote, "nor has there been any since we left Sitka." The only company was an albatross, which followed the ship for hours, soaring effortlessly and swooping toward the waves. (The frustrated hunters among the expedition, being of a literary bent, surely knew from Coleridge's poem about the ancient mariner that shooting an albatross invited trouble.) As they continued west into Prince William Sound, it would have been easy to imagine that they had left the messiness of the industrial world behind.

CHAPTER TWENTY-SEVEN:
ECO-DISASTER: A PREVIEW

Orca

"Scientific explorers are not easily managed, and in large mixed lots are rather inflammable and explosive," John Muir would write upon the death of E. H. Harriman, in 1909. After a month together, as the *Elder* neared the top of the arch formed by Alaska's panhandle and southern coast, the members of the Harriman Expedition had, according to Burroughs, "assumed the features of a large and happy family on a summer holiday cruise." Expeditions are often like military campaigns, long stretches of marching and boredom broken up by brief moments of excitement. At the point when other adventurers might be entertaining themselves by counting digits lost to frostbite or drawing straws to determine whom the cannibals would eat first, the scientists aboard the *Elder* were in the steamship's salon listening to forestry professor Bernhard Fernow play Beethoven and Schubert on the piano, posting bits of humorous doggerel on the notice board, or challenging Harriman to a round of his favorite game, crokinole. Much of the credit for high spirits belonged to Harriman, whose energetic, hyper-organized personality helped maintain the peace. "The ship was equally at the service of men who wanted to catch mice or collect a new bird, as those who wanted to survey a glacier or inlet or shoot a bear," wrote Burroughs, who by the time the *Elder* left the Inside Passage was showing less interest in any of those activities than he did in returning to his New York cottage.

Much of the good cheer was surely relief from the day-to-day drudgery of exploration. Men like Muir, Grinnell, and Dall were accustomed to living on hardtack and wild game and sleeping on the ground. Harriman not only furnished hot meals and warm beds, but had established a Committee on Lectures that provided regular postprandial entertainment. Each evening at 8:00 P.M., one of the *Elder*'s experts gave a talk. "One night it was Dall on the history or geography of Alaska," Burroughs wrote, "then Gilbert upon the agency of glaciers in shaping the valleys and mountains, or upon the glaciers we had recently visited." Daniel Elliott, who had launched the expedition by whetting Harriman's appetite for bear, spoke on the fauna of Somaliland, in East Africa. Muir, who was an even better talker than he was a writer, took his turn with a story he had been polishing for almost twenty years but had only recently published, the tale of the little dog Stickeen.

Following his trip to Glacier Bay with Hall Young and the four Tlingit guides, Muir didn't return to San Francisco until January of 1880. He had corresponded dutifully with his fiancée, Louie Strentzel, throughout his journeys yet had somehow neglected to mention the date of his return to California. Louie learned of her future husband's arrival by reading the shipping news. The two were married in April at the Strentzel family estate, in Martinez. Muir spent the next three months working tirelessly to learn the fundamentals of growing and selling fruit. Louie became pregnant. In late July, Muir departed once again for Alaska, promising to return in plenty of time for the birth of their first child.

Shortly thereafter, Hall Young was awaiting the incoming mail boat in Wrangell when, to his astonishment, he spotted a familiar bearded form on the deck. Muir, who had given Young no advance warning of his return, hopped ashore and asked his friend, "When can you be ready?"

The matter was not as simple as reassembling their crew from the previous year. A disagreement between Wrangell's Stikine Tlingit tribe and their rivals the Taku had been inflamed by the northern neighbor's heavy consumption of home-brewed hoochinoo. (The Tlingit word has been passed down in a shortened form, *hooch*.) The Taku invaded the Stikine village at Wrangell. Hoping to broker peace, Toyatte and Young stood between the two sides, armed only with the chief's ceremonial spear. When gunfire commenced, the chief was shot through the forehead and fell dead in front of the missionary. "Thus died for his people the noblest Roman of them all," Muir wrote.

A new crew of three Tlingits was recruited, and a sixth member of the party joined at the last minute. Over the objections of Muir and Young's wife, Young's dog, Stickeen, invited himself on the trip when he "deliberately walked down the gang-plank to the canoe, picked his steps carefully to the bow, and curled himself down on my coat," Young remembered. Within a week, the small white, black, and brown mongrel was

Muir's inseparable companion, joining him on his rambles and sleeping at his feet.

The party paddled north to Glacier Bay and made a quick reconnaissance of the previous year's discoveries. They devoted a full week to Muir Glacier, mapping its face and driving stakes into the ice to measure the rate of its flow. In some spots, the ice river was moving fifty or sixty feet per day, with the leading edge calving off in bergs as it reached the water's edge. After paddling across the bay in a fierce storm, they pulled into a cove. At its head was Taylor Glacier (since renamed Brady Glacier for the future governor who greeted the Harriman Expedition in Sitka). To Muir's great delight, the ice was growing rather than receding. Its main branch alone was three miles wide. The glacier was advancing so rapidly that a Huna chief who had lost a salmon stream to the encroaching ice shocked Young with the news that he'd attempted to appease the ice mountain by sacrificing two of his best slaves, a husband and wife. "They were *my* slaves," the chief replied when Young gasped. "The man suggested it himself."

Young knew that the miserable weather would not lessen Muir's enthusiasm to explore an expanding glacier. When the minister awoke early the next morning, hoping to fix a hot breakfast for his friend, Muir had already departed. He'd taken along only an ice ax, a hunk of bread, and Stickeen.

Muir ascended the east side of the ice field, using trees that stood along its edge as a shield against the blast of the storm, which was so powerful that he had difficulty breathing while facing into the wind. Newly sheared stumps and trees crushed to pulp by the advancing ice littered the ground; the rain had swollen a stream of glacial runoff into a cascading torrent. Realizing that a coat was useless in such conditions, Muir stripped his off and surrendered to a complete drenching. Having ascended several miles with Stickeen along the glacier's edge, he scanned across its body as he neared the top. "As far as the eye could reach, the nearly level glacier stretched indefinitely away in the gray cloudy sky, a prairie of ice."

Using just the ax and a compass, Muir and Stickeen traversed the relatively smooth seven miles across in three hours. At 5:00 P.M., he estimated that three hours of daylight remained for their return to camp. As man and dog started back across, they found themselves disoriented amid a "bewildering labyrinth" of deep crevasses. Some of these could be leaped. Others could be crossed only on knife-edge ridges, which Muir flattened with his ice ax and scooted across "like a boy riding a rail fence" so that Stickeen could follow. As the sky grew darker, the hungry and exhausted pair started to run whenever possible to make up time. Already soaked to the bone, Muir knew that to survive the night on the ice, he would have to jump up and down until daylight just to stay warm.

Muir halted at a forty-foot-wide crevasse that appeared impassible. Retracing his steps wasn't an option. He had barely managed to leap across an eight-foot gap from a higher spot to reach his current position. The only possible crossing point was a frozen sliver attached to the sides of the chasm, "at a depth of about eight to ten feet below the surface of the glacier." (Muir later told Young that the edge curved down "like the cable of a suspension bridge.") Stickeen looked down over Muir's shoulder into the hole and began to whine, voicing his doubts.

Muir carefully cut a series of steps down to the narrow bridge, then began scooting slowly across with his knees pinned to its sides. As he went, he leveled a four-inch-wide balance beam for his friend. At the far end, Muir cut handholds and more steps and ascended carefully from the crevasse. Stickeen continued to howl. Muir knelt at the edge and coaxed the dog into slowly walking across the bridge.

Young kept watch from camp throughout the day but could see little through the sideways rain. At sunset he told the men to build a bonfire as a homing beacon. Not until after ten did the wet and weary adventurers stagger out of the forest. Without a word, Young and one of the Tlingit guides stripped Muir naked and dressed him in dry long underwear. Stickeen, who usually bounded into camp, crawled cold and wet to an edge of blanket and curled up by the fire. Only when Muir had eaten a hot meal could he speak of the day's events. His recounting of crossing what he called "that dreadful ice bridge in the shadow of death" moved Young to tears. Muir looked over at Stickeen on his blanket. "Yon's a brave doggie," he said.

Muir, who found the process of composition excruciating, said that the short book he published in 1909 about the adventure, *Stickeen,* was the most difficult writing he'd ever done. The narrative itself is straightforward, but the parable hidden inside must have given him fits. *Stickeen* was the vehicle through which he conveyed an idea that he'd been building and revising since childhood: that animals had God-given rights just as humans had. He seemed to have absorbed the influence of his Tlingit guides, whose pantheism incorporated a belief "that animals have souls, and that it was wrong to speak disrespectfully of the fishes or any of the animals that supplied them with food," Muir wrote in *Travels in Alaska.*

Nearly twenty years after his harrowing journey with Stickeen through the crevasses, the *Elder* passed near Taylor Glacier during the final leg of its journey home. After the evening's scholarly lecture in the salon gave way to a raucous celebration with college cheers and songs, Muir quietly stepped outside to stand alone at the ship's rail in silent vigil for his canine friend.

The passengers aboard the *Elder* could smell their next stop before they could see it. As they approached the tiny fishing town of Orca, the shoreline of Prince William Sound was coated for several miles by a slick of grease "dotted with salmon heads and bodies," according to Hart Merriam. In the journals of the various team members, the subject on which all agreed most, aside from the beauty of Glacier Bay, was Orca's overwhelming stench. John Muir was repelled by not only the odors of the cannery but the "unutterably dirty, frowsy" workers within. "Men in the business are themselves canned," he wrote in his diary.

After a brief stop, the *Elder* spent a few days exploring the glaciers of Prince William Sound, then returned to Orca for repairs on a busted propeller. A hundred dolphins provided an escort much of the way. As the ship docked near the cannery in the evening, its graphophone played at full volume, attracting the attention of idle gold miners lurking near the pier. More than three thousand men from down south had departed up the Copper River the prior year "on the wildest, vaguest rumor of gold," Burroughs wrote. "Alaska is full of such adventurers ransacking the land." Scores had died from scurvy, and survivors were trickling back into Orca penniless, waiting by the waterfront and hoping that a pitying steamboat captain would front them passage back south. Orca had no need for a dry dock, due to its extreme tidal range. The propeller repair crew waited for low tide, waded out into the shoals, constructed a scaffold around the steamship's broken blade, and slipped a new one into place before high tide returned.

The hiatus for repairs gave the expedition

members a chance to take a closer look at the activity inside the cannery. Burroughs watched in wonder as Chinese laborers from San Francisco wielded blades like jugglers — slicing off unwanted bits and disemboweling innards before passing a fish on to be washed, scaled, and canned. "Every second all day long a pound can, snugly packed, drops from the ingenious invention," he wrote. Burroughs lost his appetite for salmon after seeing so much of it in one place. "It is kicked about under foot; it lies in great smelling heaps; . . . the air is redolent of an odor far different from that of roses or new-mown hay."

To George Bird Grinnell, the carnage looked all too familiar. He was so moved by what he saw at Orca that he devoted an entire chapter to the state of its salmon fisheries in the second volume of the *Harriman Alaska Series.* "If one inquires of an individual connected with the salmon industry in Alaska something about their numbers, he is at once told of the millions found there, and informed that the supply is inexhaustible." It was the same language, Grinnell noted with alarm, that he was accustomed to hearing about the abundance of fur seals, buffalo, and passenger pigeons — all species whose astounding numbers had plummeted to almost zero in less than fifty years due to hunting. Once fishermen and packers dropped their bravado, however, their private concerns showed "very clearly that the supply of Alaska salmon is diminishing, and diminishing at a rapid rate."

For untold centuries, Orca had been fished by Eyak and Sugpiaq natives. Ownership rights to certain streams were hereditary and inviolable, which encouraged caretaking. The canneries that ignored these traditions were owned by corporations in California, so profits were shipped out of the territory along with product. They relied on nets that could stretch up to a mile long across the mouth of a river and barricades that blocked fish attempting to swim upstream to spawn. In both cases, salmon were prevented from breeding. A deliberate salmon-eradication program could hardly have been more effective.

"Their greed is so great that each strives to catch all the fish there are, and all at one time, in order that its rivals may secure as few as possible," Grinnell wrote. Any unwanted bycatch was discarded, as was any surplus salmon that spoiled before it could be processed — better the fish go to waste than to allow a competitor to have it. "All these people recognize very well that they are destroying the fishing; and before very long a time must come when there will be no more salmon to be canned at a profit. But this very knowledge makes them more and more eager to capture the fish and capture all the fish." Laws restricting overfishing had been passed but were virtually unenforceable in a territory as large as Alaska. Government agents lacked boats and depended on the canneries for transportation, thus eliminating surprise visits. On those rare occasions when an inspector found violations too flagrant to ignore, Grinnell wrote, the canners would admit guilt and say, "We do not wish to do as we are doing, but so long as others act in this way we must continue to do so for our own protection." They would be happy to stop as long as their competitors did so first. "Nothing is done and the bad work goes on."

The buffalo would survive, in large part due to Grinnell's political efforts. The passenger pigeon would not fare so well. In 1831, John James Audubon had estimated that two billion of the birds lived in North America. Grinnell remembered being called from the breakfast table as a boy in Manhattan's Audubon Park to look at a dogwood tree outside the window in which "there were so many birds that all could not alight in it." In the months between the *Elder*'s visits to Orca and the publication of Grinnell's salmon essay, the last wild passenger pigeon was shot by a boy in Ohio. The species *Ectopistes migratorius* went extinct when its only surviving member, a female named Martha, died in captivity in 1914.

Chapter Twenty-Eight: Eco-Disaster: The Aftermath

Cordova

Cordova, the town that grew adjacent to the Orca Cannery, no longer greets visitors arriving by sea with salmon heads. Which is not to say there isn't plenty of evidence of fish processing. At certain hours of the day, nearly every inch of every rooftop in town is occupied by seagulls, presumably descendants of the birds that Grinnell described as "great flocks near at hand." The birds congregate in Hitchcockian numbers to feast on salmon entrails churned out by Cordova's three waterfront fish plants.

"Tourists come to town and ask, 'Where can I buy salmon?' " Kristin Carpenter, executive director of the nonprofit Copper River Watershed Project (CRWP), told me. "I say, 'Nowhere.' Everyone catches their own, so no one needs to buy it. Salmon is the lifeblood of this community." Virtually every coastal Alaska community south of the Arctic Circle is heavily dependent on salmon, but Cordova may have been the most fishing-centric town I visited. CRWP founder (and fisherwoman) Riki Ott has described Cordova as a place where "one can easily find an O-ring seal for a hydraulic motor or a U-joint for an outdrive unit, but not a bra."

In many ways, the CRWP is doing the sort of work George Bird Grinnell foresaw as necessary: restoring salmon habitat, monitoring water quality, and finding ways to balance the needs of Cordova's commercial fishermen with those of upstream communities that rely on salmon for food. The group's headquarters is in a storefront on First Street, decorated in a style familiar to residents of places like Portland and Ithaca, what might be called "Progressive Cause": paper-strewn desks in an open floor plan, earnest posters on the walls, stacks of literature — in this instance, pamphlets about fish hatcheries and culverts.

The salmon that feed small towns up and down the Copper River and serve as Cordova's shadow currency are survivors of two of Alaska's greatest ecological catastrophes. By the 1930s, historian Bob King writes, canned salmon had emerged as Alaska's top industry, "generating the vast majority of the territory's revenues." But after peaking in 1936, salmon runs began to decline so rapidly that "in the 1950s Alaska salmon were declared a federal disaster." Salmon fishing was saved by statehood. Once Alaska took control of its fisheries from the federal government, in 1959, fish traps were outlawed, hatcheries were increased to supplement populations, and the numbers of fishermen licensed to catch in particular areas were restricted for the first time. (For example, Cordova has allowed exactly 541 gillnet permits since the 1970s.) By the late 1980s, salmon fishing was once again booming. In just a few years, prices for salmon seine permits in Cordova tripled: Those lucky enough to get one paid as much as three hundred thousand dollars.

Cordova's first disaster developed over decades and required many more decades to solve. Its second occurred at 12:04 A.M. on March 24, 1989, when the oil tanker *Exxon Valdez* struck a reef in Prince William Sound. The town still hasn't completely recovered from the damage.

In *Not One Drop,* her book about the *Exxon Valdez* disaster and its aftermath, Riki Ott quotes Cordova's city manager comparing the town, before 1989, to Shangri-la. Local boosterism aside, he has a point. Like the paradise in James Hilton's novel *Lost Horizon,* Cordova is cut off from the rest of the world by high mountains, so you can't drive there. It's the sort of place city slickers from Anchorage and Juneau go to get an authentic outdoors fix: hiking trails branch off its few paved roads in multiple directions; both the Copper River and Prince William Sound are prime paddling and fishing spots; and Cordova even operates its own low-key ski area, within walking distance of downtown, serviced by the old single-chair lift from Sun Valley. I doubt any Cordovans live to be two hundred years old, like the high lama in *Lost Horizon,* though all the omega-3s in the fish consumed here presumably yield certain life-extension benefits. Shangri-la is a place of heightened consciousness. Against its will, Cordova has become perhaps the most environmentally conscious town in Alaska.

The second thing one notices when arriving in Cordova, after the gulls, is the brand-new Cordova Center. If you walk south from the CRWP (noticing on your way out that much of the informational literature concerns potential pipeline spills), past the drugstore and the intriguingly seedy Alaskan Hotel and Bar, you arrive at an enormous, modern building that would be impressive in Juneau or Anchorage and not out of place in Vail.

The Cordova Historical Museum, on the ground floor, was preparing an exhibition of gansey fishermen's sweaters, opening that evening, which had drawn yarn enthusiasts from as far as Scotland. ("At the risk of sounding slightly ridiculous, a lot of the heavy hitters in the knitting world are here this weekend," Carpenter told me.) The museum had only recently opened, and its eclectic collection was still being re-assembled from its old location across the street. Staff members were marveling at the town newspaper's old linotype machine, which resembled a church organ. Nearby were hung an Eyak canoe and a six-hundred-pound leatherback sea turtle that had taken a wrong turn somewhere far to the south and gotten tangled in a Cordova fisherman's net. A draft version of a new timeline highlighting major historic events was taped along one wall, with edits and emendations scribbled on the text. Cordova's recorded history is as old as that of any place in Alaska. Vitus Bering first set foot in the New World on Kayak Island, sixty miles south of town. Spanish explorers gave the area its Iberian name in 1790. The write-up of the Harriman Expedition's 1899 stop in

Orca had a Post-it stuck to it, flagging a minor spelling error.

"Looks like they're still making corrections," said Nancy Bird. Bird's deceptively modest official title was museum assistant. In the 1980s, she had been editor of *The Cordova Times*. She was also the former executive director of the Oil Spill Recovery Institute, established by Congress to monitor the long-term effects of the *Exxon Valdez* disaster.

Events following the 1989 catastrophe dominate the historical timeline to the same degree that the Cordova Center dominates its downtown. People remember where they were when they heard that a supertanker had run aground. By morning, when word began to spread, ten million gallons of crude oil had poured through its breached hull and into Prince William Sound. The *Valdez*'s crew was slow to report the incident, and essential spill-response equipment was in dry dock, buried under snow. The gravity of the situation was slow to sink in. Kristin Carpenter's husband, Danny, was watching the spill unfold on TV with some fellow fishermen; one of them wondered aloud if they'd be able to get back to work the next week. Hundreds of newspeople swarmed into the town of twenty-five hundred, including my father, who was working as a cameraman for the *CBS Evening News*. (His chief memory was getting up at 5:00 A.M. to take a shower, because that's when the hotel ran out of hot water.) Images of dead birds, sea otters coated in crude, and people wiping down oil-slicked rocks with paper towels were all over the national news and remained there for months.

Cordova's isolation is a big part of its charm, but during the crisis, it amplified the feeling of living in a city under siege. The dribbles of information given out by Exxon and by Alyeska, the consortium of oil companies that operates the pipeline, did not always match what people saw with their own eyes. Bird worked on a daily newsletter put out "to quell rumors," she said. "For months and months, everyone in town was working seven days a week," Bird told me. "We had oodles of bigwigs visiting — Dan Quayle, senators, congressmen. Our own Senator Stevens declared that fishermen couldn't have oil on their anchors, because oil doesn't sink. Fishermen looked at their anchors and said, 'Umm . . .' "

Day-to-day business in Cordova almost came to a halt as clerical workers, bartenders, and day care providers quit suddenly to cash in on the $16.69 an hour that Exxon was paying (plus overtime) for miscellaneous decontamination duties. Exxon promised a complete cleanup, and went to great effort to erase the spill's most obvious effects. Among other wildlife, twenty-eight hundred sea otters were killed; for some of the animals that survived, an estimated eighty thousand dollars per sea otter was spent. "Early on, the NOAA [National Oceanic and Atmospheric Administration] folks came in and said they'd do a hot-water rinse of the beaches," Bird said. The shores of Prince William Sound, some of the loveliest in Alaska, looked as if they'd been hosed down with WD-40. "I thought, Isn't that going to kill everything on the beach? And lo and behold, years later they admitted that yes, it did." The power wash killed off the microbes that form the bottom of the food chain and forced oil deeper into cracks. It still seeps out in some places.

After the busy summer of 1989, the newspeople left town, and Cordova's residents waited for things to return to normal. The 1989 fishing season was a near-total wipeout. In 1992, the population of herring, an important source of fishing income and a food source for other species (including salmon), collapsed. It has never rebounded. A pod of orcas went into irreversible decline.

Salmon eventually stabilized, but not before many fishermen went bankrupt. "One day your permit is worth three hundred thousand dollars, and the next it's worthless," Carpenter said. There were suicides, divorces, signs of PTSD. An Alaskan jury awarded five billion dollars in punitive damages against Exxon, which the company appealed all the way to the U.S. Supreme Court. In 2008, the amount was reduced to 507 million dollars plus interest.

Nancy Bird and I walked out of the rear entrance of the Cordova Center and hopped into her orange Honda Element, which had a rich scent of old dog and, like many cars in Cordova, a NO ROAD bumper sticker on the back. The road in question was the Copper River Highway, a classic Alaska megaproject that proposed to connect Cordova to the state road system. Not surprisingly, one of the project's biggest boosters was Governor Wally Hickel, famed for bulldozing his own highway to the northern oil fields. For years after the *Exxon Valdez* spill, Kristin Carpenter told me, "the road issue became a litmus test for a person's politics," revealing his or her stance toward development versus preservation. If there is any silver lining to the *Valdez* disaster, it is that the accident made it politically impossible for Governor Hickel, who returned for a second term in the early 1990s, to fulfill his dream of expanding oil drilling into the Arctic National Wildlife Refuge's nineteen million pristine acres to make up for declining yields in Prudhoe Bay.

Bird drove north, her powder-blue fingernails providing a little cheery contrast to the gray sky over the sound. Main Street quickly became two-lane Route 10, and we followed the winding coast until the pavement ended abruptly a few minutes later. The terminus was at the former Orca Cannery where the Harriman team had witnessed the horrors of salmon processing. The complex had since been converted into an adventure sports lodge and, aside from a few improvements (such as a heli-skiing pad), still looked just like the line drawing of Orca in the *Harriman Alaska Series*. We wandered the first floor, which was deserted, then returned to Bird's Element and drove back toward town. If the Copper River Highway were ever extended, we'd be able to drive on to Chitina, Glennallen, Tok, and — assuming we didn't take a wrong turn and end up in Chicken (pop. 7) — keep going all the way to Daytona Beach if we felt like it. It would be the epic road trip of a lifetime. I hope no one ever gets to take it.

CHAPTER TWENTY-NINE:
CHANNEL DISCOVERIES

Harriman Fjord

The little-known glaciers of Prince William Sound, west of Cordova, were one of the primary enticements Hart Merriam had used to lure John Muir, who'd never visited the area on his six previous trips to Alaska. The scenery from the decks of the *Elder* did not disappoint; Muir declared the view toward the Chugach Mountains "one of the richest, most glorious mountain landscapes I ever beheld — peak over peak dipping deep in the sky, a thousand of them, icy and shining, rising higher, higher, beyond and yet beyond one another, burning bright in the afternoon light." Almost no mapping work had been done here since Vancouver's voyages, a hundred years earlier. The sheer number of glaciers, most of them anonymous, came as a pleasant surprise. Faced with one of the greatest labeling opportunities since Adam named the animals in

Genesis, the boatload of academics chose to honor their favorite institutions. In a particularly fertile stretch that came to be known as College Fjord, one glacier after another was forever linked to an eastern school: Columbia, Harvard, Yale, Radcliffe, Smith, Bryn Mawr, Vassar, Wellesley, Amherst.

Even along these isolated shores, the expeditioners encountered men who'd come north looking to make their fortunes. One entrepreneur had converted an entire island into a fox farm. When he noticed his animals escaping to a nearby island, he persuaded his brother to turn that one into a fox farm as well. A log cabin spotted next to a stream was home to a Norwegian prospector, who doffed his hat and bowed to the Harriman women. The copper business was treating him kindly, and he discussed his plans to visit the Paris Exposition in 1900.

The glaciers of College Fjord were calving so violently that icebergs clogged the waters. (This was, and still is, a common occurrence; the *Exxon Valdez* was attempting to avoid a berg discharged from Columbia Glacier when it ran aground.) The thundering avalanche struck the *Elder* passengers as a fusillade aimed at driving away curious trespassers. The rocks and gravel deposited by even the smaller glaciers "dwarfed anything I had yet seen," Burroughs wrote. "They suggested the crush of mountains and the wreck of continents." A sea of ice chunks halted the *Elder*'s advance twenty miles from the head of College Fjord.

The inlets of Prince William Sound reminded Burroughs of a great spider's arms stretching out in various directions deep into the mountainous shore. Stymied in College Fjord, the *Elder* reversed course and steamed north toward the sound's farthest reaches. There they encountered the massive bulk of Barry Glacier, a great white wedge stretched across the strait. Captain Doran's U.S. Coast Survey charts confirmed that they'd reached the end of navigable waters. Harriman instructed Doran to move closer to the ice wall for a better look. A tiny slice of open water came into view at the glacier's far left. As Captain Doran slowly inched the *Elder* forward, the passage opened into an entirely new fjord, previously unknown. Passengers rushed to the deck to view the gateway into a new world of ice.

Harriman biographer Maury Klein notes that for most of the railroad man's career prior to 1899, he had been known for the prudence of his actions. Harriman's reputation as a calculating gambler stems from the period starting just before his Alaska expedition. "He had burst from the cocoon of caution to become the most daring of butterflies, as if something had pressed upon him that great things could not be accomplished without great risks," Klein writes. Harriman ordered Doran to enter the uncharted waters, declaring, "We shall discover a new Northwest Passage!"

Unlike his boss, Captain Doran was not undergoing a personal awakening. His job was to avoid damaging the ship or running it aground in one of the most out-of-the-way spots on Alaska's southern coast. In Orca, Harriman had invited on board an expert on local waters, who strongly advised against going farther. He had hit many rocks in the area and, according to John Muir, frowned upon exploring "every unsounded, uncharted channel and frog marsh." Harriman took the wheel himself, assured Captain Doran that he assumed full responsibility for any damage, and "ordered full speed ahead, rocks or no rocks."

The jarring sound of metal on rock quickly confirmed the captain's reservations; one of the *Elder*'s two propellers was lost. Harriman's instincts were correct, though. As the ship slowly steamed through the gap, a narrow fjord twelve miles long, never before seen by white men, began to reveal itself. Along its sides, ribbons of ice ran down from steep mountains. Some were tidewater glaciers extending all the way to the water's edge, looking like "the stretched skins of polar bears," one expeditioner remarked. "In the solemn evening light," wrote the poet Charles Keeler in a letter to his wife, "it was one of the grandest scenes I have ever witnessed."

Perhaps thinking of the albatross who'd escorted them, geographer Henry Gannett was inspired to quote *The Rime of the Ancient Mariner* when recounting the "magnificent" mountains and glaciers that he would have the pleasure of adding to Alaska's map:

We were the first that ever burst
Into that silent sea.

By consensus, the new inlet was named Harriman Fjord, and the ice at its head Harriman Glacier. It was the most important scientific discovery of the expedition.

After Cordova, I flew home for a month to get reacquainted with my family. In early August I returned to Anchorage, which seemed an appropriate midpoint on my journey, being equidistant from my first maritime stop, Ketchikan (about 770 air miles southeast), and my last, Dutch Harbor, in the Aleutians (about 790 air miles southwest). By this time, the luxury *Crystal Serenity*'s sold-out burst into the silent, and ice-free, seas of the Northwest Passage was just a couple of weeks away. The ship was scheduled to make some of the same stops I was planning in the wake of the *Elder,* and I'd called and e-mailed a few times to see whether they'd be interested in having a reporter on board. Perhaps, I thought, some clever marketing executive would see the parallels between the historic, but comfortable, 1899 voyage of the *Elder* and the *Crystal Serenity*'s own history-making excursion, on which I assumed no one would be camping in the observation lounge. The stops on the second half of my journey — Whittier, Kodiak, Katmai National Park, Nome — were spread out along a couple thousand miles of almost roadless coast, only part of which was covered by sporadic ferry service: the three-day end-of-the-line run out to the Aleutians. The *Serenity* was making the same voyage, and the idea of traveling on a ship with its own casino and driving range sounded a lot more appealing than my other option: three days on the

Alaska Marine Highway's oldest ship, the fifty-year-old *Tustumena,* aka the "Trusty Tusty," aka the "Rusty Tusty."

One of the optional stops planned for the *Crystal Serenity* was Shishmaref, on the small barrier island of Sarichef, along the Pacific coast near Nome. Shishmaref had been in the news lately as one of several Alaskan villages that were in danger of falling into the sea due to erosion caused by climate change. *Crystal Serenity* passengers had been offered what sounded like a rather tone-deaf extracurricular activity, a six-hundred-dollar day trip called "Flight to Shishmaref: A Study in Global Warming." Promotional materials promised that participants would have four hours to soak in the pathos of the situation. By unfortunate coincidence, the same day the *Serenity* departed, the residents of Shishmaref were voting on whether to stay and build another seawall — they had already lost two — or move the village to a new location farther inland.

The *Serenity* folks evidently had no interest in the pleasure of my company and set sail without me. The next day, I had coffee in Anchorage with Esau Sinnok, a Shishmaref native and sophomore at UAF, who, as news of the landmark vote spread across the country and then the globe, had become something of a spokesman for his village. (He texted a last-minute apology for pushing back the time of our meeting, but he had a good excuse — he hadn't finished packing for the fall semester, and the BBC wanted to interview him.) The voting results were due in at any time, and Esau wasn't sure about the outcome. "The people who want to go are the younger generation like me," he said. "The people who want to stay are the ones who've been here all their lives. Most of us in Shish are family. But if we stay, we have to keep moving our houses. My grandparents have a big blue house on a cliff, where there used to be an actual beach." He sipped his drink and checked his phone. "Shish might be underwater in two or three decades."

Later that afternoon, Esau texted me with the referendum results. The village had voted 89 to 78 to relocate.

CHAPTER THIRTY: WEIRD

Whittier

If you are fortunate enough to travel to various parts of the world, you may eventually begin to notice that some places feel a lot like other places, even if they're thousands of miles apart. There are blocks in Madrid that could be transplanted to the Bronx without causing a stir. The marshes of central Botswana and the Amazon jungles of Peru look (and smell) like the Everglades. Whittier, which is frequently referred to as the Weirdest Town in Alaska, could be the sister city of Pago Pago, in American Samoa. Both are situated on lush, horseshoe-shaped harbors, enclosed by steep green mountainsides that rise nearly vertically from the sea. Both contain a lot of decaying infrastructure left behind by the U.S. military. Both get a lot of rain almost daily. And both are home to a lot of Samoans.

This last thought occurred to me as I sat

in the lobby of Whittier's one large residential building. While I waited for my laundry to dry down the hall on a blustery gray summer day, three different women walked past wearing traditional Samoan lavalava wrap skirts. I asked the last of them if there was a Polynesian-themed party going on, perhaps a luau for a visiting cruise ship. She told me that, no, a couple of dozen people had made the move from American Samoa a few years back, starting with a pastor who had felt called to serve the Lord in Alaska. It was a classic case of lighting out for the Alaskan territory, though in this case the pioneers had traveled five thousand miles northeast, from a South Seas paradise where I had swerved to avoid coconuts in the road to a town that owes its existence to the strategic value of its crappy weather. She said she was getting used to it and gave me the name of a store in Anchorage that sold taro root.

Whittier may or may not be the Weirdest Town in Alaska — I'm guessing that none of the people who make that claim have been to Yakutat — but it's certainly unusual. Its deepwater port doesn't freeze during the winter, which made it a prime spot for a far-north Pacific military base during World War II. Two mountain ranges converge near Whittier, trapping a semipermanent cloud cover that hid its waterfront from Japanese bombers. Those same mountains sequester Whittier from the rest of Alaska like a geographic safe room. To establish access, the U.S. military had to carve a 2.5-mile-long tunnel that accommodated a single rail line. Until 2000, the train was Whittier's only land access to the rest of the world. Since then, it's been possible to drive through, but since there is space for only one lane of traffic, cars are allowed through just once an hour in each direction.

Since the tunnel is the sole road out of a town that can feel a little claustrophobic, its schedule is the hourglass by which time passes in Whittier. People say things like "I'm out on the next tunnel," and the other person understands that this means "I'm leaving in twenty minutes." The passageway is closed from 11:00 P.M. to 5:30 A.M. (longer in winter), making the last openings of the day in and out a little stressful to anyone who stops for dinner and a movie after commuting to Anchorage (sixty miles away). For some residents, a tunnel run feels like crossing Checkpoint Charlie, in West Berlin, except the wall is six thousand feet high and, instead of smuggling microfilm in their socks, Whittier's citizens carry trunkloads of cheap toilet paper from

Target. "I see the tunnel as a portal between two worlds," Ted Spencer, curator of the museum located on the first floor of the Anchor Inn, told me. "I get a sense of calm as I emerge into all this natural beauty."

Spencer isn't exaggerating, about the scenery anyway. One genuinely weird thing about Whittier is the juxtaposition of its cracked asphalt, abandoned fishing boats, and hideous buildings (including, truth be told, the Anchor Inn) against a backdrop that anywhere else in America would merit national park status. When the sun is shining, which happens only 133 days per year, you can stand in the center of the large parking lot that constitutes much of downtown and see glaciers, cascades, green mountainsides, snowy peaks, and the deep blue waters of Passage Canal.

Aside from its access limitations, the primary reasons for Whittier's oddball reputation are a pair of buildings left from the Cold War era. The Buckner Building, built in the 1950s as housing for a thousand enlisted military personnel, was known as "The City Under One Roof" because it included a movie theater, a bowling alley, a shooting range, a bakery, and even a jail. When the military pulled out of Whittier, in 1960, the Buckner was abandoned to Whittier's notorious weather, which is terrible even by Alaska standards: an average of sixteen feet of snow on top of all the rain and winds that frequently top fifty miles an hour. The abandoned Buckner now looks like a set from a postapocalyptic movie, filled with graffiti and water and toxic sludge. It's a favorite of urban explorers and the backdrop to countless hours of poorly lighted GoPro footage. Some skiers shot a slick Warren Miller–inspired movie of themselves slaloming the Buckner's snowy stairwells and jumping out of its broken windows. When I walked past, two excited European tourists were taking pictures of each other as they slipped through a hole cut in the flimsy chain-link fence.

Whittier's other relic of military housing is the fourteen-story Begich Towers, built at the same time as the Buckner. The Begich is still very much alive; it was getting a new boiler and a fresh paint job in cheerful pastel colors when I was there. The exterior could pass for one of the nicest buildings in Pyongyang; the interior is a 1950s time capsule. (The pink bathroom in the condo I rented was nearly identical to the one in my grandmother's ranch-style house, except for the earthquake crack in one wall.) The Begich is also famous for being self-contained, and is home to not only most of Whittier's population but its post office (where I inquired about sending a package Priority Mail and also the location of the laundry room), police department, mayor's office, and medical clinic, plus a mini-mart and, in the basement, a church. The building is connected underground to Whittier's school, to shield children from the snow and wind. In winter, it isn't uncommon for everyone to stay inside for days at a time. Begich Towers is perhaps one-eighth occupied — it was built to house a thousand people, and Whittier's current population is just over two hundred — and even on a busy day it's eerily empty. One resident I met said she frequently runs for half an hour up and down its staircases and hallways without seeing anyone.

My primary purpose in coming to Whittier was to get a look at Harriman Fjord. I booked a charter with Ben Wilkins aboard the *Explorer*. Wilkins was young and bearded and cool in the way one can be only after years of captaining boats in Hawaii. (To answer the obvious next question, the money is a lot better in Alaska.) Ben knew all about the Harriman Expedition. He told me that so many landforms in the area were available for naming in 1899 that even the less famous members of the *Elder* crew saw themselves immortalized on maps. Point Doran honored the poor captain whose warnings to stay away from the rocks left him cast as the Chicken Little of the expedition.

"I don't blame Doran *at all,*" Ben said as we made our way into Prince William Sound. "That is some sketchy water. There are spots near Barry Glacier" — the ice mountain that had initially appeared to block the path to Harriman Fjord — "where the water might be a mile wide and six inches deep." Wilkins had a depth finder on his console and checked it constantly. Varying measurements were represented by vivid contrasting colors, and the closer we approached a receding glacier, the more the onscreen swirls resembled one of Peter Max's trippier paintings. "They haven't updated the charts yet," Ben explained when the coordinates briefly indicated that we had taken flight over a promontory. "There are places on this GPS that show us two miles inland."

We passed a petrified forest that was younger than the state of Alaska; when the '64 earthquake hit, the ground dropped several feet, and trees calcified from absorbing salt water. A solitary lump of rock that served as a puffin rookery appeared to have hosted a violent paintball battle. The weather was typical for the Whittier region — lousy verging on terrible — so we decided to skip College Fjord, where visibility was close to zero. "There's been so much calving off of Columbia Glacier that you can't get within five miles of it anyway," Ben said.

As we headed northwest, the numbers on the depth monitor kept sliding up and down, dipping to twenty feet and then surging to two hundred. "This is where Doran freaked out," Ben said. "Every time I come through here, I wonder how they did it in a giant steamship." Barry Arm, which had once been nearly cut off by the glacier of the same name, was now wide-open. A sixty-foot-high rock island rose out of the water near Barry Glacier's face. "Ten years ago, that was under ice," Ben said. "This is the fastest-retreating glacier in Prince William Sound right now."

We finally entered a long fjord obscured by low clouds. At its terminus was a very wide, very flat, very blue mass. "There's Harriman Glacier," Ben said.

Until the 1990s, the Harriman had been one of those rare glaciers that was still advancing a century after the end of the Little Ice Age. A decade ago it seemed to be stable. Over the past several years, Ben said, it had been retreating two hundred yards a year.

Because the Harriman was relatively low and less prone to catastrophic calving, it was possible to approach much more closely than I had at any other glacier. The ice had the cracked face of a Sun Belt centenarian. New soil peeked out around the edges of the glacier where it had recently withdrawn onto land. "Do you see that dirt underneath?" Ben asked, standing and wiping fog from the window for a better view.

The Harriman had been the last serious glacier seen from the deck of the *Elder* before the steamship turned for home, and I suspected it might be the last one I'd get a good look at in Alaska. I opened the front hatch and stepped out onto the bow with binoculars. A river of silty water gushed out from the glacier's underside.

"We might be some of the last people to see this glacier while it's still tidewater," Ben said, meaning the ice soon would no longer reach the water's edge. He plopped back down into his captain's chair. "That's nuts."

CHAPTER THIRTY-ONE:
WARMING TRENDS

Harriman Glacier

Around the time I was staring at the Harriman Glacier's dirty face, the *Alaska Dispatch News* published a six-page photo essay with the headline GLOBAL WARMING DOUBTER? COMPARE THESE IMAGES. In before-and-after shots spanning a century or more, some of Alaska's most famous ice was shown to have melted away like unwanted belly fat in a Weight Watchers ad. One spread contrasted a 1905 picture of the robust Toboggan Glacier, just a few miles northeast of the Harriman, with a recent shot. The modern image showed a frozen puddle tucked into an otherwise green valley.

Bruce Molnia, the man who'd assembled the photo pairs, calls his image-comparison methodology "repeat precision photography." Molnia is a research geologist at the U.S. Geological Survey, based in Reston,

Virginia, and the author of a very thick book titled *Glaciers of Alaska*. He's one of the few people who've spent more time flipping through the *Harriman Alaska Series* than I have. Glacial behavior is an excellent indicator of slight changes in climate. The thousands of photos Molnia had collected demonstrated overwhelmingly that Alaska's glaciers have retreated in the past century. A few, like the Johns Hopkins in Glacier Bay and the Hubbard, near Yakutat, showed growth, though. What did it mean if glaciers were both advancing and retreating?

Not surprisingly for a geologist, Molnia takes a very long view of what he calls "the frozen part of the hydrosphere": glaciers, sea ice, and permafrost. Glaciers are not eternal fixtures of the landscape; over the past two-plus billion years ("as long as the Earth has had an atmosphere") they have come and gone on a continental scale hundreds of times, in cycles that have lasted millennia. Coastal cities such as New York, Miami, and Norfolk are bracing for a predicted sea level rise of up to three feet by 2100, which would inundate their lowest-lying coastal areas and cause hundreds of billions of dollars of infrastructure damage. Molnia reminded me that 125,000 years ago, sea levels were probably twenty feet higher than they are today. When global temperatures fell and the ice sheets advanced, these levels fell to more than *four hundred* feet lower than they are now, exposing the Bering Land Bridge. "I hear people say, 'It's never been this warm,' or, 'Sea levels have never risen this fast,' " Molnia said. "Let's put this in perspective. Twenty-one thousand years ago, if there had been an Empire State Building and you stood on the top floor and looked east, you would not have been able to see the Atlantic Ocean, because the shoreline was sixty to seventy miles further away."

I'd heard guesses as to how many of Alaska's large valley glaciers are shrinking that ranged from half to 90 percent. The correct answer, Molnia said, is greater than 99 percent. The few that are growing — not even a dozen, depending on local conditions — aren't evidence refuting climate change. Advancing glaciers such as the Hubbard and the Johns Hopkins have fluctuated over time as others have. The Hubbard is more than fifty miles long and draws from an extremely high source area (that is, its maximum elevation exceeds ten thousand feet above sea level) with heavy precipitation. Some of the ice that cruise ship passengers see calving off its front probably fell as snow before Columbus piloted the *Santa Maria* across the ocean.

The recent retreat of Alaska's glaciers seems especially dramatic, Molnia said, because many expanded so significantly during the cooling period of the Little Ice Age. "Greenhouse gases are a major factor in causing the recent changes in earth temperatures and the extent of glaciers, but the Little Ice Age started less than a thousand years ago and ended in some places as early as 1750," Molnia said. "In some cases, the volume of ice lost between 1750 and 1850 in places like Glacier Bay greatly exceeds that lost in the past hundred years in the same areas." Today, most of Alaska's valley glaciers would still be retreating without the effects of global warming, just more slowly.

Near the end of the nineteenth century, the Swedish chemist Svante Arrhenius attempted to uncover the cause of ice ages. He calculated that the level of carbon dioxide in the atmosphere had the effect of a thermostat; if CO_2 levels declined, an ice age resulted. If levels rose, temperatures would rise, too. (As a resident of frosty Sweden, Arrhenius saw this potential warming as a positive development.) The vast majority of the world's climate scientists now agree that global warming is primarily the result of increased concentrations of gases in the atmosphere, especially carbon dioxide, which is emitted during the burning of fossil fuels. Starting around 1850 with the late Industrial Revolution, atmospheric concentrations of CO_2 have accelerated. Humans have been cranking up the earth's thermostat ever since.

For some time now, Alaska has been warming twice as fast as the rest of the United States. The effects of this change are so obvious that even the state's most anti-environmental politicians — a rather non-exclusive club — had to admit that something was going on. The same legislature that couldn't agree on how to balance a budget without upsetting oil companies or reducing Permanent Fund dividend checks nevertheless established the Alaska Climate Change Impact Mitigation Program in 2008 to assist the state's many communities dealing with erosion, flooding, and thawing permafrost. (As a sort of global-warming multiplier, thawing permafrost also releases huge amounts of CO_2 and methane into the atmosphere when long-frozen organic matter decomposes. Methane has a more powerful effect on human-induced warming than CO_2, but atmospheric concentrations of CO_2 are much greater.) The growing season of interior Alaska expanded by 45 percent in the past century and is expected to continue lengthening. Plant and animal species have migrated north. The number and intensity of forest fires have increased. A patch of warm water nicknamed "the blob" has parked in the Gulf of Alaska, with devastating effects on the marine food web.

Faced with overwhelming evidence, the Alaska coalition in Washington, DC, has adopted the position that, while climate change is definitely occurring, no radical steps should be taken to fight it, because, to use a favorite phrase, "the science isn't settled." As George Bird Grinnell said about the overfishing of salmon, nothing is done and the bad work goes on.

The rising temperatures that launched the Holocene epoch, around 11,700 years ago, spurred the growth of agriculture, cities, civilization, and, eventually, the Industrial Revolution and coal-burning railroads that closed the American frontier. Nomadic tribes adapting to the end of the last ice age could migrate when sea levels rose too high. You can gas up your Escalade and escape a flood, but you can't pick up and move the Empire State Building, or Bangladesh, or Shishmaref.

I e-mailed Molnia a photo I'd taken of the Harriman Glacier to get his prognosis. He said that, unlike its neighbor the Toboggan Glacier, the Harriman looked pretty healthy. What I'd thought was exposed bedrock turned out to be moraine — debris pushed forward by a moving glacier that can actually slow its melting by protecting it from seawater.

"People ask me all the time, 'When are Alaska's glaciers going to be gone?' " Molnia said. "The simple answer is, never" — for those at the highest and coldest elevations, anyway — " 'never' being millions of years." For tidewater glaciers like the Harriman, however, which have shrunk in number from about two hundred, at the end of the Little Ice Age, to fewer than fifty today, the trend line is definitely pointed in the wrong direction.

"I can't imagine the Hubbard or the Johns Hopkins being gone in the next century," Molnia said. However, warming temperatures cause ocean temperatures to increase, which accelerates the rate of melting and ice loss at lower elevations. "If you want to see glaciers that are easily accessible from the deck of a ship before they're gone, you need to get moving."

Chapter Thirty-Two:
Loaded for Bear

Kodiak

After a roundabout four-hundred-mile trip southwest from Orca to Kodiak Island, the passengers of the *Elder* "swarmed out of the ship, like boys out of school, longing for a taste of grass," John Burroughs wrote. Compared with the cold monochrome austerity of Harriman Fjord, disembarking at a place covered in green fields and rolling, flowering slopes was like emerging from a fever. Even John Muir, for whom glaciers were the entire point of the voyage, had to admit that "no green mountains and hills of any country I have seen, not even those of the Emerald Isle, can surpass these."

The island's main village, St. Paul (known today as Kodiak), was in 1899 a melting pot of cultures. Russians had subjugated the island's Alutiiq population during the initial fur frenzy and had since intermarried with them. A scattering of Americans had moved in since the handover. Burroughs found the village nearly as enchanting as the surrounding countryside: frame cottages with small gardens, grassy lanes instead of streets (the island had neither horses nor wheeled transport of any kind), and a shop with a large sign reading CHICAGO STORE, where he purchased some fresh eggs.

The *Elder* had arrived in Kodiak ahead of schedule because Harriman had learned that the island was prime bear country. After five weeks in Alaska, he was growing impatient with his failure to land his trophy. Hart Merriam, who was engaged in a decades-long project at the U.S. Biological Survey to classify the varieties of brown bear, surely knew that once the ship departed Kodiak and made its way into the Aleutians and beyond, the chances of finding a bear to shoot were slim. Merriam sought out an old Kodiak hunter named Fischer, who'd sent him some skulls in Washington, DC. Fischer told the scientist that the largest sample he'd forwarded had belonged to a bear shot by his wife not far from town. Merriam rushed back to share the promising news. By that evening, Harriman was speeding in a steam launch to a campsite eight miles away.

Muir was cranky as ever about all the

hunting, grumbling to his journal, "Everybody going shooting, sauntering as if it were the best day for the ruthless business." But he, too, succumbed to Kodiak's verdant charms, joining a party that wandered the wildflower-covered foothills outside of town. Poet Charles Keeler and John Burroughs sneaked away with a picnic of beer and sandwiches to lounge beneath a giant spruce tree on Wood Island. Keeler counted the robins and warblers he recognized from their winter visits to Berkeley as Burroughs took a snooze on the grass. At the request of Mrs. Harriman, the young mineralogist Charles Palache helped supervise the Big Four girls on "their first taste of outdoor life," which included rowing a boat upriver and cooking their own pancakes and bacon. When Palache spotted a bald eagle's nest in a cottonwood, he impressed the ladies by shinnying up and snatching a young bird with feathers as soft as beaver fur.

While the rest of the *Elder* passengers savored Kodiak's rustic pleasures, Merriam waited alone anxiously for the expedition patron's return. At around 8:45 P.M. on July 3, Harriman roared into camp and announced — to Merriam's "immense delight" — that he had bagged "a real big genuine Kodiak bear." Even in the scientist's scant notebook jottings from the day, one can sense his relief.

It is perhaps for the best that George Bird Grinnell had gone off hunting elsewhere on Kodiak Island, for the tale of Harriman's feat didn't exactly rise to the Boone and Crockett Club's standards of fair play. Harriman had come across a mother brown bear with her cub, munching grass "like a cow," he said. The team of hunters drove the two bears into a narrow gorge, where Harriman was waiting with his Winchester. The odds were heavily stacked in the railroad man's favor, since he was encircled by men "with enough firepower to tear the bear to pieces," should his nerve fail him, one participant recalled. Harriman dropped the sow with a single shot. Guide Yellowstone Kelly completed the ambush by dispatching the cub.

The specimen was not quite as impressive as originally believed. She was a little undersize for a Kodiak bear and, judging from Edward Curtis's photo of the kill, rather mangy. Nonetheless, a taxidermist was immediately dispatched to prepare Harriman's trophy. The skulls of both animals wound up in the archives of the Smithsonian, deep in whose bowels they may still reside today.

The next day, the Fourth of July, dawned

warm and clear. "The celebration began by the firing of the ship's little brass cannon," Burroughs wrote, which the crew stuffed with rags and blasted repeatedly for an hour. "The Stars and Stripes Forever" blared from the graphophone. Botanist William Brewer delivered a rousing speech praising the United States' entry into the Spanish-American War as evidence of its dedication to freedom. Charles Keeler rebutted with a poem condemning the intervention.* Someone picked up a fiddle, and a pair of middle-aged scientists danced a jig to an old Christian hymn. The afternoon concluded with "a boat race and general merriment," Burroughs wrote. A final cheer went up when the team that had been dispatched to collect the dead bears

* Keeler, while a respected naturalist, was quite likely the strangest of the *Elder* guests. His best-known book, *The Simple Home,* was essentially an interior design and landscape architecture manifesto. Late in life, he attempted to formulate a universal religion by founding the First Berkeley Cosmic Society. He is also known for writing the Cremation of Care ceremony, performed annually at the private Bohemian Club assembly, which conspiracy theorists believe is a powerful satanic ritual but is actually ridiculous.

returned with the trophies.

John Muir took a dissenting view of the gaiety, recording Harriman's sporting feat in his journal as the killing of a "mother and child." It was aboard the *Elder* in Kodiak, however, that Muir's resistance to Harriman's magnetism finally crumbled. While some other members of the party were assembled on the front deck awaiting another fine meal, several praised the "blessed ministry of wealth" that had made the expedition possible. Ever the gadfly, Muir interrupted the laudations, saying, "I don't think Mr. Harriman is very rich. He has not as much money as I have. I have all I want and Mr. Harriman has not."

Word filtered back to Harriman, who took a seat next to Muir after dinner. "I never cared for money except as power for work," he told Muir. "What I most enjoy is the power of creation, getting into partnership with nature in doing good, helping to feed man and beast, and making everybody and everything a little better and happier." A most unusual friendship was born, one that would last until the end of Harriman's life.

The accord between conservationist and capitalist did not prevent Muir from getting the last word, as he almost always did. In a long letter he wrote to the Harriman children upon returning to his farm in Martinez, he concluded, "Remember your penitential promises. Kill as few of your fellow beings as possible and pursue some branch of natural history at least far enough to see Nature's harmony. Don't forget me. God bless you."

CHAPTER THIRTY-THREE: LIFE AMONG THE BRUINS

Uyak Bay

Kodiak Island is enormous, more than twice the size of Long Island and larger than Crete or Corsica. On maps, it sits just south of the point where the tusk formed by the Alaska Peninsula and the Aleutian Islands starts to jut out toward Asia; Kodiak looks like a puzzle piece that could be picked up and placed into the gap of Cook Inlet, to the north. I flew in from Anchorage and spent a day poking around the main town, Kodiak, which is fairly large by Alaska standards. (It has a McDonald's and a Walmart, both of which appeared to be very popular with personnel from Kodiak's enormous Coast Guard station.) The next morning I caught a propeller plane flight across the island to Larsen Bay, a small village near the mouth of Uyak Bay, on Kodiak's northwest coast. The other passenger and I seemed to be afterthoughts on a cargo

353

run; boxes filled virtually every inch of space not occupied by human flesh. The aerial view confirmed Burroughs's verdurous raptures: Kodiak was wet and hilly, with few trees and, in late summer, little snow or ice except at the highest altitudes. Pools of water and rocky brown spots took the shapes of golf hazards; all else was fairways. This year was the third in a row on Kodiak that had qualified as warmest ever. Berries that usually appeared in late July had popped out in mid-June. Bears were gorging so much on fruit that some scientists wondered if they'd have any interest in salmon once the fish returned to spawn.

Like Harriman, I'd come to Kodiak after getting a tip that this was prime country for getting close to big brown bears — on my own terms — and had put myself in the hands of a specialist. Harry Dodge III picked me up at the tiny airport. From what I could see, the town of Larsen Bay consisted of the gravel airstrip, a cannery, a couple of sportsman's lodges, and a small school. After a quick stop for supplies at the cannery's sparsely stocked general store, we boarded Harry's skiff and motored into the wide green mouth of Uyak Bay.

Harry was uniquely qualified to discuss the topic of bears on Kodiak Island. He'd worked for years as a wildlife biologist and master hunting guide and now ran a company with his wife, Brigid, offering bear treks. The service was similar to guiding hunting clients, minus the guns: Kodiak Treks tracked bears so their clients could shoot them with Nikons and Canons. He was the first outdoor guide I'd met with an MFA in creative writing.

"As far as the East Coast of the United States is concerned, the Harriman Expedition really put Kodiak and its bears on the map," Harry said as we cruised south. Now in his early sixties, Harry had spent a year in Vietnam during the Cambodia campaign, and had a vaguely John Muir–ish beard. He tended to nod distractedly when asked a question or not respond at all, which I took to be Alaskan taciturnity until I realized he was a little hard of hearing. (You can practically hear your heartbeat during an awkward silence in Uyak Bay.) He wasn't the type to boast about his accomplishments. It was only after he mentioned one of Harriman's hunting guides by name that he admitted he'd written a book titled *Kodiak Island and Its Bears: A History of Bear/Human Interaction on Alaska's Kodiak Archipelago*.

Before the arrival of muskets with the Russians, killing a bear was a much more serious undertaking, and not merely because a hunter's arsenal against an animal that could weigh fifteen hundred pounds consisted mainly of sharp objects attached to sticks. "Many early cultures considered the bear as intermediary between man and the sacred powers of nature," Harry writes in *Kodiak Island.* "Most ancient hunting societies observed pre-hunt traditions, such as avoiding certain activities, seclusion or abstention from sexual relations, and ceremonial sweat baths." The Russians had little interest in bears except as a nuisance, but "after the sale of Alaska, the Americans killed *everything,*" Harry told me. By the time the *Elder* arrived, in 1899, with sea otter populations dwindling, many hunters had turned their attentions to bears.

In the decades after Harriman's much publicized visit, Kodiak was established as *the* place to kill a brown bear. Hart Merriam completed his ursine taxonomy in 1918 and categorized the Kodiak bear as a subspecies, in part because of its great size. Of the twenty largest trophy bears of all time, as tallied by the Boone and Crockett Club in the 1990s, seventeen of them had been bagged on Kodiak Island. Hunting is still a major business in Kodiak; Harry estimated that at least 150 adult male bears are harvested each year, a kill that costs an out-of-state sportsman at least twenty thousand dollars, between permit, guiding fee, and expenses. Mothers and cubs are off-limits, unlike in Harriman's day. "There are more bears here now than when I got here forty years ago," Harry said. "They seem to be at capacity."

For decades, Kodiak's guiding business was in conflict with an unlikely foe. We were deep in the Kodiak National Wildlife Refuge, in what looked to be primeval forest, but Harry said that homesteading had actually been attempted in the area starting in the 1920s. "Some ranchers came here and saw all this grass and thought it would be a good place for cattle," he said. Livestock and bears don't mix, for obvious reasons. Several cattle ranchers pushed for the complete eradication of bears. In 1963, Alaska's governor approved a secret program to deal with the perceived problem. The Alaska Department of Fish and Game mounted a semiautomatic rifle onto a Piper Super Cub, which patrolled for bears. When a target animal was spotted, the pilot circled above until the copilot could get a clean shot. One rancher recalled, "If a bear hid in the alders, firecrackers were dropped in the bushes and the bear would come running out." The aerial slaughter ended a year later, but a few ranchers still raise cattle on Kodiak, which, as Harry notes in his book, with typical understatement, "has proven to be a challenging enterprise."

Harry and Brigid own several acres on a small island in the middle of the bay — an island tucked inside a remote nook of a larger island separated from the mainland by a twenty-five-mile-wide strait. Uyak Bay is not a great place to go looking for action on a Saturday night, but it is an excellent place to go looking for bears. An estimated three hundred live in the wildlife refuge. Every year, more people come to Alaska wanting to see bears, primarily from airplanes and buses. Harry and Brigid promote a more low-impact, sustainable approach that requires a little more patience.

We slowed and pulled into a small cove. Harry jumped into the shallow water and tied up the boat. His black Lab, Loyal, chased Harry ardently until he spotted the new visitor, at which point he smothered me with paws-on-the-chest attention. A path through a rocky slope ran up from the pebbled beach, leading to a red house, around which were arranged a few outbuildings where guests slept. In the kitchen I met Brigid, who offered me a cup of coffee and introduced me to some of the other guests, all of whom were speaking French. Brigid speaks several languages, and Kodiak Treks sees a lot of business via European travel agents. She told one of the other guests that I was staying in a room *à côté de la serre,* which sounded extravagant but meant a small room attached to the greenhouse — cozy accommodations that most gardeners would identify as a potting shed. (The Dodges had squeezed me in during a busy week.) The setup was actually pretty close to perfect: The camp bed was comfortable, and just outside my door stood a thicket of wild salmonberry bushes, their fruit at the peak of ripeness. Everyone else had eaten so many already that no one objected when I stood and gorged myself until my fingers were stained red.

After dinner, we all piled into two boats and rode deeper into the wedge of the fjord. I went with Harry in an open aluminum boat with an outboard motor. Everyone was dressed in enough rain gear to work on a trawler. At the Kodiak airport, I'd checked the forecast in New York: ninety-eight degrees and sunny. In Uyak Bay it was fifty-five and drizzling. I asked Harry, who'd interviewed dozens of Kodiak hunting guides for his book, if he'd gleaned any time-tested techniques for staying dry. He mulled it over for a few seconds. "You just sort of get used to being wet a lot of the time," he said.

Before long the sky cleared, revealing the high green sides of the scooped-out valley. After ten miles, we landed in a wooded area where Harry and Brigid kept their satellite camp. We sat around a big fire talking for an hour or two, most of which I didn't comprehend. Brigid tried to explain the phrase "Who cut the cheese?" to one young Parisian, a question that not only lacked a direct analogue in French but seemed to imply negligence when performing an essential duty. We went off to sleep in our tents. Harry said not to worry about bears, so I didn't, and slept like a stone.

Our bear hunt commenced after breakfast the next morning. We moved single file like an army patrol, starting down the beach because that was the clearest path. The tide had just gone out, and moon jellyfish littered the shore like giant contact lenses. Harry and Brigid walked in front, her tight blond ponytail providing a beacon amid our earth-toned clothing. (Bears don't like bright colors.) They wore rubber hip waders and had the sort of lean and sinewy builds that one earns from carrying a heavy pack through hilly country for several hours each day. (They had once hiked ninety miles from near their Uyak Bay home to the town of Kodiak for a music festival, a feat I learned about only later back at their house while eating a cookie, because I happened to pick up a book of essays Harry had written.) Where Harry was reserved unless someone asked a question, Brigid was gregarious, demonstrating how to estimate the size of a bear by its paw print, pointing out otter holes and creepy ancient burial sites — one of which had a set of human teeth in it — while passing around binoculars so that everyone could see the goats on the far shore. (*"Voilà, chèvres!"*) Occasionally Harry would say something fascinating about bears in a low voice and Brigid would shout, "Please say that again a little louder, sweetie, so everyone can hear you."

We filled water bottles from a fast-running stream (no purification needed this far out), crossed a mudflat and joined a bear trail leading up a hill. The tall grass had been matted down along a path about a foot wide and paved with scat. Bears did not merely shit in these woods — they asphalted them with fish bones and salmonberry seeds. The air smelled of rotting seafood, which I took as a good sign that the year's early berry crop had not converted Kodiak's famous omnivores into half-ton fruitarians. Brigid indicated a very large, very fresh bear bed ("This thing's like an impact crater") and some bits of brown fur clinging to trees adjacent to the trail. I tried to keep in mind what I'd come to think of as Harriman's Rule: Just because you travel a long distance doesn't mean you're guaranteed a bear at your convenience. We parked ourselves on a slope overlooking a pond for about fifteen minutes, hoping that someone would turn up.

"What is that gun you are carrying, 'Arry?" asked Bernard, one of the two men in the French group. Harry kept a rifle lashed to his gigantic rectangular pack. From behind he looked as if he were hauling an enormous transistor radio. As usually happens in mixed-language groups in neutral territory, initial embarrassment about linguistic limitations had quickly collapsed against the human urge to communicate, and Bernard and some others spoke decent English. Combined with extravagant hand gestures that Marcel Marceau might have considered overwrought and some intermediate Spanish verbs on my part, we'd settled into a fairly effective mode of communication. Bernard was the sort of Frenchman whose charms were difficult to resist — funny and handsome, with a fondness for American popular culture. He sang snippets of Harry Belafonte songs as we walked.

"That's a .338 Winchester," Harry said, pulling a cartridge out of a side pocket and handing it to Bernard. "It's not loaded, obviously."

Bernard rolled the brass cylinder between his fingers and gave a Gallic nod of approval. "This is very good quality. When I am hunting, I also prefer the *plomb* to the plastic."

We were walking above the bank of a river half an hour later when Brigid suddenly dropped to one knee, put her finger to her lips, and gave the signal for everyone to hunker down. All eight of us crawled behind a bush and tried to sneak glances into the shallow pool below. Dozens of salmon were swimming slowly in circles, making light splashing noises as they leaped and spasmed. "This is nothing," Harry said. "Sometimes it's like popcorn popping down there."

"Are they, you know, doing their business before they die?" I asked Brigid quietly as she passed around a bread bag filled with sandwiches. I assumed this was the final chapter in the life cycle of the Pacific salmon: Swim upstream to where you were born, spawn, expire.

"Not yet. The males are waiting for a female to turn on her side, which indicates she's making a nest," Brigid said. Once the female had prepared the gravel just so, she and the dominant male would swim past to release their eggs and milt together, in a romantic crop-dusting. Some of these fertilized eggs would hatch, migrate to the sea, and (should they avoid predators and fishermen) return to this stream one day to sustain the cycle.

A lot of fish were definitely dying a little further downstream, because a mother Kodiak bear and two cubs had edged into view and were enjoying what looked like a beat-the-clock salmon-eating contest. The cubs would pick up a fish in their mouths, drop it, then pick up another one. "There must have been fifty pink salmon in that pool and those cubs caught every one," Harry said. "That's how they learn: by playing." Their mother barked. The two abandoned their fish and ran to her.

"The mother can give all sorts of vocal commands," Brigid said. *"Come. Stay. Go climb that tree."*

We continued down the bear highway through chest-high grasses. Brigid told me she'd first come to Kodiak Island during college, one summer in the 1980s, because a friend working at a Minneapolis restaurant had waited on a customer who said it was a nice place. The two of them flew to Anchorage, hitchhiked south to the end of the Kenai Peninsula, caught the ferry to Kodiak, and got cannery jobs the day they arrived. "Ask Harry to tell you the story of how he got into the guiding business," she said.

Harry had also come to Kodiak for a summer job, in 1975. That September, an opportunity came up to join a crew transplanting red salmon from one location on the island to another in an old amphibious Grumman Goose, an airplane designed with a wide, boatlike hull.* The move required carrying adult fish in a portable wooden tank. Bad weather rolled in, trapping six men in a lakefront cabin for three days. On the fourth day, things cleared enough for

---

* The original Grumman Goose was commissioned as a commuter craft by a group of businessmen, including Roland Harriman, also known as the toddler who walked up and down the decks of the *Elder* with his father, pulling a toy on a string. The other Harriman son on the expedition, Averell, would go on to serve as U.S. ambassador to the Soviet Union and governor of New York.

Harry and the pilot, Hal Derrick, to attempt a run. But rains had raised the lake level, and water now slopped against the fuselage. "By the time I got the door closed, the water was above the floorboards of the plane," Harry said. The first fish drop went okay, though the Goose "felt a little tail-heavy."

The second takeoff was more sluggish. The lake was still too high to drain the water from the plane, but Hal finally got the Goose airborne. "We got about five hundred feet up in the air and the water rushed to the back of the plane," Harry said. "The plane just stood straight up, with the nose pointed at the sky. Hal somehow got the plane down to about forty-five degrees. We hit the water hard." As water poured into the cockpit, Harry remembered an old episode of *Sea Hunt* in which Lloyd Bridges had survived a similar crash by sticking his head into an air pocket near the cabin ceiling. He took a lungful of air but couldn't open his window, which he later learned had been wired shut. He followed Hal out the pilot-side window. The two stood on a wing and considered their options. "Then we started sinking."

Hal's back had been wrenched by the crash, and he was in too much pain to swim. "I'd had lifeguard training, so I jettisoned my big boots to get us both to shore," Harry said. Hal was a large man, and the cold water sapped Harry's strength, but they finally reached the shallows, where they could stand. "Hal told me to follow the lakeshore to a creek that led to an old cannery," four miles away. "I was so glad to be alive, I didn't care that I was barefoot."

Harry followed a bear trail, his feet going numb from the autumn cold. He finally spotted smoke rising from the cannery's chimney. When he knocked on the door, he was greeted by Bill Pinnell, one of Kodiak's bear guiding legends. Pinnell sat Harry down by the fire and poured him a whiskey. A rescue party set out to find Hal, but he managed to reach the cannery on his own. Pinnell and his guiding partner, Morris Talifson, were evidently impressed with Harry's tenacity, because they offered him a job working as a packer on bear hunts that fall. "I never imagined I'd be working for them for the next seventeen years," Harry said. "They taught me a ton about bears."

The Grumman Goose was salvaged from the lake bottom and rehabilitated. "Hal started his own flying business later on," Harry said. "He and four passengers died in a crash."

It turned out to be a very good day for

tracking bears. We hiked from one spot to another, crawled on hands and knees until we were caked with mud, reached into one another's backpacks for cameras and sunglasses and binoculars. Sitting on a slope above one stream, we munched Pringles until a male brown bear strolled past about fifty yards away, slowing slightly to give us an over-the-shoulder double take. (Harry and Brigid disagreed over whether he'd smelled us or spotted someone's fuchsia-and-aqua jacket. Bernard and I theorized he'd heard the Pringles.) Another stream dead-ended like a cul-de-sac in a shallow pool where a mother and cub were vacuuming up the unfortunate salmon who'd swum from the ocean expecting to spend their final moments triumphantly propagating the species. As the sun began to set, we sat on a hillside above the beach, waiting for the tide to go out. A feeling of immense gratitude descended upon me, not so much for the perfect day of bear watching — though it had, as John Burroughs described his time in Kodiak, been both epic and lyric — but because I realized that Alaska's savage biting insects had closed up shop for the year.

Loyal the Lab had been trained to keep calm in the presence of bears. He had more trouble staying cool in the presence of a fox that kept popping out of the woods every hundred yards or so to shriek at us as we walked down the beach toward camp. I had never heard a fox before and was unaware that its yelp is one of the most irritating noises in nature. "He'll probably follow us all the way to camp," Harry said. "If you hear something during the night that sounds like an old lady being skinned alive, that's a fox."

We were carrying on several loopy end-of-day conversations in Franglish when Brigid spotted a very large mother bear and two cubs in the distance, ambling slowly in our direction along the crescent of the waterline. Our only option was to crawl into the foliage behind the beach and wait for them to pass. The three walked past in single file, maybe fifteen yards away from where we were spying on them. I got a very good look at the distinctive shoulder hump and in my excitement took about three dozen blurry photographs that were so uniformly terrible, Brigid cried laughing when we reviewed them later. The cubs ran into the water and splashed each other playfully. We'd just started exchanging wide-eyed *Can you believe this?* looks when the same fox popped out of the forest to confront the cubs with its ululations. The mother bear growled, the fox ran away. Show over.

It was 10:00 P.M. before we got back to camp. Bernard brought out a flask of home-made Armagnac from his farm in Normandy and some charcuterie. Brigid and Harry busied themselves with dinner, and I fell into the temporary role of spokesman for America, trying to answer questions as best I could: Why do Americans eat so much processed food? Why do they get so little vacation time? (Everyone in our group had more or less taken off the last month of summer.) Why do they love guns? Having been placed in this situation frequently during my travels, I blamed everything on the Republicans, which always satisfies Europeans. Brigid said she and Harry were looking forward to spending the winter in one of Iowa's Mississippi River towns, which at that moment seemed as far away as the moon. We stayed up past midnight and went to bed only when people started nodding off around the fire.

The fox returned around 3:45 A.M., with a friend. They both evidently had a lot to discuss. I was starting to understand the appeal of fox hunting.

The morning was cold. Harry was up early at the camp stove, making coffee. "Leaves on the ground, a little chill in the air," he said, warming his hands over the gas flame. "Feels like summer's coming to an end." It was mid-August. Not everything about Alaska's climate had gone haywire.

We had a long, leisurely breakfast, at which details of real-world lives emerged over instant oatmeal. Bernard was not just a cutup who liked to hum the "Banana Boat Song"; he was also a major exporter of automobiles and a major political figure in one of France's eighteen *régions*. His partner, Natasha, was a geologist. Jean-Michel, who looked a little like one of the elves in Santa's accounting department, was a former alpinist who'd climbed in the Himalayas. Brigid told a story in two languages simultaneously, about how, the year before, she and Harry had helped rescue three cubs whose mother had been killed by a hunter.

While Harriman had been stalking his prize near town in 1899, George Bird Grinnell and a team of hunters prowled the shores of Uyak Bay. In four days, they never spotted even a sign of bears. On our second day out at the Uyak Bay satellite camp, we enjoyed a gorgeous sunny day, walking for hours. The highlight was probably when Brigid coaxed me into climbing on top of a beaver dam that could've plugged a decent-size river. I said something about admiring their engineering. "To be honest, these beavers are kind of assholes," Brigid said. Each year, their architectural creations seemed to block another salmon stream without regard for their neighbors in the ecosystem. The forests of Kodiak were infested with bucktoothed John Galts.

We never came close to seeing another bear. That night we took the boats back to the island. In the morning, a yellow de Havilland floatplane buzzed overhead and glided to the beach. We soared above the green hills to the city of Kodiak. With a few hours to kill at the airport, I pulled out my phone to check on some details about my bear hunt while they were still fresh in my mind. Among the results was a news story from Dayton, Ohio, describing an orphaned Kodiak bear cub who'd recently been adopted. His name was Dodge.

CHAPTER THIRTY-FOUR: BLAST FROM THE PAST

The Valley of Ten Thousand Smokes

The *Elder*'s visit to Kodiak Island was book-ended by two stops in Kukak Bay, a mainland spot directly across the Shelikof Strait. A team of scientists had asked to be dropped off to conduct wildlife surveys while Harriman pursued his bear. The reconnaissance mission of those who went ashore in what is now Katmai National Park is a rare part of the Harriman Expedition that was not well documented in words or photographs. Burroughs, sounding like a reporter dishing secondhand information, writes that a group of men "who wished to spend a week collecting and botanizing on the mainland" pushed off from the *Elder* into the darkness (which at that time of year probably meant after midnight), many miles from shore, in a small boat. The unusual circumstances of departure perhaps hint at both Edward Harriman's haste to reach Kodiak and the scientists' desire to go anywhere but. Burroughs tallied "five or six" men in the boat; the Smithsonian Institution collections hold birds and plant fossils gathered by at least seven individuals. "Their days spent there were in every way satisfactory," Burroughs summarizes hastily in the *Harriman Alaska Series*, as if he, too, was eager to move on to topics more interesting than insects of the Eocene epoch.

Burroughs could never resist musing earnestly on the splendors of nature, however, and a few pages later in his chronicle, he doubles back briefly to Kukak Bay, unable to shake the scientific party's beguiling account of something they saw there:

They described one view that made the listener wish he had been with them: they had climbed to the top of a long green slope back of their camp and had suddenly found themselves on the brink of an almost perpendicular mountain wall with a deep notch, through which they had looked down 2,000 feet into a valley beneath them invaded by a great glacier that swept down from the snow-white peaks beyond. The spectacle was so unexpected and so tremendous that it fairly took their breaths away.

What fascinated me about this verdant alpine dreamscape was that much of it no longer existed. Thirteen years after the indeterminate number of specialists from the *Elder* marveled at the scenery behind Kukak Bay, everything they'd seen was obliterated by the biggest volcanic explosion of the twentieth century.

If you split Alaska into four quadrants, the lower right quarter — which includes the Inside Passage and has Fairbanks and Kodiak Island as its rough northern and western borders — would account for at least 80 percent of the state's population. Technically, any territory in Alaska that can be reached only by plane or boat can be considered "bush," but the sparsely populated areas in the remaining 75 percent of the state are where the bushiest bush is. Reading descriptions in the journals of the Harriman Expedition members, one can almost sense that an invisible line is being crossed once they leave Kodiak and spot the smoking peak of Mount Iliamna. No more quaint towns or breathtaking glaciers lay ahead. The mountains set back from the coast, which reach heights of six thousand to ten thousand feet, are spectacular, but less impressive if you've just sailed beneath eighteen-thousand-foot Mount St. Elias. These are the volcanic peaks of the Aleutian Range, formed where the Pacific Plate subducts beneath the North American Plate, causing magma to rise toward the earth's surface. The Aleutian Range's growth has been stunted because its mountains occasionally blow their tops off.

The specimen collectors who rowed away from the *Elder* in the wee hours visited what is now Katmai National Park. In 1898, according to Katmai historian John Hussey, a geologist visiting the area had "ascended the lush green valley of the Ukak River" and recorded "earthquakes and other evidences of volcanic activity" that included hot springs, tremors, and a report from local Natives that one of the mountains sometimes smoked. On June 6, 1912, a twenty-mile-high column of smoke began rising above Mount Katmai. Two hours later came an enormous explosion, heard as far away as Juneau, 750 miles to the east. A cloud of ash billowed in the sky and, carried by the wind, began to fall like snow over hundreds of square miles. Kodiak Island was paralyzed by sixty hours of darkness and a blizzard of ashfall deep enough to collapse roofs. (Harry Dodge described the dirt in his Kodiak garden as "four inches of topsoil above ten inches of ash.") The blasts from Katmai continued for three days. By the time the violence ended, more than three cubic miles of ash and pumice had been ejected — thirty times the volume released during the Mount St. Helens eruption of 1980. When the air cleared, several hundred feet of Mount Katmai's summit had vanished.

The 1912 explosion coincided with a heyday of exploration funded by the National Geographic Society, which had recently sponsored Robert Peary's race to the North Pole and was funding Hiram Bingham's excavations at Machu Picchu. In 1916, the Society dispatched botanist Robert Griggs, who had made previous trips to the area to study its revegetation, to have a closer look at Mount Katmai's truncated peak and the formerly lush Ukak River valley. Atop the mountain he found a deep crater, two miles wide and filled with water. Griggs was pursuing the source of a mysterious steam cloud when he climbed a hill and caught a glimpse of what had been, until four years earlier, the thickly forested valley.

The sight that flashed into view as we surmounted the hillock was one of the most amazing visions ever beheld by mortal eye. The whole valley as far as the eye could reach was full of hundreds, no thousands — literally tens of thousands — of smokes curling up from its fissured floor. . . . It was as though all the steam engines in the world, assembled together, had popped their safety valves at once and were letting off steam in concert. . . . We had accidentally discovered one of the great wonders of the world.

The vents from which the fumes escaped were fumaroles, hissing up through hundreds of feet of volcanic ash. Griggs would return three more times to explore the area, but his first impression gave this wonderland its name: the Valley of Ten Thousand Smokes.

Approximately one hundred years and two weeks after Griggs made his life-altering discovery, Kyle McDowell visited me at a condo I'd rented for a few nights in Anchorage. Kyle was going to guide me on a trip to Ten Thousand Smokes, the preservation of which had been the primary reason for establishing Katmai National Park. The slow-motion catastrophe of Alaska's melting glaciers was too slow to observe except in photos; I was too timid to try to visit the scene of Lituya Bay's seventeen-hundred-foot mega-tsunami; and the effects of the 1964 Good Friday Earthquake have faded over time. But the evidence of the biggest recorded cataclysm in America's most natural-disaster-prone state is still very much on display.

The fumaroles had died out by the 1930s as the valley's floor cooled, but their extinction had left behind a haunting moonscape of ash and painted rocks. There are no roads or rangers in Ten Thousand Smokes, nor any enforceable restrictions; if you want to hike up and touch the massive volcanic dome of Novarupta, site of the 1912 blast, no one is likely to be there to stop you. "There's so much ash, it looks like the explosion happened last week," Alaska state seismologist Mike West had told me excitedly when I asked him about Ten Thousand Smokes. "It'll take a little bit of logistics work to get there, but if you can? Go! Absolutely."

Logistics were Kyle's specialty. He'd booked our flight to King Salmon and hired a bush pilot to fly us into Ten Thousand Smokes, and had asked to stop by the condo to review our itinerary and triple-check that I had all the gear we'd need for our four-day excursion. He had a crew cut, taught firearm safety, and liked to talk about "contingencies." As we knelt on the floor going through my rain gear and examining the soles of my boots, he said, "I always like to have a preliminary agenda for the day, with A, B, and C contingencies based on what we see out there."

Kyle collected me in his pickup truck the next morning at five sharp and we drove off to the Anchorage airport. Kyle was a relative newcomer to Alaska. He'd grown up in Michigan, spent time building houses in Arizona, and had moved his family north four years earlier looking for a sense of community that he'd never been able to find in the Lower 48. He loved the state's ethos of pioneer self-reliance; he and his wife home-schooled their kids, and their freezer was filled with meat Kyle had hunted. At the airport, we gave our tightly packed gear one more pass — "I didn't give you a giant summer sausage, did I? Oh, wait, there it is" — Kyle checked his .45 at the reservations desk, and we flew off to King Salmon.

Because so much of Alaska is hundreds of miles from the road system, the state has six times as many pilots per capita as the rest of the United States. Bush pilots are essential to keeping the remote parts of the state functioning. Much in the way you'd hail a taxi or call an Uber in a big city, if you need to move people or supplies into or out of the Alaska backcountry, you call up a bush pilot, fix a price, and go. Equipped with the right landing gear, bush pilots are willing to touch down on almost any flattish surface — glaciers, tundra, lakes, riverbeds, valleys coated in volcanic ash. Unpredictable weather and unconventional landing conditions require Alaska's bush pilots to rely on instinct and experience as well as instruments. Alaska also leads the nation in plane crashes, averaging close to a hundred per year, and in per capita aviation deaths (by a wide margin). Ted Stevens Anchorage International Airport was named after Alaska's most famous politician, who died when the floatplane he was riding in collided with the side of a mountain. In 1972, a plane carrying two U.S. congressmen vanished while flying from Anchorage to Juneau; it has never been found. In Alaska, the old maxim about flight safety is simply a statement of fact: There are old pilots, and bold pilots, but no old, bold pilots.

Our bush pilot, Dave, gathered us at the King Salmon airport and drove us over to his company's hangar, which was filled with airplane parts, ramshackle furniture, and a couple of desks with computers. His flying uniform included a long-sleeved camouflage T-shirt, rubber boots, and wraparound shades. The plane was an old Cessna 206 with plywood covering the floor in the back. Dave pointed out the exit doors for use in case of emergency, the seven days' worth of provisions in case of an emergency touchdown in a remote area and the Mossberg .540 shotgun "in case we need to walk anywhere" after an unscheduled landing. The plane was loud, and we talked through headsets. Kyle ran through the now familiar list of dos and don'ts with regard to bear encounters — do make noise, don't run — and I have to admit I zoned out a bit, as one tends to do while hearing safety instructions prior to takeoff for the thousandth time. Kyle's enhanced bear safety techniques left me more concerned about any animal's potential welfare than my own anyway. "Obviously, I do have a firearm and I'll fire a warning shot," he said. "If that doesn't work, I'll use deadly force."

The skies were clear in King Salmon, and our destination was less than fifty miles away. That told us little about what to expect on the ground, since Katmai's weather was legendarily unpredictable. "Yesterday was sort of a mess with the wind and the rain," Dave said. "I was flying about five hundred feet off the deck all day." He promised to text Kyle on his satellite phone if conditions started to turn ugly. "It'd have to be *pretty* bad for me not to make it back out to get you guys."

For the first part of the trip, the scenery below was the opposite of scorched earth. Enormous blue lakes met a sidewinding river that sliced through greenery as thick as anything in the Mekong Delta. This was Brooks Camp, a spot so rich in salmon that its brown bears were frequently too busy fishing or too full to pay the slightest mind to the humans who flew in to observe them. Kyle pointed out a road used once a day by a Park Service tour bus that shuttled visitors out from the lodge at Brooks Camp to an overlook at the lip of Ten Thousand Smokes — our plan B for returning to civilization if a flight out became impossible. (Kyle had packed his own reserve of extra food, so the hypothetical plan C was walking all the way back.) John Muir once wrote that "between every two pines is a doorway to a new world." Here, we flew between two low mountains and might well have slipped through a wormhole. We entered a wide plain, a wasteland from which all signs of life had been scrubbed. The Valley of Ten

Thousand Smokes.

Dave brought the plane down in the middle of the bleak vastness. As we stepped out, the ground underfoot felt like a graham cracker crust. We were ringed by what looked like extremely tall and steep sand dunes, decapitated halfway up by foamy cloud cover. In all directions, everything appeared charred, forty square miles of emptiness.

"Planet Katmai!" Kyle shouted. "No trails! We can go wherever we want. There's places here that the USGS and park rangers haven't even been." Fewer than two hundred people had applied for backcountry permits in Ten Thousand Smokes the previous year, and that included the volcanologists. After Dave flew off, a pair of hikers appeared briefly on the distant horizon, then vanished. They were the last people we would see for three days.

"What don't you hear?" Kyle asked. "Birds! Where else can you go in Alaska where you don't even hear birds?" He took in the 360-degree view. "I don't think I've ever been out here when it's so calm." Katmai is infamous for its williwaws, a type of violent windstorm that kicks up suddenly in places where the mountains meet the sea. When geologist Josiah Spurr came through the area in 1898, he reported that "gusts are so powerful that stones of considerable size are carried along by them." Robert Griggs had doubted reports of such winds until he was scooped up by one and flown into a mudbank. Kyle pointed out some USGS cabins on top of a mountain. "The wind can get up to a hundred miles per hour down here," he said. "We can go up there if we really need to."

The only sound other than the wind was the low roar of the River Lethe, named by Griggs for the river of forgetfulness in Hades. Over the years, water originating as glacial runoff had carved a slot canyon through the ash and rock. The ravine was sixty feet deep, with boulders and raging whitewater — actually, sort of pinkish brown water — at the bottom. "People say, 'We could jump over that,' " Kyle said as we peered over the side. "And we could, but we're not going to. Because if you fall, no one's coming after you. Five people have disappeared down there, and none were ever found."

We walked with poles to keep our balance on the unstable ash, following the Lethe toward an enormous blue hanging glacier high on the mountainside ahead, which roughly marked our destination for the day.

Kyle pointed out a mountain that had never been climbed, one of thousands of such peaks in Alaska. The next valley over was green, he said, completely regrown since the 1912 blast. "It looks like Hawaii." On the floor of Ten Thousand Smokes, the only visible flora was small clumps of grass, maybe one per every few acres. The old forest that once grew along the Ukak River was seven hundred feet below us, buried in ash.

In some spots, the pumice appeared to have melted into stone. These were the fumaroles that had enchanted Griggs in 1916, so hot at the time that his team had cooked corn bread in them. Now they were ghosts, deep holes encircled by small piles of red, orange, and yellow rocks, like crumbled and melted crayons.

The River Lethe's canyon leveled as we advanced, the water forking off in one direction as a swift-running blue stream, which we followed. Twice Kyle stopped to probe the depth of the water with his walking pole, edged toward the center of the stream, and retreated when he couldn't find the bottom. When he finally located a suitable spot to cross, I rolled up my pants and followed. Not long before — hours? days? — the water had been glacial ice. Its temperature hadn't changed much.

We stopped for a late lunch, and Kyle pulled out the summer sausage, which was the size of a tennis ball can. A crack in the clouds created a shaft of light that bounced around the valley like a spotlight. Finally the beam settled on Mount Katmai. Griggs believed that this mountain was the source of the 1912 eruption, and pointed to the missing cubic mile of rock from its summit as evidence. "There's an eight-hundred-foot-deep lake at the top in the caldera," Kyle said as we polished off the last few inches of the sausage. Griggs was baffled by Mount Katmai's near-total lack of rock debris, which he hypothesized should lie sixteen feet deep for miles around. It was not until decades later that volcanologists determined why: The mountain hadn't exploded; it had collapsed when the magma at its core was drained and ejected through a new vent located six miles away. This newborn volcano was christened Novarupta, a name that means "new eruption" in Latin. In photographs, it looked less like a stereotypical volcanic cone than the woofer in a high-end car stereo; it was low and circular, its crater plugged with an enormous black Superdome of lava rock more than two hundred feet high and a quarter mile across. Supposedly you could still find live fumaroles steaming in its fissures. I was dying to see it up close.

Our campsite was a pumice beach on a turquoise meltwater lake, tucked behind a wall of rocks and fed by a cascade that poured down from the glacier far above. It may have been the most secluded spot I'd ever seen. Aside from the vanishing hikers and some scattered animal tracks and plants, we hadn't seen any signs of life since we arrived. Kyle was just starting to set up the stove when I noticed something crossing the far shore. A bear. Why he was wandering a foodless wasteland when, thirty miles away, his brethren at Brooks Camp were gorging themselves insensate on salmon, I don't know. The bear turned and went over the mountain, perhaps to see what he could see. Kyle fetched his gun and holstered it.

Over dinner, we chatted a little bit about Chris McCandless, the twenty-four-year-old whose disappearance and death in the Alaskan wilderness was the basis of the book and movie *Into the Wild.*

Kyle had recently gone hunting with some buddies near Healy, the closest town to the spot where McCandless died. Park Service rangers in the area complain about the naïve visitors who come from around the world hoping to re-create the famous photo McCandless snapped of himself, seated and grinning outside the Magic Bus. For many, that picture encapsulated the escape-to-Alaska fantasy. Unfortunately, a lot of tourists seek to commune with their rebel hero's unfettered spirit without taking into account the dangers of the bush. They turn their backs on Alaska. Every year, at least one ends up needing to be rescued. In 2010, a Swiss hiker drowned.

"I see stories about people who get lost — the trail ends and they're not prepared," Kyle said as we ate. Every few minutes, one of us walked up to the ridge to scan for the bear. "They should just turn around, but they go on. Sometimes they come back, sometimes they don't. I admire the spirit of a guy like McCandless, I understand the DIY idea — that's why a lot of us come here. But there are situations where you're not ready for the what-ifs and the unknowns in the wilderness."*

* The story of Chris McCandless resonated particularly with me, because it nearly got me fired. A quarter century ago, despite having zero journalism experience or training, I managed to talk my way into a magazine internship by somewhat overstating my Macintosh computer skills.

Kyle had a low tolerance for such ambiguities, and woke up every two hours through the night to patrol the beach. I was proud to have more or less conquered my bearanoia, though the presence of a trained marksman likely contributed to my peace of mind. The morning was rainy and cold, but Kyle downed water as if a heat wave were approaching. He liked to overhydrate when water was plentiful, and I tried to match him ounce for ounce. "Always good to keep an extra liter in your belly," he said. We each put away three liters before departing. "I got a message overnight from Dave, the

---

The Friday of my first week on the job, word came down that a last-minute cover story was being crashed in, and that I was to talk to the writer of the emergency replacement — Jon Krakauer — and retrieve his manuscript file over the modem. (This was 1992.) A task that should've taken minutes instead devoured half of the day as I tried to hide my ignorance of how to get two computers to talk to each other and surreptitiously speed-dialed a friend who subscribed to *MacUser*. Even the editor in chief, whom I knew only from his photograph, eventually poked his head over the wall of my cubicle to inquire about the delay. McCandless's tragic story was so compelling that everyone quickly forgot about my incompetence.

pilot. The weather today is anyone's guess, same tomorrow. Wednesday could get a little hairy. I've got a couple contingency plans."

We crossed the stream again — still beer-cooler cold — and faced a decision whether to hike uphill in the direction of Mount Katmai on crumbly dirt or hard-packed snow that hadn't melted over the summer. "The dirt's a little soft," Kyle said. "The snow is faster, but you can't fall. No, really, you *can not fall.* Once you get going, your momentum can take you into those rocks headfirst."

We ascended slowly and carefully toward a ceiling of angry, dark clouds. Once again the sun broke through for a few minutes, and I looked back to see our beachfront campsite far below, disappearing in an encroaching fog. The snow eventually petered out, revealing a gorge filled with ash and boulders. Near the top of our ascent, one lone purple flower whipped in the wind. A rotten-egg whiff of sulfur blew by. We were high enough to look out onto an undulating valley spread out before us like the sands of Arabia. Kyle pointed north with a walking pole, identifying the ash-coated mountains of Ten Thousand Smokes.

"From left to right, that's Cerberus, Katmai Peak, and Trident," he said. "Trident was the most recent eruption. That's where the sulfur smell comes from. That black patch" — a wrinkled charcoal-colored tumor stuck on the side of the mountain — "that's all lava."

As we continued upward, the veneer of ash and stones began to fall away, revealing frozen chunks buried beneath. It was quickly becoming clear that we were hiking up a single massive slab of ice. "You know what this is?" Kyle asked excitedly. "It's an ancient buried glacier. No one ever comes up this way — I've certainly never come up this way. We might be the first people to see this." The glacier probably hadn't been visible since 1912, and had reappeared only when a century of williwaws had skimmed off enough ash. Kyle pondered the possibility that we'd made a genuine discovery. "How many explorers are finding new things nowadays?" he asked, poking a pole into a frozen crevice.

"Well, Harriman already has his glacier," I said. "Maybe we can call this McDowell Glacier in your honor until someone tells us otherwise." Kyle liked that idea.

The wind was intensifying again, so we camped next to a stream in a boulder-filled gorge just above McDowell Glacier. In several places where we stepped, we immediately fell into sinkholes up to our knees, a possible sign of subterranean thawing. The night was quiet, but when I woke in the morning, the valley below had disappeared behind a veil of fog. Rain poured down, and the air was cold and clammy. I felt a chill coming on and passed the time trying to remember the names of Victorian maladies exacerbated by damp conditions: catarrh, croup, consumption.

After two days of camping, my tent looked as if someone had emptied an ashtray inside, and it was starting to smell like a locker room, body funk mixing with the scent of baby wipes and Purell. Kyle slept in a sort of tepee whose immaculate interior resembled a Bedouin sheikh's lodgings. He made me a cup of coffee and some surprisingly good freeze-dried eggs while he tried to get a sense of where the weather was heading. The closest weather station was back at King Salmon, which, considering the meteorological idiosyncrasies of Ten Thousand Smokes, might as well have been in Anchorage. Kyle was forecasting the weather using methods George Vancouver would have used in 1794, monitoring the barometric pressure and checking the sky. Neither seemed promising. Kyle said we'd stay put for a while, since, if we broke the tents down in the rain, everything would get wet and stay wet until our scheduled pickup the following evening.

"I like to say there's three types of fun," he said as we settled in for a second cup of coffee and a second liter of water. "Type 1 fun is stuff that's fun to do and fun to talk about later." Hiking through the smoldering fissures of Novarupta on a clear day would be classic Type 1 fun. "Type 2 fun is stuff that's not fun to do, but it's fun to talk about later because you survived it." Walking through ice-cold rivers was Type 2 fun. "Type 3 fun is stuff that's not fun to do and not fun to talk about later." Sleeping in a wet tent as a cold front approached was archetypal Type 3 fun.

The wind and rain slacked off a bit late morning, and we decided to take our chances descending into the badlands below to get a closer look at Novarupta before any storm came. As we rounded the base of Mount Cerberus, a tremendous gust flung ash into our faces. We took a quick stab at a shortcut up an ice field even steeper than the prior day's — Kyle warned that we were in "a *serious*, I mean a *serious*, no-fall zone" — but after a couple of nervous minutes he turned and said, "I'm sorry, let's backtrack, this is just too dangerous." For the first time, Kyle seemed to be rushing, and had to pause every few minutes to allow me to catch up. We scrambled over a field of deep crevasses that unfurled ahead of us like corduroy, an activity that might have been enjoyable if we hadn't been in a hurry, and traced the crumbly edge of Falling Mountain, named by Robert Griggs "on account of the frequent rock avalanches." Boulders were perched at the top like bowling balls. We were the pins. "Yell 'Rock!' if you see a rock coming," Kyle said.

We stopped for a break and sipped the last of the water we'd brought. "How badly do you want to see Novarupta?" Kyle asked. "You think you can climb Baked Mountain to those cabins if we have to?"

I very much did want to see Novarupta and very much did not want to climb Baked Mountain. "Why?"

"Look behind you," Kyle said. The sky toward the Gulf of Alaska looked like it was psyching itself up for a fight.

"I guess it depends on how long until we're in a serious situation."

"Mark, I would say this is already a serious situation," he said. Kyle was not a stranger to dramatic pronouncements, but a tempest was definitely brewing on the horizon, and we hadn't seen any water sources since leaving camp. With a little prompting, Kyle conceded that the squall might have stalled temporarily. We pushed on around Falling Mountain and located a tiny pool of meltwater, which Kyle dammed with rocks to slowly fill our bottles as he sought places to shelter in place.

As Kyle monitored his waterworks, I walked up to the top of a small ridge and saw the black bulge of Novarupta. It looked close enough to hit with a rock — which, come to mention it, there seemed to be a lot more of, now that we'd gotten close to the epicenter of the 1912 blast. Kyle estimated we were twenty minutes' walk away.

"You really want to go over there, don't you?" Kyle asked, and already knew the answer. "All right, let me check the sat phone to see if there are any messages from Dave, and if things get hairy we can either make our way to the cabins, which should take a few hours, or hunker down somewhere."

The sat phone took a couple of minutes to find a signal. There was a message from Dave. "Low pressure coming up east side of Aleutians," he'd written. "Problems all around!" By the time of our scheduled pickup the next day, Katmai, Kodiak, and everywhere else on the southern coast of

Alaska was likely to get slammed. A storm like that might trap us in Ten Thousand Smokes for four days. Or more.

Dave gave us a drop-dead cutoff of 9:00 P.M. to make it back to the spot where we'd landed near the River Lethe. If we blew that, our best hope was a long, steep hike up Baked Mountain in the wind and rain, after which we could look forward to several damp days in an empty one-room plywood hut. Type 3 Alaska fun in excelsis. Also, I had a boat to catch to the Aleutians; they weren't going to hold the *Tustumena* for me.

"Your call, buddy," Kyle said. "I'm still game for Novarupta if that's what you'd like."

"Let's bail," I said.

I took a last, longing look at Novarupta's black dome and we hoisted our packs to speed-walk back to the rendezvous point. We made it in just over two hours. Kyle called Dave on the sat phone to let him know we were ahead of schedule, which was a good thing, because storm clouds were advancing quickly from the east. A fierce wind was whipping through the valley and we had to shout to hear each other. "As long as he's here in fifteen to twenty minutes, we should make it!" Kyle yelled at seven thirty.

A few minutes after eight, when I'd just

about given up hope, a glint appeared on the horizon. Five minutes later, Dave was on the ground. "Woo, that doesn't look good," he said, facing the direction of the storm. (It was almost dark, but he still had his shades on.) We tossed our bags into the Cessna and sped off. Dave pressed PLAY on a Third Eye Blind cassette. The first song had just finished when we broke through into sunlight, the brown ash below alchemizing into greenery. By nine we were at the King Salmon airport, warm and dry. I wanted to kiss the ground.

We did have one small problem: It was the height of the fishing season and, as might be expected in a town named after the most prized species of salmon, no hotel rooms were available. Dave offered to let us sleep on the floor of his apartment. We begged off and he suggested that if we were going to pitch tents, we might do so behind the hotel next to the airport that had closed suddenly at the start of summer — so suddenly, according to Dave, that people had been arriving with suitcases all season, unaware that their reservations would not be honored. As we waded through the uncut grass behind the main building, something about the place gave me a bad feeling. Perhaps it was the empty liquor bottles on the picnic tables or the papered-over windows of cabins whose doors appeared to have been kicked in. Kyle didn't seem especially concerned, but then, he was packing heat. We crossed the street with our packs to Eddie's Fireplace Inn to discuss our options.

We sat down at the bar and ordered beers. Kyle struck up a conversation with the guy next to him, who heard about our escape and nodded his head. "Alaska will kill you quick enough if you don't pay attention," he said.

"That's so Alaska!" Kyle said, and bought the guy a beer. Then he bought beers for the couple at the end of the bar and bought me another, though I'd taken only two sips of my first.

I would have asked the patron on the other side of us his thoughts on the subject, but the seat was occupied by a Labrador who was drinking beer out of a highball glass. I offered to buy him another, to preempt Kyle's generosity, but his owner said his limit was one because he had a tendency to overindulge. Kyle asked the bartender, whose name was Mike, if he knew any place we could camp out for the night.

"Just set up in the grass in back of the

parking lot," Mike said, turning to look out the window behind him. "You see that old boat? Go behind there and no one will bother you."

I couldn't help but notice that Kyle's beer consumption habits mirrored his morning hydration, and in spite of my own thirst, he was putting down two pints for each of mine. He'd made friends with the cook at Eddie's and was trying hard to cajole him into grilling a steak, but his new drinking buddy had punched out at nine and wouldn't budge. So, we had beer for dinner. After four or five pints had flushed any lingering adrenaline out of my system, I walked a little unsteadily out to the parking lot and tried to set up my tent in the grass behind the boat, which was up on blocks and hadn't seen the water in a long while. In my compromised state, I couldn't remember a key step, and kept assembling and disassembling it for twenty minutes. I had curled up on the ground, using the tent as a blanket, when Kyle came out, shook his head disbelievingly at my ineptitude, and set it up for me. In the morning, I found him fast asleep under the boat.

CHAPTER THIRTY-FIVE: ENDANGERED

The Pribilof Islands

"Green, white, and blue are the three prevailing tints" of the eight-hundred-mile run west from Kodiak Island to the Aleutians, John Burroughs writes in the *Harriman Alaska Series.* "Blue of the sea and sky, green of the shores and lower slopes, and white of the lofty peaks and volcanic cones — they are mingled and contrasted all the way." As mile upon mile of tritone scenery scrolled past, mirages appeared in the distance. Islands seemed to hover in the air; Greek temples materialized atop rocky plateaus; an old abbey, complete with belltower, appeared along the shore, "bathed in the soft light of the afternoon sun."

A thick fog rolled in and activity aboard the *Elder* slowed nearly to a standstill. Botanist William Brewer tried to reconstruct his rousing Fourth of July speech from memory. Someone delivered a lackluster presentation about insects. During a brief stop at Sand Point, in the Shumagin Islands archipelago, the expeditioners found a village that was deserted except for a single resident. Back on board, Burroughs, who had lectured the ship's ornithologists about the evils of shooting birds, quietly approached Merriam, offering to trade a sparrow's nest with four eggs he'd snatched at Sand Point for a bird skin he coveted. The teasing that ensued when Merriam spilled his secret to the other passengers provided some much needed entertainment.

On the morning of July 8, the *Elder* docked at the port town of Dutch Harbor. They had finally crossed into the Aleutian Islands. For thousands of years this had been Aleut country, until the arrival of the Russians, who made the area their nexus of fur trading. The Harriman expeditioners found a newly rebuilt church on the site of the original constructed by Father Veniaminov (later resident of the Russian Bishop's House, in Sitka), and not much else. No bears lived in the Aleutians. The only trees on the island were a small grove of miniature spruces, transplanted decades earlier by the Russians, their growth hindered by the fierce wind of the island chain. Dutch Harbor was a hub for the Northern

Commercial Company (NCC), which operated a coaling station and used the town as the base of operations for its lucrative seal-harvesting operations.

The *Elder*'s stay lasted less than a day, far too brief for Burroughs. In his official account, he describes a longing to while away some days amid the flowering hills above Dutch Harbor, "following its limpid torrent streams, climbing its lofty peaks, and listening to the music of the longspur." The truth was that, having had more than enough sea travel, Burroughs had arranged to stay at a local woman's home while the *Elder* steamed off to the remote Pribilof Islands and Siberia. He packed a small bag and was walking down the gangplank when he was spotted by John Muir and Charles Keeler, returning from a stroll. "Where are you going with that grip, Johnny?" the suspicious Muir asked. Burroughs waffled, then confessed that he feared the tempestuous Bering Sea. Muir insisted that the sea was "like a mill pond," and that the best part of the journey lay ahead — surely Burroughs wouldn't want to miss the famous fur seal breeding grounds of the Pribilof Islands? Burroughs buckled under peer pressure and returned to the ship.

If anything, Muir was underplaying the

fame of the Pribilofs, which Eliza Scidmore noted in her 1885 guide to Alaska were "too small to be marked on an ordinary map" but "have had more attention drawn to them than to any part of the territory." The pelagic seals of the Pribilofs had been perhaps the most valuable resource in all of Alaska when the United States purchased the territory in 1867. The NCC held the exclusive license to harvest the animals.

Merriam knew the Pribilofs and their valuable occupants well. He had visited the islands in 1891 as part of a commission to establish rules to maintain a steady seal population, and coauthored a report that recommended pragmatic solutions. A ban on pelagic sealing (killing in the open sea) would limit the number of animals slaughtered each year and prevent the culling of pregnant mothers, who migrated long distances to feed. Since the Pribilof rookery was essentially a harem in which a small group of dominant bull seals impregnated the females, restricting hunting to males would maintain the essential breeding stock. As the *Elder* sailed north, Merriam delivered a post-dinner lecture on what to expect at the government-sanctioned rookery.

Muir's description to Burroughs of the gentle Bering Sea, however well intentioned, was a complete falsehood. During the night, as the boat approached the Pribilofs, the winds increased. Frederick Dellenbaugh reported that when he woke, the ship was "pitching and rolling a great deal," rocking that intensified throughout the morning. He downed a homemade seasickness remedy of coca leaf extract mixed with whiskey, which he quickly deposited over the ship's rail. Other passengers fared worse. Keeler, who had helped Muir corral Burroughs back onto the *Elder* at Dutch Harbor, recorded remorsefully that "Mr. Burroughs lay in his berth and groaned." Keeler atoned for his guilt by sitting at Burroughs's bedside, "reading Wordsworth to him."

The seas had settled sufficiently by early afternoon to allow the expedition members to row out from the *Elder* and meet their hosts from the NCC. The team wandered a mile across a grassy meadow to a rocky shore where the animals assembled. Merriam was shocked by what he saw. In just the eight years since his last visit, the population had been hunted down by at least 75 percent. The carcasses of skinned seals lined the rocky beaches. No one had enforced Merriam's pragmatic regulations from 1891. Not only was the NCC ignoring its own government's quotas — possible because of the lack of oversight — but pelagic hunters from Russia, Japan, and Canada were shooting or harpooning thousands of females.

George Bird Grinnell recognized that the situation mirrored that of the vanishing salmon in Orca. He estimated the species that had been the backbone of Alaska's economy for a century would be extinct in four years. "There is but one remedy for this decline, and that is the total prohibition of pelagic sealing," he wrote in a scathing *Forest and Stream* editorial upon his return. Grinnell's experiences with passenger pigeons and the buffalo of Yellowstone had taught him a painful lesson. Any lasting solutions to Alaska's creeping eco-disasters would need to be political.

CHAPTER THIRTY-SIX:
THE ALEUTIAN LOCAL

Aboard the Tustumena

Up until Kodiak and Katmai, I'd made every important stop the Harriman team had. To continue to do so beyond Ten Thousand Smokes would have required my own steamship. Many of the most remote places visited in 1899 sounded like the least interesting, both then and now; the less accessible they were, the more they cost in time and money. Uninhabited Bogoslof Island was intriguing — it had just sprouted a new lava addition when the *Elder* paused there — and I found a group of marine biologists headed there whose ship sounded like a nonsmoking update of Jacques Cousteau's *Calypso.* They considered allowing me to join them, which seemed promising until I learned that Bogoslof's sensitive sea lion habitat prohibited me from setting foot on shore. St. Lawrence Island, where Harriman mistakenly thought he might bag a

407

polar bear, was marginally more promising. Its few visitors today were mostly birdwatchers and artifact hunters, who were permitted to pillage ancient gravesites as a source of revenue.

Muir had visited St. Lawrence in 1881 as a member of a search party aboard the cutter *Thomas Corwin*. The expedition was a rescue mission dispatched by the U.S. government to hunt for survivors of the USS *Jeannette*. That vessel had set out for the Arctic two years earlier and was believed to have been trapped in pack ice. The *Corwin* party failed to find any survivors (most of the *Jeannette*'s crew perished in the cold), but details of the journey were assembled from Muir's writings, after his death, into *The Cruise of the Corwin*. The travelogue is, among other things, a snapshot of the cultures of Bering Sea natives during a period of rapid disruption.

On St. Lawrence, Muir encountered devastation. Two-thirds of the island's fifteen hundred Yupik natives were dead, victims of a famine two years earlier. The surviving Yupik had drunk themselves into a stupor on liquor supplied illegally by American traffickers. Natives had long hunted slow-moving walruses for food. Newly acquired rifles enabled them to increase their kills exponentially, and, in turn, stockpile valuable ivory from the tusks. American whalers had harvested many tens of thousands more. Walrus populations collapsed. Amid St. Lawrence Island's flowering tundra, which Muir wrote "swept back to the snow-clad volcanoes," beneath "the wide azure sky bent kindly over all," the *Corwin* crew saw heaps of shrunken corpses. Some were piled atop kitchen garbage still clad in their rotting furs. Others had been picked clean by crows. Muir saw further disaster ahead for the Natives of the Bering Sea. "Unless some aid be extended by our government," he wrote, "in a few years at most every soul of them will have vanished from the face of the earth."

According to Burroughs, the Harriman Expedition had initially planned to turn toward home after visiting the seal rookeries on the Pribilofs. To his regret, Harriman's wife, Mary, had expressed an interest in seeing Siberia, so the *Elder* set off across the Bering Sea. A thick fog had rolled in, and an hour after departing, the ship came to a sudden halt when it slammed into a reef. Burroughs reported that "some of us hoped this incident would cause Mr. Harriman to turn back," but resistance to Harriman's will was futile. He stood up from his dinner, confirmed with the crew that the *Elder*'s hull wasn't damaged, and ordered them to continue via a slightly altered course. Within minutes he was frolicking with his children "as if nothing had happened," Burroughs recalled.

The *Elder*'s stop in Plover Bay, on Siberia's Chukchi Peninsula, was brief. Muir had visited there with the *Corwin* in 1881 and recorded finding a happy Native village whose hospitable residents eagerly shared their uncooked food — wood being extremely scarce — and slept "perfectly nude in the severest weather," swathed in layers of furs. Merriam was the first Harriman team member to land ashore. He was immediately repulsed by the appearance of the local Eskimos, whose heads were scarred with open sores, signs of syphilis that had been carried by Russian sailors. The expeditioners snapped some photographs, engaged in a little trading, and poked their heads into the Eskimos' houses, which Dellenbaugh recorded were "smoky and dirty and foul-smelling," filled with blubber and bloody whale parts. A strong wind chilled everyone but Harriman, who wore a reindeer coat he'd purchased in Dutch Harbor as he handed out tobacco and glass beads to his Siberian hosts. Merriam called Plover

Bay "the most barren and desolate place of its size I ever saw." He had once spent a season in Death Valley.

The Harriman Expedition endured nearly two days of rough travel to earn two hours in Asia. Nowadays, no American gets in and out of Siberia in forty-eight hours. A small airline in Nome offers infrequent charter flights, but between the interminable Russian visa application process and waiting for a seat to open up, it would've been easier to fly to Siberia via Anchorage, Frankfurt, and Moscow. Awaiting me on the far end of such an odyssey was the crumbling Soviet provincial city of Petropavlovsk, which one leading travel website enticingly described as "a necessary evil."

Instead, the day before the *Tustumena* was scheduled to depart for Dutch Harbor, I flew to Homer, the town at the tail end of Route 1, on the southern tip of the Kenai Peninsula. A kid from the rental-car agency greeted me outside the front door of the airport in my vehicle, a 2003 Subaru Outback with a cracked windshield. "You can drive a stick shift, right?" he asked as he handed me the keys.

In lieu of visiting Siberia, I drove north to Nikolaevsk, home to a religious sect called the Old Believers. Originally from Siberia, they split with the Russian Orthodox Church in 1666 and had settled in Alaska after stints in South America and China. Many of the villagers still wore traditional clothing — you could see women in long dresses and headscarves in Homer, which was a fairly progressive town — and spoke Russian. The Old Believers were a closed community, and thus the source of much speculation. One Alaskan told me Nikolaevsk was the second-wealthiest zip code in the state; Kyle McDowell, who lived nearby, thought the men all drove suspiciously expensive cars. I found Nikolaevsk's onion-domed church fairly easily but saw no sign of the alleged riches. The roads were deserted, and the only business appeared to be the aggressively kitschy Samovar Cafe, which was closed, depriving me of an opportunity to sample the borscht while stocking up on local intel and wooden nesting dolls.

At the Land's End hotel, my alarm went off at three o'clock the next morning. I grabbed my backpack and walked in the chilly dark across a strip of asphalt that represented the final few feet of the American road system. The *Tustumena* was already buzzing two hours before departure. I stopped at the purser's office to put my name on the waiting list for a cabin. Prospects didn't look good — a travel club from Anchorage had booked most of the beds all the way to Dutch Harbor — but she told me she'd announce my name over the loudspeaker if something became available. "Once," she said, not looking up from her clipboard.

The forward observation lounge on the main level had already been colonized with sleeping bags and coolers, so I resigned myself to a spot in the open-air solarium upstairs. Again, the chaise lounges touted by guidebooks proved to be fictional. I inflated my mattress on the non-skid deck under the canopy and unrolled my sleeping bag. The *Tustumena*'s engines thrummed loudly, but heat lamps above kept the space warm and dry, conditions I appreciated acutely because Kyle had called to let me know that the storm we narrowly escaped in Ten Thousand Smokes had drenched the entire southern coast of Alaska for days. We'd probably *still* be trapped in that cabin atop Baked Mountain, eating powdered eggs and playing rock-paper-scissors. Two other unlucky souls joined me in the solarium: a snowboarder who had approximately five hundred pounds of gear in two wheeled trunks (he was moving to Kodiak Island "to find a real job") and a scruffy recent college graduate in overalls, whose tiny knapsack of belongings could have fit in a bandanna tied to a stick. I propped my head against my backpack, checked the Internet for what would be the last time for a few days, and saw that the *Crystal Serenity* and its five-star amenities had just departed Nome for the Northwest Passage. Then I rolled over and fell asleep on the floor.

When I woke, my hair was wet. We were at sea in a drizzling rain that streaked across the plexiglass roof and dripped intermittently onto my sleeping bag. I dragged my stuff to a drier spot and went downstairs. Other than the tiny *Lituya,* which I'd taken from Ketchikan to Metlakatla, the *Tustumena* was the most austere ferry I'd seen. The state had been discussing a replacement for years, but with the current budget crisis, the future of the Aleutian run itself (which was heavily subsidized) was in jeopardy. There was no urn of free-refill coffee on the *Tustumena,* just a two-dollar Keurig machine. The food service was different, too, more like a truck stop diner than a cafeteria. Meals were served for only one hour, three times a day. You sat at a table with metal flatware and ordered from a waitress, who shouted to the short-order cook in the kitchen. Signs were posted to remind passengers that tipping onboard was prohibited by state law.

The booths in the observation lounge were so full of sleeping bodies that their collected mass radiated humid warmth. I took my coffee back up to my goose down cocoon and ate handfuls of trail mix, standing up occasionally to look for signs of land.

We had a layover that afternoon in the town of Kodiak, where I picked up a shatterproof bottle of bourbon and some sleeping pills. Overnight, the seas grew rougher as we moved into the open ocean. The swaying — from inside a sleeping bag, anyway — was less like the ups and downs of a teeter-totter than being slowly swirled around a washing machine. Every couple of hours, my solarium neighbor in overalls would slip into the men's room for a few minutes. When the door opened, a cloud of pot smoke wafted out. We exchanged pleasantries whenever one of us caught the other's eye — he was celebrating his liberation from the educational system with a big Alaska adventure — but each casual conversation quickly veered into a stoner-logic monologue. The *Elder* crowd heard lectures from some of America's finest minds. I got soliloquies from a twenty-two-year-old about how science and history were "total bullshit, no offense."

Around lunchtime on the second day, we arrived at Chignik. Having spent almost two months in coastal Alaska, I should have known to moderate my expectations, but the phrase "fishing village" had lodged in my unconscious, so as we approached the cluster of buildings nestled among some steep green hills, I was somehow anticipating the American version of a Portuguese coastal town: fishermen in thick wool sweaters and caps, drinking rough *vinho tinto* over plates of grilled octopus. It seemed a promising sign that a crowd of parents and kids were waiting with excited faces for the ferry to dock. Maybe this was the sort of warm welcome you could expect in bushiest Alaska, where everyone felt like extended family.

Actually, they were eager to come on board and purchase takeout hamburgers and fries, because Chignik had no restaurant. The biweekly ferry stop was a special treat. I wandered around the tiny town for an hour. The school was empty — students, teachers, and parents were busy ordering burgers — and the only commercial establishment was a shop selling candy bars and cheap trinkets.

"I just came in on the ferry," I said to the woman behind the counter.

"I sort of guessed that," she said.

"Anything interesting I should see while I'm here?"

"Not really."

In the afternoon, the *Tustumena*'s captain, John Mayer, stood at the front of the observation lounge and answered questions from passengers, as if holding a press conference. He explained that we'd left Chignik a little late because he'd been moving ballast around the ship to maintain balance. "We've got a whole dump truck full of sand for the airport at Sand Point," he said. (Captain Mayer, whose knowledge of maritime matters verged on omniscience, did not know why the town needed to import the granular substance with which it shared a name.) He talked about the challenges of the open ocean ("That scares the bejeezus out of some captains, but I never get bored") and what would happen if the GPS system went out ("Don't worry, we're still tested on celestial navigation"). I asked if sailing here was much different than it had been in 1899. "Just look out there," he said. To one side of us was the ocean, and to the other empty hills with snowy mountains in the distance. Green, white, and blue were still the prevailing tints of the run to Dutch Harbor. "Very little has changed since Captain Cook was here."

As Burroughs had been reminded when he attempted to trade his pilfered nest to Merriam, secrets are hard to keep on a boat. I was sitting in the observation lounge when a woman with a long white braid and a batik headband approached, introduced herself as Judy, and asked if it was true that I was a writer. I reluctantly admitted I was. When such information spreads around a group that's traveling together, people tend to start acting like they're the pilgrims of *The Canterbury Tales* and I'm Chaucer: *As we find ourselves on a long journey, kynde scrybe, I shall tell you why I'm here and perhaps share an interesting story or ten to pass the time. Hey, why aren't you writing this down?*

Judy said, "Oh, good, I'm a writer, too," and showed me a spiral-bound notebook she was carrying. My gut reaction was *Oh no, cat poetry,* but I offered to take a look. Three sentences in, my gut stood at attention. Judy could write! She'd sketched a prose portrait of the Alaskan coast that was easily good enough to publish in a travel magazine.

"This is terrific stuff, Judy," I said.

"Oh, I know."

Judy and her husband were from Maine, vagabonding around Alaska. Happy wanderers accounted for maybe a third of the passengers. Another third were residents of the tiny towns along our route, returning home from Anchorage and Outside with new trucks and supplies to get them through the oncoming winter. The final third was the travel club: mostly women of retirement age who'd signed up for the round-trip excursion to Dutch Harbor. The sun was shining and the shore views were lovely as we passed between an island and the mainland, but after two days at sea, a tour seemed approximately 50 percent more Aleutian maritime fun than was strictly necessary. When the purser announced, "We're going to put on a movie about smoking fish in the entertainment lounge," twenty people crowded into the room. About halfway through, the DVD skipped back to the beginning. No one complained. It wasn't like we had anything better to do.

The further west we traveled, the flatter and more sparsely forested the land became. Rows of volcanic mountains stood in the distance, one of which, Mount Pavlof, was smoking, just as it had been in 1899. Passengers went out to the bow to snap photos. Judy handed me her binoculars. The pointy peaks of Pavlof and its twin, Pavlof Sister, resembled the silhouette of a Chihuahua's head, a clever observation I couldn't resist sharing with a fellow writer.

"More like an owl, don't you think?" Judy said.

By the third day at sea, a pervasive languor had enveloped the ship. People fell into deep naps wherever they happened to cease locomotion. I'd boarded with two rolls of quarters, hoping to stash my valuables in a locker as I had on other ferries, but the *Tustumena* had no lockers and, I soon understood, no need for them. As we neared the end of the Alaska Peninsula, I was leaving my backpack unattended and my iPad charging in the men's room like everyone else. (The quarters went into the Keurig machine.) We stopped at more lonely little towns: King Cove and Cold Bay and False Pass, where locals lined up to come on board for burgers. The *Tustumena*'s crew took obvious pride in providing what amounted to a public service. They were a tight-knit bunch, and extremely fond of Captain Mayer. I once snuck around the side deck of the boat to peek into their tiny private dining room, which had two round tables covered with white cloths. The diners seemed to be enjoying one another's company tremendously.

The number of passengers disembarking to explore the limited tourist opportunities at each stop dwindled, until no one got off for the 6:00 A.M. stop at Akutan on our final day at sea. We had crossed into the Aleutians, into the land beyond bears. The dawn was so beautiful that even previously unseen *Tustumena* crew members in coveralls emerged from the bowels of the ship to take photos. Three African men who boarded at Akutan told me they'd come to the United States as Somali refugees and worked summers in the cannery. Two were going to Dutch Harbor because sailing three and a half hours each way beat hanging around Akutan on their day off. The third was flying out to see the dentist and showed me his aching tooth.

"You should visit Mogadishu sometime," he told me. "It's a nice city if you know how to avoid the violence."

CHAPTER THIRTY-SEVEN:
THE FORGOTTEN FRONT

Dutch Harbor

Europeans had been drawn to Dutch Harbor's sheltered waters for more than a century before the *Elder* arrived in 1899. Captain Cook had anchored nearby in 1778, just before departing for his fateful visit to Hawaii. His crew found that in a single generation, the Russian traders had suppressed the area's Aleut population. The Alutiiq of Kodiak Island and the Tlingit of the Alexander Archipelago would maintain their independence for a few years yet, but the era of gold rushes had begun.

By the time he arrived in Dutch Harbor, Cook had begun to doubt the existence of his expedition's primary objective, the Northwest Passage. He had sailed into the Chukchi Sea, between the northernmost regions of Alaska and Siberia, and encountered an impassable wall of ice that "seemed to be ten or twelve feet high at least." Cook followed the ice west all the way to Siberia, hoping to find a breach, but eventually gave up. University of Washington mathematician Harry Stern recently studied ships' records since Cook's frustrating voyage and determined that this Chukchi Sea ice formed more or less regularly around seventy degrees north until the 1990s, when it commenced a retreat of hundreds of miles. The Northwest Passage was now navigable for a brief but lengthening period each year. The *Crystal Serenity* had stopped in Dutch Harbor a week before I did and was now docked at the tiny Canadian town of Ulukhaktok, first seen by white men in 1911, when the explorer Vilhjalmur Stefansson arrived by dogsled.

As I walked down the ramp of the *Tustumena,* Jeff Dickrell was waiting for me at the dock. He was attired in shorts and sunglasses, as if we were headed to the beach. By the usual climatic standards of Dutch Harbor, or Unalaska, as it is alternately called, we probably should have been. (Dutch Harbor is a port inside the city of Unalaska, but the names are used more or less interchangeably by people who don't live there. The name Unalaska means "Island Next to the Mainland" in the Aleut language, Unangan.) Unalaska is known for its Category 5 winds and pea-soup fog, but the temperature was in the mid-sixties and the sky was clear. "Don't bother buckling up," Dickrell told me as I slid into his passenger seat. "This is definitely a no-seatbelt, leave-the-keys-in-the-ignition kind of town."

Dickrell was the history teacher for the Unalaska City School District and had written extensively on the town's past. "There were probably just a few buildings when Harriman got here," he told me, including the Orthodox cathedral built by Father Veniaminov in the 1830s, with the help of the Aleut Natives. For decades, the all-powerful fur-trading companies used Dutch Harbor as a base for their Alaska fiefdom, Dickrell said. As seal and sea otter numbers declined, a pattern of boom and bust in Unalaska was established. The posh tourist clientele aboard the steamer on which E. B. White traveled couldn't hide their disappointment at the melancholy scene they encountered on their Dutch Harbor stop in 1923: "A few deserted houses, a family of Indians, a sow and her three young ones — hardly a place made to order for San Francisco ladies bent on sightseeing."

Unalaska's doldrums continued until 1940, when the U.S. military, concerned about the expansion of the Axis powers, selected Dutch Harbor for the Aleutians' major naval base. "Every bit of infrastructure in this town came from World War II," Dickrell said, including all the roads and the power station still in use, a gray slab next to the ferry terminal, built with five-foot-thick reinforced concrete walls to withstand aerial bombardment. "This is actually a terrible place for a naval port — there's no place to turn a ship around and no place for an airfield."

Driving around Unalaska today is like taking a magnifying glass to one of those recycled medieval parchments on which a monk calligraphied some dogmatic drivel over a poorly erased ancient text. At first glance, one sees an industrial fishing town, with several processing plants larger than any I'd seen in Alaska. Bald eagles congregate like pigeons on stacks of enormous crab pots. Unalaska consistently ranks as the biggest fishing port in the United States, and the boats in its fleet were two or three times the size of those in places like Cordova. Cranes capable of hoisting forty-foot shipping containers towered over the docks. "That big one there came down in a gust of 175 miles per hour," Dickrell said as we crossed from the harbor to the main island. "If you drive across this bridge on a windy day, you definitely feel the car moving horizontally."

A closer look at Unalaska reveals that the treeless green hills that once called out to John Burroughs are carved with zig-zag defensive trenches and dotted with rusting Quonset huts; near the shore, it's easier to find a World War II–era pillbox than a U.S. mailbox. Dickrell handed me a guidebook to the area's historic sites, which I flipped through as we drove. Visiting hikers were cautioned to keep an eye out for pointy metal antipersonnel stakes installed in tall grass seventy-five years ago. Not that anyone in Unalaska was expecting huge growth in its travel economy anytime soon, Northwest Passage cruises or not. "Nobody in this town could give two shits about tourism," Dickrell said. "A one-way airplane ticket, in or out, is five hundred dollars whether you buy it a year in advance or an hour before." You weren't guaranteed to get in or out even with a confirmed seat. Local lore dictated that fog could cancel flights for days, and that the only way to know whether planes were flying was if the top of sixteen-hundred-foot Mount Ballyhoo was visible.

Mobilization all through Alaska accelerated after the Japanese raid on Pearl Harbor, in December 1941. Dutch Harbor is roughly equidistant from Tokyo and Seattle. Admiral Yamamoto, planner of the sneak attack on Hawaii, was planning a major offensive in the northern Pacific.

"The Americans had broken the Japanese code," Dickrell said as we pulled into the parking lot of my hotel, the Grand Aleutian, easily Alaska's finest lodging whose name is a homophone for a Styx album. "They knew they were getting bombed, they just didn't know when." Shortly after the early Alaska sunrise of June 3, 1942, Japanese bombers and Zero fighters attacked. Finding no airfields to destroy — Unalaska's scarcity of flat land had required locating air bases on nearby islands — their pilots instead targeted the army barracks at Fort Mears, killing thirty-five soldiers. "The bombs fell right here, where the hotel is," Dickrell said. The next day the Japanese raided again, inflicting additional casualties but relatively minimal material damage.

Almost no one remembers the Battle of Dutch Harbor today other than World War II buffs, because it transpired at the exact same time as the Battle of Midway, the crushing defeat of the Japanese that marked the turning point of the Pacific War. As that battle raged, Japanese forces withdrawing from the Dutch Harbor raids occupied the islands of Attu and Kiska, at the far western end of the Aleutians. (Longitudinally, Attu is further west than Auckland, New Zealand.) A radio operator was killed; his wife and forty-four Aleut residents, including children, were shipped to a prison camp in Japan, where more than a third of them died from malnutrition and disease. Ten Americans were captured on Kiska. The battle to retake Attu, in May 1943, was one of the fiercest and bloodiest of the war as Japanese soldiers fought to the death rather than surrender. Japan lost 2,351 soldiers; only twenty-eight were captured. Once again, news from the Aleutians was overshadowed by simultaneous military action elsewhere, this time at Guadalcanal.

For the Aleuts, Japanese attacks were only the beginning of their wartime misery. "You know how Japanese Americans were 'interned,' during the war," Dickrell said, making air quotes. "They did the same thing with the Natives here. It was one of the most messed-up things in American history." A month after the Japanese attack on Dutch Harbor, 881 Aleuts living in Unalaska and elsewhere — who were American citizens — were informed that they would be evacuated within twenty-four hours. They were allowed to take one suitcase, containing clothes only, no personal effects. Unalaska's whites were allowed to remain. The Aleuts were deposited at abandoned canneries in the southern Alaska panhandle, where they lived in squalor until the war's end. "After three and a half years, they were brought back and dropped off here in Captains Bay," Dickrell said. "Of course, while they were gone, ten thousand GIs had been here kicking in doors and pissing on everything." Dutch Harbor's cathedral, which the army had used for storage, was severely damaged from rain, snow, and wind. When Attu's survivors returned from Japan, they were prohibited from returning to their home island because it was too expensive to provide government services there.

After another period of decline following the war, Dutch Harbor's fortunes were reversed again, in the 1960s, by a new method of quick-freezing king crab, which rebranded what had been a cheap canned food as a luxury item. Crab fishermen suddenly had more money than they could spend. "There are stories of guys coming up in the 1970s and making a million dollars in a couple of years," Dickrell said. For years, Unalaska was rife with the sorts of bad behavior that occur when young men make too much money too quickly — drinking, drugs, the occasional stabbing. Then, in 1983, king crab populations plummeted and the season was canceled. Stocks still haven't fully recovered.

Once again, Unalaskans beseeched the Deity with what Dickrell called "the age-old Alaska prayer: 'Please, God, send us another boom.' " The wish was granted in the 1990s, when bottom-fishing for species like pollock took off. Unalaska's enormous processing plants convert most of it into fillets for fish sticks or a paste called surimi, much of which is frozen in blocks and shipped off to Japan to be reconstituted into budget sushi. "By the time they're done, it's odorless, tasteless protein," Dickrell said. In a century, the local economy had evolved from fur to war to king crab to fake crab.

The next day was a beautiful Sunday and, while I probably should have been out exploring the hiking trails that Dickrell had recommended, I recovered from the *Tustumena* by lounging in a king-size bed with clean sheets, watching political talk shows, and gorging myself at the Grand Aleutian's famous buffet. I was scheduled to fly out midafternoon, and the possibility of my flight being canceled hadn't crossed my mind, until someone told me what happened when a famous astronaut visited Dutch Harbor. A man who'd calmly walked on the moon almost snapped when his flight out of the Aleutians was canceled by fog for five consecutive days.

Sure enough, while I wasn't looking, the fog rolled in. My flight was canceled. I felt a twinge of envy the next day when I ran into the ladies' travel club from the *Tustumena*. They were departing in the Grand Aleutian shuttle van for the morning flight to Anchorage, on which I hadn't been able to get a seat. An hour later they returned with their luggage. Their flight had been grounded at the last minute due to fog.

"I wouldn't plan on getting out tonight," said the waitress who served my lunch.

"Supposedly, there's a fog coming in from Cold Bay," said the agent at the ticket counter when I checked in later that afternoon.

"They won't fly unless you can see the top of Ballyhoo," said everyone in the airport bar, which was doing a brisk business in shots.

Ticketed passengers could stand at the plate glass window and stare straight out at Mount Ballyhoo. For an hour, people scanned the horizon to the east, watching the world's least thrilling duel, fog versus mountain.

This time, the mountain won.

CHAPTER THIRTY-EIGHT: THE NEW GOLD RUSH

Nome

When John Muir arrived in the Alexander Archipelago for the first time, in 1879, the Tlingit he met referred to Americans as "Boston Men." The name derived from the sailors who'd come from New England to capitalize on the riches of Alaska's waters. "Boston" became an all-purpose adjective to describe non-Native behavior. "When we entered and passed the regular greetings," Muir writes of his and Hall Young's first stop at a Tlingit village after their visit to Glacier Bay, "the usual apologies as to being unable to furnish Boston food for us and inquiries whether we could eat Indian food were gravely made." Boston Men had initially been lured west by the furs in places like the Pribilofs, but sailors from New Bedford and Nantucket quickly realized the Bering Sea's potential for commercial whaling, too.

From Siberia, the *Elder* steamed east to Port Clarence, a whaling depot on the Alaskan mainland. Ten ships were secured in the harbor as the *Elder* anchored offshore. Harriman, perhaps indicating that the novelty of Alaskan culture was waning, invited the whaling captains aboard for drinks and cigars but declined to extend the offer to the Eskimos who approached, paddling umiaks.

One visitor who joined the group swapping stories on the *Elder* was the manager of a U.S. government reindeer station. (Reindeer are not native to Alaska — the missionary Sheldon Jackson had begun importing them from Siberia as a food source.) The reindeer man confided that animal husbandry was merely a sideline for him. His true calling was gold mining. Just fifty miles down the deserted coast, at Nome, ships filled with hopeful prospectors had in recent weeks begun arriving on the beaches.

Port Clarence was one of the last redoubts of America's dying whaling industry. By the end of the nineteenth century, whale populations had been drastically reduced, and whale oil, which until the Civil War had been the primary source of fuel for lamps, had been replaced by other sources, including kerosene derived from petroleum. As ever in Alaska, the end of one boom left the door open for another.

In September 1898, a trio of Scandinavian prospectors — forever to be known as the "Three Lucky Swedes" — had found gold deposits along Anvil Creek. By the time word leaked out, the Swedes had locked up virtually every mining claim in the area. They had not accounted for the fortune in tiny flecks of gold that littered the beaches of Nome, deposits left in part by the advance and retreat of long-gone glaciers. Claims could not be staked on the beach. Unlike in Skagway, prospectors in Nome did not need to transport two thousand pounds of provisions across a steep pass littered with horse carcasses. All they had to do was step ashore and start sifting. As the *Elder* sat off Port Clarence, stampeders by the hundreds were revising plans to strike it rich in the Yukon and booking passage to Nome. By the end of 1899, the population had grown from a handful to two thousand. A year later, it was estimated at twenty thousand, most of them living in tents that stretched for miles along the beach.

Had they learned this news a month earlier, the *Elder*'s shipboard mineralogists would surely have asked to explore Nome and its impending gold rush. But Port Clarence was the northernmost stop of the Harriman Expedition, and the turnaround point. Its patron's thoughts had already begun to wander back to Wall Street and the important railroad business that awaited him there. Several days after leaving Port Clarence, the steamship once again passed beneath the majestic fifteen-thousand-foot peaks of the Fairweather Range, this time on a rare clear day. Hart Merriam went to fetch Harriman, who was sitting with his wife on the opposite side of the ship.

"You are missing the most glorious scenery of the whole trip!" Merriam shouted.

"I don't give a damn if I never see any more scenery" was Harriman's curt reply.

Two distinctive landmarks are visible during the five-hundred-mile flight from Anchorage to Nome: Denali and the Yukon River. On the day I flew, America's tallest peak was shrouded in its own slowly swirling bad-weather system. The twisting Yukon, cloudy with glacial silt carried as far as two thousand miles from the Juneau Icefield, turned sharply south as we approached the middle bulge of the three that protrude from Alaska's west coast into the Pacific Ocean. This is the Seward Peninsula, which twenty thousand years ago was part of the Bering Land Bridge. It's now a stub of tundra completely exposed to the fierce winds coming off the ocean.

I was carrying a map of Alaska superimposed over the continental United States, on which Ketchikan and Metlakatla sat near Jacksonville. Anchorage aligned with Kansas City. Dutch Harbor floated somewhere in southwestern New Mexico, and Attu Island matched almost perfectly with San Francisco. The Seward Peninsula — roughly the size of West Virginia, with a population of perhaps ten thousand — straddled the state line between South Dakota and Nebraska. And about halfway between Omaha and Denver was the very small city of Nome, clinging to the edge of the continent.

The novelist Joy Williams once wrote that if one looks past Nome's obvious lack of palm trees — and all the other absent varieties of arboreal flora — there is something about the place that evokes Key West, its antipodal twin dangling from the other end of the North American landmass. Both are small places with big reputations; both are known for heavy drinking; both feel vulnerable, since they are composed largely of late-Victorian wood-frame buildings that could be washed away like chalk drawings if the ocean ever lost its temper. Other than the weather, the biggest difference between Nome and Key West is the solitude. Unless you're driving in from one of its handful of outlying villages, no roads lead to Nome.

The Nome visitor center is an octagonal building next to a liquor store on Front Street, a hundred or so feet from the ocean. Across the street stands the wooden arch that Iditarod finishers triumphantly mush through in March. When I called the visitor center from Dutch Harbor, inquiring about meeting Nome's mayor, the person answering the phone had suggested stopping in when I got to town. "He's not exactly hard to find," I was told.

When I arrived at the center, a few locals were seated at a round table drinking coffee and talking about the search for a Nome resident whose car had been found parked by a roadside several miles outside of town. So many people used to disappear in Nome that the FBI was called in a decade ago to investigate the possibility of a serial killer. The truth was sadder. People were coming to the Sin City of the North, getting blitzed, and wandering off into the waves or the cold. (In early January, when the sun doesn't rise in Nome so much as it appears for a few hours around lunchtime and rolls across the horizon like a pinball, overnight temperatures can plummet below minus forty degrees.) Late-night safety patrols had since all but eliminated the problem but had not completely ended speculation about another possible cause, alien abduction.

I'd been hoping to meet Mayor Richard Beneville, who doubled as Nome's number-one booster and tour guide. He'd been all over the Alaska news for two weeks, talking about what impact the *Crystal Serenity*'s visit to Nome would have on the future of the city. No one could locate the mayor, so one of the guys hanging around the office — I'll call him Robert — offered to take me for a spin. Unlike Dutch Harbor, Nome was still coasting, sort of, on its first big boom, the gold rush.

"Robert" requested that I not use his real name because he transacted much of his business in gold and considered the Internal Revenue Service illegitimate. He wore a trucker cap on which he had cellophane-taped a handwritten message: INFOWARS — WAKE UP AMERICA YOUR GOVERNMENT IS CORRUPT. His truck was an early-eighties Chevy Custom Deluxe, slowly dissolving from road salt and oxidation. "I got a break on the price because you have to jiggle it to make it start," he said, his left hand agitating the steering column as his right turned the ignition. His very large mutt, named Nome, rode in the back seat and rested her head between us as we took off down Front Street.

Robert worked half the year in Nome, dredging its frigid waters for gold. "The season is ice to ice, roughly May to October," he said. "We take a ten-inch vacuum cleaner and just start sucking." If he and his partner were lucky, they'd sift through several tons of sediment and find a little bit of gold. "There's an old saying in prospecting, 'The sluice box doesn't lie.' "

Though Nome's population of thirty-eight hundred is only a fraction of what it was during the stampede, it's still a gold town. Within a block of my hotel, the Nome Nugget Inn, I spotted two businesses offering assaying and refining services. As Robert drove into the foothills back from the coast, mining sites, mostly one-man operations, dotted the bleak landscape. "This guy here is *killing* it," he said, pointing at one spot. "These guys over here hit twenty-nine hundred ounces in six weeks." We passed a gigantic hole like a sunken football stadium, with tiny trucks rolling around its dusty bottom. "That's an open-pit mine. I hear their workers get a hundred and fifty thousand dollars per season." That money didn't go as far in Nome as it did elsewhere. Gas cost twice what it did in Anchorage. "Lunch here is twenty dollars."

We followed a dirt road uphill toward Anvil Creek, where the Three Lucky Swedes had made their discovery. "This mountain right here was the big one in the gold rush," Robert said. The hills were scored with dried-out water trenches and littered with piles of rubble from gold rush mining operations. "Watch your step if you get out of the truck," Robert said. "There are hundred-foot-deep shafts all through here." Herds of shaggy wild musk oxen, with enormous horns, stood along the roadside. On the top of Anvil Mountain stood four enormous white antennas, each like a weathered drive-in movie screen, Cold War remnants of the Distant Early Warning System pointed at the Soviet Union.

Coming back toward town, we passed an old guy shoveling mud into three tiny sluices. In the wake of a popular reality TV show (on which Robert had declined to show his face due to privacy concerns), Nome had struck up a decent trade in gold tourism. The sorts of dreamers who arrived by steamship in 1899 now flew in during summer vacation. Robert reversed the truck and rolled down his window to ask how the prospecting was going.

"Been out here a week, nothing so far," the man said. "Got another week to go."

"You never know when you're gonna hit it," Robert told him.

"That guy could pull up a nugget today," Robert said as we pulled away. "It's absolutely hit or miss — the gold could be three feet over and you don't see it."

We stopped at Robert's cabin, which was in Nome's version of a subdivision: a small congregation of plywood shacks and container cars. Each home had a dredge boat parked in front, vacuum arms hanging off the sides like Doctor Octopus. Inside the cabin were arranged a rusty stove, a fridge running off a gas generator, and a lot of canned goods. I stepped outside and Robert followed a minute later, holding something that he slapped into my palm. It was two small ingots of pure gold, slightly irregular in shape, each the size of a mini Hershey bar and worth about seven thousand dollars. "Twelve ounces between the both of them," he said. "I do my own refining and molding."

His cabin wasn't exactly Fort Knox. I asked if he ever worried about theft. He shook his head.

442

"Anyone who's carrying gold in Nome is armed," he said. "And everyone knows it."

The next morning I stopped by the visitor center to see if the mayor had picked up the message I left. He hadn't, which seemed a little odd. Nome wasn't a very big place, and judging from the hundreds of photos I'd seen online, Richard Beneville was not a man who ducked attention. The front page of the current *Nome Nugget* showed him performing for the guests of the *Crystal Serenity* with a native dance troupe. I was about to cross Front Street to try my luck at the city offices when a large white van pulled up. "Mayor's here," someone said.

A small, very thin man with a shaved head and large, deep-set eyes stepped out; he looked a little like a middle schooler in a skeleton costume. I introduced myself and said I was hoping to talk to him about the future of Nome. "The future of Nome? Hello, Central!" Beneville shouted. "Get in!"

In a state that honors its unusual characters, Beneville is summa cum laude: a chatty, gay, ex-alcoholic liberal who'd grown up as a military brat idolizing Ethel Merman and ended up in deepest Alaska after bottoming out in New York City. In the 1970s he'd had a successful musical theater career — "Upper West Side, tenor voice, chorus, a hair's breadth from working on Broadway" — but drank so much that his phone eventually stopped ringing. "I was a mess." His brother, who worked for Merrill Lynch in Anchorage, helped arrange a sales job in Barrow, the biggest oil town on Alaska's North Slope, as a sort of intervention.

"I arrived in the middle of the night, forty degrees below zero, snow blowing everywhere," Beneville said as we sped down the two-lane coastal highway. "I stepped out of the jet in a camel hair wraparound coat, three-piece suit, tie, and a fedora like Indiana Jones. Boom! As I looked at the terminal, the fine Eskimo people are wiping the steam off the window, looking at me, saying, What the hell is that?"

Somehow he managed to sober up only after settling in booze-soaked Nome, eventually finding a niche in teaching. "I've put on more than thirty plays since I got here," he said. "Unfortunately, I have a gap in my repertoire because I left New York in 1982. *Cats* had just opened on Broadway."

Beneville's cell phone rang every few minutes — constituents looking for help with minor problems that ranged from needing a ride to the hospital to agony aunt personal matters. Between calls, Beneville explained that after retiring from teaching the prior year, running for mayor seemed the natural next step. "Hello, Central!" he said. "The grass doesn't grow under my feet!" ("Hello, Central," it took me about twenty minutes to deduce, was Beneville's multipurpose exclamation. He once hosted a local TV show called *Hello Central*.) The timing of his victory was fortuitous, he said, because after a century-long gold hangover, Nome was once again a town "on the brink," ready for its next phase.

Beneville pulled the van off the road and pointed out to sea, where a large ship was anchored. The ship was part of a project that was taking advantage of the ice-free Northwest Passage to lay an undersea fiber-optic cable from England to Asia. Nome would serve as the connection point to Japan.

"This is all about a shrinking planet and the accessibility of the Bering Strait," he said. "Everything is changing, and it's happening so quickly. Ice that once formed in November is forming in late December. It's breaking up in mid-May as opposed to June." Climate change wasn't forcing Nome to search for its next boom. In Nome, climate change *was* the next boom. "This is the new Arctic," he said.

Keeping in mind that I was driving around with an elected official who was an actual song-and-dance man, I listened as Beneville touted the mostly good things that were coming for the people of Nome as temperatures rose. Project Chariot, the late-fifties plan to create a deepwater port a couple hundred miles north of Nome by exploding multiple atomic bombs, had been scrapped in part because there was no need for a port in the Bering Sea. Due to the thinning pack ice, that is no longer the case. Chinese companies have already started shipping goods to Hamburg via the Bering Sea, Beneville said, circumventing the Suez Canal and lopping more than three thousand miles off a trip. In the past decade, traffic at the Port of Nome had increased fivefold. As the ice-free season continues to grow, more traffic will surely follow. Both Nome and the old whaling hub Port Clarence were being considered by the Army Corps of Engineers as sites for a new deepwater port. The plan this time was to dredge rather than detonate.

"Climate change isn't the herald of what is happening," Beneville said. "It's already happened. It's here. And it's an opportunity."

I asked the mayor if any of the *Crystal Serenity*'s nine hundred upscale tourists had objected to being shuttled around in the Nome district's yellow school buses. "Not all of them were absolutely filthy rich," Beneville said. "Some of them were retired teachers, people who wanted to be a part of an historic event." The *Serenity*'s owners hadn't melted the ice. They were merely taking advantage of its disappearance to provide something people wanted. "My mantra about tourism is: If you can get there, people will go, period," he said.

We drove out to the Port of Nome, and Beneville noted recent improvements, such as the third dock, added to relieve overcrowding. A deepwater port would allow fuel tankers and large military vessels to moor. Cruise ships like the *Serenity* could pull right into port, as they do in Skagway and Ketchikan. "The military, diplomats, everybody is referring to the Arctic Ocean as a new ocean," Beneville said. "Everything about this is new and exciting." With the Arctic warming twice as fast as most of the world, some scientists were predicting that within fifty years, cargo ships would be making regular trips across the North Pole.

"Hello, Central! I feel like we're living in the times of the great explorers — like

Portugal with Vasco da Gama, you know?" We stepped out of the van and walked to the edge of the dock, staring out into the infinite blue sea. "One guy said it's like stumbling on the Mediterranean all over again."

Chapter Thirty-Nine: Green Men

Washington, DC

The return of the Harriman Expedition to Seattle on July 30 was national news. *The New York Times* ran a front-page story, surrounded by dispatches about a deadly yellow fever outbreak in Virginia, rioting in Paris over the Dreyfus affair, and a daylong race in which two automobiles averaged the blistering speed of almost thirty miles an hour. The *San Francisco Chronicle* called the *Elder* a "curiosity shop" that was "stocked with everything Alaskan from a totem pole five feet through and sixty feet high to the minutest insect."

Totem poles were last-minute additions to the ship's cargo. At Kodiak, an old gold miner had given Frederick Dellenbaugh a crude hand-drawn map showing the location of an abandoned Indian village near what is now Ketchikan. As the homebound *Elder* approached the Alaska–Canada border, Harriman compared the miner's map against Captain Doran's charts and ordered a stop at a settlement called Cape Fox Village. When the *Elder*'s launches landed on shore the next morning, the expeditioners encountered a ghost town. Just behind the beach stood a row of traditional Tlingit houses. In front of the houses stood nineteen totem poles.

The scientists were ecstatic. Clothing, blankets, masks, carvings, and other artifacts were so plentiful that the *Elder* docked off Cape Fox Village for two days to allow each expert to maximize his haul. As they rummaged, the expeditioners speculated on the fate of the missing residents. "It was a question with us as to why the village had been so completely deserted and apparently all at once," Dellenbaugh wrote.

The top prizes were the massive poles, several of which the crew and scientists alike labored, in unusually warm weather, to dig out and float to the ship. Celebratory beers were opened, and a program of songs performed in Harriman's honor. The patron gathered his entire party on the beach for a final all-star-team photograph in front of the remaining totems. Long into the night, the quiet Inside Passage echoed with the Harriman Alaska Expedition cheer: "Who are we? Who are we? We are, we are, the H.A.E.!"

Two members were absent from the photograph: Edward Curtis, who was standing behind the camera, and John Muir, who had wandered off in a huff. Muir was infuriated by the theft of the totems, and also displeased that a family of squirrels living atop one pole had been preserved as specimens. On his 1879 visit to Alaska, some of the Presbyterian missionaries with whom he was traveling had cut down a pole belonging to the family of Kadachan, the Tlingit chief who was among those who guided him to Glacier Bay. ("I heard a chopping going on at the north end of the village, followed by a heavy thud, as if a tree had fallen," Muir writes in *Travels in Alaska*.) In spite of having recently converted to Christianity and presumably forsaking pagan idols, Kadachan looked the missionary party's leader squarely in the face and asked, "How would you like to have an Indian go to a graveyard and break down and carry away a monument belonging to your family?"

If Muir feared that his fellow Harriman expeditioners were making a mistake, he was correct. Cape Fox Village hadn't been abandoned. Its occupants had moved a few miles away, probably to avoid a smallpox epidemic and almost certainly so that their children could attend a new school.

A month after the *Elder* arrived in Seattle, a consortium of local business leaders sailed to the village of Tongass and chopped down another Tlingit totem pole, which they carried back to be erected in Pioneer Square. This time, the Natives appealed to Governor Brady and a grand jury indicted eight of the businessmen. They were fined a total of five hundred dollars. Seattle kept the pole. After an arsonist vandalized the original in 1938, Tlingit craftsmen carved a replacement, the same pole beneath which I first learned about the Harriman Expedition from a national park ranger in a Smokey Bear hat.

After stepping off the *Elder* in Seattle, the Harriman Expedition's luminaries gave newspaper interviews, lingered for a few days, and dispersed. Harriman, pleased with his burst of positive press, departed immediately to deal with a brewing railroad crisis. John Burroughs and others returned east on another Harriman special train. William Dall, having wrapped up his fourteenth and final trip to Alaska, sailed for a new chapter in Hawaii. Hart Merriam spent three months in the Bay Area, tracking mammals and fretting about the work ahead editing the *Harriman Alaska Series,* which would consume more than a decade of his life.

George Bird Grinnell returned to *Forest and Stream* and published a series of reports on the expedition, highlighting the problems Alaska's wildlife faced and the need for government intervention. The fur seals of the Pribilofs would eventually be saved by the first international treaty to protect wildlife, 1911's North Pacific Fur Seal Convention. Aboard the *Elder,* Grinnell had invited photographer Edward Curtis to join him the following summer in Montana to observe a Blackfeet Indian ceremony. That journey would launch a project that became Curtis's twenty-volume opus, *The North American Indian,* one of the twentieth century's masterworks of photography and ethnology. Like his photographs of the melting giants of Glacier Bay, Curtis's images of Native Americans and their rituals are in some cases all that remains of a vanished world.

John Muir returned to his fruit farm in Martinez, where over the coming months he hosted a swarm of visitors from the expedition, everyone from Merriam to Captain Doran. His two months at sea had solidified alliances with some wilderness defenders and created new ones with others. In a letter to Harriman's daughters written upon returning home, he described his time aboard the *Elder* as "a floating university in which I enjoyed the instruction and companionship of a lot of the best fellows imaginable, culled and arranged like a well-balanced bouquet."

The nascent environmental movement was itself evolving, and hardening into two general groups. The utilitarians believed that America's natural spaces should be managed for their potential resources, chiefly logging. The preservationists, led by men such as Muir and Grinnell, wanted wilderness to be maintained in its original state for its own sake, and for the sake of future generations. Muir's lyrical nature writing took on a sharper edge. The famous introduction to 1901's *Our National Parks* shows a touch of manifesto seeping into the pastoral sweetness and natural light: "Thousands of tired, nerve-shaken, over-civilized people are beginning to find out that going to the mountains is going home; that wildness is a necessity; and that mountain parks and reservations are useful not only as fountains of timber and irrigating rivers, but as fountains of life."

The American conservation movement,

like the First World War, built slowly over decades and then seemed to burst forth suddenly with an anarchist's bullet. By the spring of 1901, Boone and Crockett cofounder Theodore Roosevelt was in Washington, DC, serving as the new vice president to William McKinley and eagerly reading early drafts of reports from the Harriman Expedition that his friend Merriam had sent over. Under other circumstances, the peripatetic Roosevelt would have been an ideal member of the HAE. He had known Grinnell and Merriam for years, wrote authoritatively on the outdoors, and dined frequently with his literary hero, John Burroughs. He envied their adventures aboard the *Elder*. Upon reviewing Merriam's writings on bears, "Roosevelt hatched a plan to take a steamer to Alaska and then hunt with an Aleut guide along the salmon streams of Kodiak," writes historian Douglas Brinkley. "He even ordered rubber boots and rainproof slickers in anticipation of the journey."

Roosevelt was returning from a hike in the Adirondacks on September 13, 1901, when he received word that McKinley, who had been shot in Buffalo, was near death. McKinley died the following day and Roosevelt was sworn in as president. The new president's status as both unelected to the highest office in the land and the youngest chief executive in American history, at forty-two, did nothing to diminish his legendary confidence. Suddenly the defenders of America's wilderness had an ally in the White House. Just six weeks after Roosevelt took the oath of office, Hart Merriam wrote to John Muir, in California, that the new president "wants to know the facts and is particularly anxious to learn them from men like yourself who are not connected with the Government service and at the same time are known and esteemed by the people."

Roosevelt knew well from Grinnell's lobbying efforts to preserve Yellowstone that getting Congress to support progressive conservationist projects over the interests of wealthy businessmen was no easy task. As president, he instead chose to save wilderness largely by executive fiat. In August 1902, he issued a proclamation setting aside the Alexander Archipelago as a forest reserve. The same year, influenced by Grinnell and other fellow members of the Boone and Crockett, he pushed for the first comprehensive law protecting game animals in Alaska. Moose and brown bears now fell under the jurisdiction of the Division of

Biological Survey, where Merriam was chief. In 1907, Roosevelt enlarged the Alexander Archipelago reserve to create the seventeen-million-acre Tongass National Forest reserve, the largest in U.S. history. A few weeks later he set aside 5.4 million acres, including College Fjord and other areas he'd read about in the *Harriman Alaska Series,* as the Chugach National Forest. Almost all the glaciers seen by the passengers of the *Elder* were now federally protected.

By 1903, the enormously popular Roosevelt was planning his Grand Loop tour, a two-month working vacation that would take him through most of the states west of the Mississippi. Mutual acquaintances inquired if Muir might be open to guiding the president in the California Sierras. Though the two men had never met, Roosevelt had been deeply influenced by *Our National Parks.* "I do not want anyone with me but you," Roosevelt wrote to Muir in March 1903. "I want to drop politics absolutely for four days and just be out in the open with you."

Muir had his own agenda for the president's visit. The Yosemite National Park, established in 1890, was still a quadrilateral doughnut, with the state of California retaining its control over the spectacular Yosemite Valley, at the park's center. Lumbermen and sheepherders continued to exploit the state's lax supervision. Muir and the Sierra Club repeatedly asked the state legislature to consider ceding the valley back to the United States government, without success.

Roosevelt's Yosemite visit went even better than hoped. The president largely ignored the slate of formal events organized by California politicians, slipping away to pass four days camping with Muir. The two men slept beneath the sequoias and rode horses to Glacier Point, where snow fell onto the valley and Half Dome. Muir felt comfortable enough with the president that he chided him for his love of hunting.

"Mr. Roosevelt, when are you going to get beyond the boyishness of killing things?" he asked.

"Muir, I guess you are right," he replied.*
Roosevelt readily agreed that Yosemite Val-

* While it would be nice to imagine that Roosevelt never again took up arms against fauna, he seems to have been only momentarily under Muir's spell. Just weeks after his presidency ended, in 1909, Roosevelt embarked on the Smithsonian-Roosevelt African Expedition, on which more than eleven

ley needed to be saved, but the California legislature would not vote to return control to the federal government without the approval of the Southern Pacific Railroad, the most powerful lobbying force in Sacramento. Fortuitously, the Southern Pacific had been acquired by a reinvigorated Edward Harriman after his return from Alaska. Muir's unusual friendship with Harriman had continued to flower, and he somewhat reluctantly asked for the mogul's help. Overnight, the Southern Pacific switched its position on Yosemite from opposition to support. In Washington, DC, the budget-conscious speaker of the House was slow to ratify the move. Harriman had a word with him, too. President Roosevelt gladly signed the legislation into law.

Perhaps the most powerful weapon in Roosevelt's preservationist arsenal was the Antiquities Act of 1906, which gave him the power to protect "historical landmarks, historic preservation structures, and other objects of scientific interest."* Over the next two and a half years, he designated Devils

---

thousand animal specimens were collected for the museum.

* The Antiquities Act had been pushed through by one of the unsung heroes of Capitol Hill

Tower, the Petrified Forest, the Grand Canyon, and other western wonders as national monuments. In 1908, a wealthy businessman donated a tract of nearly three hundred acres of Northern California redwoods to the government; Roosevelt, honoring the donor's request, named the monument Muir Woods. In 1925, President Calvin Coolidge would use the Antiquities Act to set aside Glacier Bay.

For a hundred years following the 1867 purchase of Alaska, the question of Native land rights remained in legal limbo. The 1968 discovery of massive oil fields lurking beneath Prudhoe Bay changed everything. The state of Alaska quickly sold nine hundred million dollars in drilling leases. Vari-

---

conservation, Iowa congressman and fellow Boone and Crockett member John Lacey. He had previously cemented the B and C's reputation as a political force by shepherding the Lacey Act of 1894, "to protect the birds and animals in Yellowstone National Park." He'd been convinced of Yellowstone's lawlessness when his stagecoach was robbed there at gunpoint. Lacey also wrote the Lacey Act of 1900, a wildlife protection bill that, when passed, became the first comprehensive federal law dedicated to preserving the environment.

ous tribes laid claim to the land through which the major petroleum companies planned their eight-hundred-mile pipeline. It was soon apparent that no oil would flow until the land rights issue was settled. The solution was the Alaska Native Claims Settlement Act (ANCSA), which divided forty-four million acres and 962 million dollars among twelve regional corporations and more than two hundred village corporations.

In 1978, facing a deadline to determine the fate of the U.S. government's remaining Alaska land holdings following the ANCSA settlement, President Jimmy Carter used the Antiquities Act to designate fifty-six million Alaska acres as national monuments. During his final weeks in office, Carter signed into law the Alaska National Interest Lands Conservation Act of 1980, widely considered to be the most important environmental legislation passed since Theodore Roosevelt's administration. The move vastly expanded the dimensions of the Arctic National Wildlife Refuge, doubled the size of National Park Service lands, and elevated several monuments to national park status. Among them were Glacier Bay National Park and Katmai National Park.

CHAPTER FORTY:
LAND'S END

Shishmaref

A freshly skinned seal looks like an oversize beef tenderloin with a cute whiskered face stuck on one end. I know this because the first person I met after dropping off my bag in Shishmaref, Annie Weyiouanna, was scraping the fat from a spotted seal she had hunted that day with her husband. "I'll feed this to my sled dogs," she said, separating the greasy fat layer with her curved ulu knife. "The skin will make a hat and a couple of pairs of mittens."

Weyiouanna is Shishmaref's relocation coordinator. Two weeks had passed since the town's historic vote to move to the mainland. The handwritten ballot results were still posted on the door of the city office building. Shishmaref has about six hundred residents and is the sole settlement on Sarichef Island, which is essentially a long sandbar, an elongated peanut two and a half miles long and less than a half mile wide at its narrow waist. The island sits five miles off the coast of the Seward Peninsula, about 120 miles north of Nome. The Arctic Circle is thirty miles north. As Alaska heats up, weather patterns that have been reliable as long as anyone in Shishmaref can remember — that is, bitterly cold — are becoming increasingly less predictable.

"The seasons have changed," Annie told me. "We get an earlier spring. It's taking longer for the ocean to freeze. Traditionally, it freezes in October. Last year it froze in January."

Shishmaref was my final stop in Alaska, and probably the most traditional of all the villages I visited. Its residents are Inupiat, a subgroup of northern people once known as the Eskimos. (The term Eskimo is considered derogatory by some Natives and was eliminated from federal government use in 2016.) For thousands of years, the nomadic Kigiqtaamiut — the name translates as "people of the island" — have occupied the coastal areas surrounding Shishmaref. In response to the debauchery of the Nome gold rush, which was starting up as the *Elder* sailed by in 1899, missionaries led by Sheldon Jackson pushed for the Kigiqtaamiut to settle permanently in one spot so that a school, church, and post office could be built. Sarichef Island, with its year-round availability of food, was the obvious choice for a village. Annie Weyiouanna estimated that 90 percent of the town's food still came from subsistence hunting and gathering: bearded seal, caribou, duck, moose, fish, walrus, greens, berries. "The ocean is our supermarket," Annie said. "We can't just get up and go to Walmart."

The thinning ice that promises a potential boon for Nome's economy and global shipping companies dooms Shishmaref to near-certain disaster. The ice is too dangerous to hunt on; Esau Sinnok, the UAF college student from Shishmaref I'd met in Anchorage, told me that an uncle had drowned after falling through late-spring ice that should have been frozen. In autumn, violent storms blow in from the Chukchi Sea. The protective buffer of ice that once solidified along the seashore in October no longer keeps the most powerful waves at a safe distance. Rising temperatures have thawed the permafrost beneath the island. Since the 1970s, the fall storms have increased in frequency and intensity, eating away at the loose sand and taking houses with it.

After a summer spent weighing Alaska's past against its present, Shishmaref offered an opportunity to end my travels with a glimpse of the state's likely future. If the town's recent history was any indication, I probably wouldn't get another chance.

I slept in a classroom at the Shishmaref School. Inspirational signs on the walls encouraged HARD WORK and RESPECT FOR OTHERS, along with HUNTER SUCCESS and RESPONSIBILITY TO TRIBE. The school is one of only three buildings in the village with treated running water, along with the washeteria (for laundry and showers) and the medical clinic. Thick hoses ran on the ground, connecting the three. The morning drop-off routine was pretty similar to the one in my New York suburb, except all the vehicles parked out front were sport quads with knobby tires to churn through the soft sand.

To most of the world, polar bears are mascots of climate change. In Shishmaref, I was informed by a gaggle of curious second and third graders who assembled around the stranger they encountered in the hallway before school began, all bears are dangerous nuisances, regardless of color.

"My dad had to chase away a polar bear with his snow machine," said one boy.

"A brown bear can kill a white bear," said

another, to dubious reactions from his companions.

"There were seven brown bears here, because a dead orca washed up on the beach and they smelled it," said a third. A walrus carcass had landed ashore the day before, which promised more unwelcome visitors as it ripened.

William Jones is Shishmaref's policeman, a job he's had since 1980 and clearly enjoys. (The town also has a village public safety officer, or VPSO, a jack-of-all-trades functionary, trained by the state, whose job portfolio includes law enforcement, fire protection, and emergency medical services.) Jones was a little more ambivalent about the new civic duties that had been thrust upon him shortly before I arrived. "I was appointed acting mayor last week," he told me when we shook hands in the city offices, on the second floor of the town hall. The previous mayor had resigned suddenly. Jones had been selected by the council as a temporary replacement.

Jones had a goatee and wore a T-shirt and jeans. If he possessed a firearm or handcuffs, I did not see them in the several hours we spent together. His eyes were puffy from lack of sleep. He'd been awakened at 3:00 A.M. when some folks who'd snuck a few bottles of cut-rate R&R whisky onto the dry island got a little out of hand. (Jones, who said that he could usually sense within a few hours when someone had smuggled liquor into Shishmaref, did have a single-occupancy jail cell at his disposal; on busy nights like New Year's Eve, the better-behaved drunks were allowed to sit with him in his office.) We filled two Styrofoam cups from the Mr. Coffee machine and went into the conference room next door. Its walls were plastered with maps showing where erosion had taken place and where it would likely take place soon.

"We've lost quite a bit of land," Jones said, scanning the maps. "The beach is eroding on the west side. There used to be houses over here." One storm in 2013 carved off fifty feet of beach, including a chunk of the main road. The Army Corps of Engineers has built a series of seawalls, each more formidable than the last, but none has been completely effective at neutralizing the effects of the waves.

Another map showed two possible mainland locations to which Shishmaref could be moved. Contrary to breathless international media reports, the Shishmaref diaspora was not exactly imminent. Both potential sites for a new town were deep in the bush on the mainland. If and when it rose from the tundra — "They haven't even built a road yet," Jones noted — Shishmaref II would be an Arctic Brasilia. The cost of the move would likely be in the tens of millions of dollars, approximately none of which had yet been arranged. The state of Alaska had an office to deal with such potential moves, and a dozen communities threatened by climate change were considering relocating. The August vote wasn't even the first such referendum in Shishmaref. The first one had been held in 1975, and residents had already voted, in 2002, to relocate.

"Were you surprised by the results?" I asked Jones, who'd voted to stay.

"I was pissed off," Jones said. "We voted forty years ago and we're still here. Talk, talk, talk, talk. We're gonna be talking for another forty years. This island is home. They should just get a barge and move the sand around to protect it."

Shishmaref didn't look like a town holding a going-out-of-business sale. A new liquid-fuel tank farm was being planned, and housing for teachers (almost all of whom are non-Native) was under construction. The island's main road had just been tarmacked for the first time a few weeks earlier. Jones walked me over to the latest and greatest seawall, a wide strip of large rocks piled neatly along the waterline.

"There used to be sand dunes here, all along the coast," Jones said. "People used to sit and enjoy the water." Waves splashed onto the rocks, and onto the dead walrus. Jones said walrus meat is a delicacy but that you have to bury it for a while so it can ferment properly. "It's oily, but it's delicious," he said. "It tingles when you eat it." He had already admitted to a fondness for teasing reporters who parachuted in to collect a few sound bites from Alaska's newly famous climate refugees — he'd recently told a radio host from Los Angeles that he lived in a two-story igloo and was unfamiliar with the word "electricity" — but insisted that walrus was the real culinary deal. Ideally, it was followed up with a bowl of Eskimo ice cream, a dairy-free treat whose key ingredients are local berries and seal oil.

In real estate terms, everyone in Shishmaref has a house that is either "beachfront" or "walk to beach." Where other Alaska towns might have a cannery and a marina filled with trawlers, Sarichef Island's mainland-facing side was filled with small wooden boats and drying racks where meat and fish could cure in the salt air. A few times, I asked someone what the protocol was during particularly dangerous storms, expecting to hear about evacuation plans and helicopters, but everyone said the same thing: When it gets bad, they make sure everyone's boats and meat racks are secure, and then they hunker down. In an emergency situation, residents took shelter at the school or the church.

Jones suggested we have a look around the island and visit some of his neighbors. He drove his four-wheel ATV and I sat on the back, clinging to the rear rack. The day was cold and drizzly. On the ocean side of the island, you could see the top few inches of yellow bulldozers and other retired heavy equipment that had been buried in the sand as bulwarks against the waves. The wind shifted direction and we were hit with a foul blast. Because homes in Shishmaref lack flush toilets, household waste is collected and deposited into a cesspool, which, Jones had insisted with a smirk, was an essential part of the tour.

"Is that stink the cesspool?" I shouted over my shoulder.

"Nope, walrus. Smells a little like that when you eat it, too."

If the number of doors we knocked on or entered unannounced is any indication of

Jones's investigative methods, I doubt there are many unsolved crimes in Shishmaref. I met Esau's grandfather Shelton Kokeok, whose house was perched at the edge of a sand bluff. He'd already lost one home to erosion. "I'm always looking out that window and watching that beach in bad weather," he said. Howard Weyiouanna — every other person I met in Shishmaref had the last name Weyiouanna — reminisced about the long-gone sand hills that children would sled down on sealskins in winter.

Clifford Weyiouanna served us his famous sourdough pancakes and talked about how he'd taught himself to fly a plane and had spent seventeen years as an unlicensed bush pilot. "I found seven people alive and two dead on search-and-rescue missions," he said. "The ones I found alive always said they wanted a cup of coffee or a cigarette." Clifford had a fondness for both. Like Jones, he thought the relocation vote had been a waste of time but admitted he likely wouldn't be around to see how things turned out. "This move will happen more slowly than the Second Coming of Jesus Christ," he said.

Our last stop was at the small house of Ardith and Johnny Weyiouanna. We sat at the kitchen table as Ardith cleaned moss-berries she'd gathered that morning. "I came here in 1958 by dogsled," she said. "No one spoke English except me and my brothers and sisters. Everyone spoke Inupiaq. We used to have Eskimo dancing every week, to celebrate a hunter catching a polar bear. The last time one of these young men killed a polar bear, I suggested we bring the dancing back one time, but there were too many things going on. Like bingo."

Ardith had voted to move. "It's hard to leave the place you've lived all your life. But you have to sacrifice for younger people." She offered me a mossberry, which looked like a tiny blueberry but was more bitter than I expected. I grimaced. "I guess this means you won't be staying for Eskimo ice cream," she said.

Several people in Shishmaref told me that according to oral tradition, Shishmaref is a "floating island," with water running underneath. I asked Ardith what she thought the story meant.

"The elders a long time ago used to say, 'Shishmaref built up from the sea and one day it will return to the sea,'" she said. "I think that means we're doomed."

Jones and I went back to his small house to wait for my plane to Nome. I bought him a pack of Marlboros at the general store as a thank-you gift. He gave me a mastodon tooth he'd found on the beach. Clifford Weyiouanna, the sourdough man, met us at the airport in his pickup truck, one of two full-size vehicles I saw in Shishmaref. He had a twenty-pound box of fish he'd asked me to deliver to his sister in Nome. Jones unwrapped his Marlboros and offered one to Clifford.

"There used to be sand dunes all along that side and this side, some as tall as a two-story building," Clifford said. "Big beach out here where you could land a plane." He took a deep drag of his cigarette and flicked the butt. "Gone, all gone."

EPILOGUE

New York City

John Muir struggled for years to write his autobiography. In 1908, Edward Harriman invited him to his family's summer home near Crater Lake, in Oregon. Harriman was by that time fighting stomach cancer, his condition exacerbated by a dispute with his former friend Theodore Roosevelt. The progressive president had singled out the railroad tycoon as one of the immoral businessmen whose monopolies needed to be broken up for the good of the country. Efficient to the end, Harriman arranged for a secretary to follow Muir around his estate for three weeks, recording Muir's every utterance in shorthand until he had dictated a thousand pages of memories, which later formed the core of *The Story of My Boyhood and Youth*. A year later, Harriman was dead. "I feel very lonesome now my friend Harriman is gone," Muir wrote to John Burroughs. "At first rather repelled, I at last learned to love him."

On Christmas Eve 1914, Muir, suffering from pneumonia, died alone in a Los Angeles hospital bed at age seventy-six. It seems probable his last thoughts were of glaciers. Scattered around him on the bed were the manuscript pages of what would be his final book, his recounting of his early trips through the Inside Passage with Tlingit guides, *Travels in Alaska.*

In the essay "General Geography," published in volume two of *The Harriman Alaska Series,* geographer Henry Gannett gives a quick overview of the things that still make Alaska unique more than a century later: its immense mountains, extreme climate, majestic glaciers, towering forests, and mysterious interior. After providing a summary of Alaska's resources, he finishes with a rather radical suggestion. Alaska's chief asset, "more valuable than the gold or the fish or the timber, for it will never be exhausted," is its scenery. Echoing his *Elder* shipmate John Muir, the father of American mapmaking notes that, for the one Yosemite in California, "Alaska has hundreds."

He concludes by offering a "word of advice and caution" for anyone considering a trip to Alaska. "If you are old, go by all means, but if you are young, wait. The scenery of Alaska is much grander than anything else of its kind in the world, and it is not wise to dull one's capacity for enjoyment by seeing the finest first."

A few months after I returned to New York, a new administration was voted into the White House. With regard to the environment, the forty-fifth president was no Theodore Roosevelt. Among his first proposals were slashing the national parks budget, lifting a federal ban on hunting hibernating bears and withdrawing from an international climate accord that was the world's best hope for slowing the effects of global warming. The year 2016 ended as the third in a row of record-breaking heat in Alaska. The new chief of the Environmental Protection Agency, who had spent the last several years at his previous job suing the EPA to loosen regulations on the oil and gas industries, declared that carbon dioxide is not a major contributor to climate change. The new secretary of the interior, boss of the national parks, announced that drilling for oil in the Arctic National Wildlife Refuge — the Serengeti of the North — was one of his first priorities. Alaska's representatives on Capitol Hill, while paying lip service to the effects of climate change on their state, pushed to make their dream of drilling in ANWR come true.

A year after my visit to Juneau, the price of oil had risen only slightly. Economist Scott Goldsmith had seen little sign that it would again approach a hundred dollars a barrel. The Alaska State Legislature sat through three special sessions, still trying to close its enormous budget gap. After much debate, a state income tax was again rejected and the annual Permanent Fund Dividend was raised back to eleven hundred dollars per person. Included in the budget was twenty-two million dollars to build a replacement for the *Tustumena,* which had canceled most of its sailings for the summer after cracks were found in its hull. Since the full cost of the new ship was 244 million dollars, the federal government chipped in the remaining 90 percent. The *Crystal Serenity* once again departed on a monthlong Northwest Passage cruise, stopping at Dutch Harbor and Nome before continuing into the Arctic.

The winter was surprisingly cold, and Shishmaref survived intact. A new mayor was elected, and plans for the relocation continued to be discussed. William Jones happily returned to full-time police work then lost his job due to budget cuts. On Kodiak Island, the harsh winter minimized the summer's wild berry crop, but Harry and Brigid Dodge reported that a strong salmon run had resulted in favorable conditions for both hungry bears and those who love to watch them. Sitting at my desk beneath my enormous map of Alaska, I felt a pang of bruin envy. Then someone forwarded a video of a massive brown bear bursting out of the woods to chase an automobile along the same two-lane Yakutat road I'd blithely bicycled down a year earlier, and I got over it.

In and around Gustavus, the corner of Alaska to which I most often found my mind wandering, the ice continued to melt and the land continued to rebound slowly like bread dough. David and Brittney Cannamore purchased a plot next to Kim and Melanie Heacox, where they planned to start building their own home once kayak season wound down. The Heacoxes sketched out plans to convert their homestead into the John Muir Alaska Leadership School, which would tutor future generations of environmentalists. Kim churned out another novel in the winter gloom. Melanie trained another batch of interpretive rangers to enlighten cruise ship passengers with the story of Muir and his Tlingit guides, though she fretted that an even rainier-than-usual summer would scare many away from returning.

One half of Henry Gannett's caution about visiting Alaska — his warning that its spectacular scenery will ruin anything that follows — still holds true, to an extraordinary degree. The lands set aside during Theodore Roosevelt's benevolent conservationist dictatorship have aged remarkably well. Some scenes from the *Harriman Alaska Series* are largely unchanged since 1899. I have seen the sun rise over Paris, above the ruins of Machu Picchu, and on the horizon of an elephant-dotted African savanna, and none of them can equal the dawn breaking in Glacier Bay.

The other half of Gannett's warning, that potential visitors should wait until later in life to witness Alaska's wonders, may be rapidly approaching its expiration date. I don't worry that a trip to Alaska will dull my sons' capacity to appreciate natural beauty elsewhere. I do worry that if current climate trends prevail, the spectacle will become a little less spectacular with each passing year.

Shortly after returning from the Harriman Expedition, John Muir wrote, "Fortunately,

Nature has a few big places beyond Man's power to spoil — the ocean, the two icy ends of the globe, and the Grand Canyon." Muir's hopefulness resonated with George Bird Grinnell, who in 1902 published the quote on the front page of the year-end edition of *Forest and Stream.*

The optimism of men like Muir and Grinnell helped preserve Alaska for generations that followed. As I type this, however, the ocean is warming and clogged with millions of tons of plastic. The frozen poles are melting into the sea at an alarming rate. America's new president is reviewing monuments preserved under the Antiquities Act and considering lifting a ban on uranium mining in the area surrounding the Grand Canyon, which could contaminate its waters.

If you are old and want to see the finest scenery in the world, there's no time like the present. And if you are young, what are you waiting for? Check the ferry timetable, grab a sleeping bag, and go. Stay for a while. Believe me, it could be the event of a lifetime.

ACKNOWLEDGMENTS

A number of people in Alaska kindly responded to an Outsider's unexpected phone call or e-mail by offering to share their expertise in person. In Anchorage: Diane Benson, Scott Goldsmith, Stephen Haycox, and Esau Sinnok. In Fairbanks: Terry Chapin, Vladimir Romanovsky, Ned Rozell, Martin Truffer, and Michael West. Kim and Melanie Heacox not only helped me retrace John Muir's original route through Glacier Bay prior to my Gustavus visit, but provided room and board and later flagged several embarrassing errors in my manuscript.

When reporting books that combine travel and history, I have always depended on the kindness (and chattiness) of strangers. Aboard the *Kennicott:* Beau Bailey and Paul Rambeau. In Metlakatla: Naomi Leask. In Ketchikan: Dave Kiffer. In Wrangell: Lawrence Bahovec, Lydia and Mike Matney, and Eric Yancey. In Haines: David Nanney.

In Sitka: Charles Bingham, Harvey Brandt, Peter Gorman, and Andrew Thoms. In Gustavus: David and Brittney Cannamore. In Yakutat: Jim Capra, Jack Endicott, and Marcia Suniga. In Cordova: Kristin Carpenter, Nancy Bird, and Karl Becker. In Whittier: everyone at Lazy Otter Charters, especially Kelly Bender and Ben and Kerry Wilkins. On Kodiak Island: Harry and Brigid Dodge. In Katmai National Park and King Salmon: Kyle McDowell and the team at Kenai Backcountry Adventures, Dave the pilot, Mike the bartender, and whoever owns that beer-drinking Labrador. In Unalaska: Jeff Dickrell and Bobbie Lekanoff. In Nome: Richard Beneville and Leon Boardway. In Shishmaref: Donna Barr, Barret Eningowuk, Dottie Harris, William Jones, Shelton and Clara Kokeok, Susie Kokeok, Harold Olanna, Darlene Turner, Annie Weyiouanna, Ardith and Johnny Weyiouanna, Clifford Weyiouanna, and Howard Weyiouanna.

Several people provided essential counsel, connections, and/or ideas during my research, including Mark Bryant, Rab Cummings, Daniel Coyle, Maurice Coyle, Mique'l Dangeli, Jen Kinney, Tom Kizzia, Nancy Lord, Elizabeth Marino, Bruce Molnia, Riki Ott, John Reiger, Dan Ritzman,

David Roche, Marin Sandy, and Ted Spencer. Kay Sloan mailed a large box of pre-Internet research materials saved from her own book on the Harriman Expedition, which included copies (with typewritten transcriptions!) of the journals kept by several members of the party. Once again, the extraordinary staff at the Pelham Public Library kept me stocked in reading material. Special thanks to the employees of the Alaska Marine Highway System and to the knowledgeable booksellers and librarians whom I encountered in Alaska's bountiful and excellent bookstores and libraries.

In New York City, the usual behind-the-scenes magic was performed by the usual suspects at Dutton: Jessica Renheim, Amanda Walker, and Emily Brock. Ben Sevier got the ball rolling. John Parsley kindly devised a catchy title. David McAninch, Maura Fritz, and Jason Adams read unedited passages and suggested crucial course corrections. Gillian Fassell read the whole thing twice and once again provided the necessary doses of carrot and stick. Will Palmer copy-edited the book with the skill and care of a soap opera surgeon. My agent, Daniel Greenberg, offered steadfast support, sometimes in the form of lunch. Olivia Notter preserved my sanity by transcribing many hours of interviews.

An incomplete list of those owed special gratitude would include: David Adams and Mary McEnery, Robert Corbellini and Barbara Miller (and cats), Natividad Huamani, Fred and Aura Truslow, and Veronica Francis. As ever, my deepest thanks go to my dear wife, Dr. Aurita Truslow, who yet again maintained order in the household while I ran away for most of a summer. Honorable mention to Alex, Lucas, and Magnus for not driving your mother crazy in my absence.

NOTES ON SOURCES

Scientists have demonstrated conclusively that the most powerful force in the universe is the urge to inform an author that you've found an error in his or her book. If you have corrections, thoughts, or moose recipes you'd like to share, feel free to e-mail me at turnrightmp@gmail.com.

Anyone interested in learning more about Alaska's history and environment, and the Harriman Expedition's relation to each, will find the following sources useful:

The Harriman Alaska Series, vols. I–V, VIII–XIV

This twelve-volume collection, edited by C. Hart Merriam, is available online. (Confusingly, numbers six and seven were never published.) The first two volumes, which include the most interesting essays — especially John Burroughs's travelogue and George Bird Grinnell's proto-ecological essay on Alaska's threatened salmon — can also be found in various paperback editions.

Looking Far North: The Harriman Expedition to Alaska, 1899, by William H. Goetzmann and Kay Sloan

The Harriman Alaska Expedition Retraced: A Century of Change, 1899–2001, edited by Thomas A. Litwin

Green Alaska: Dreams from the Far Coast, by Nancy Lord

Goetzmann and Sloan's is the most accessible history of the 1899 voyage. Litwin organized a 2001 expedition à la Harriman, which included a boatload of multidisciplinary experts who faithfully followed the original route of the *Elder* (and arranged to return several of the totem poles stolen from Cape Fox during the 1899 expedition); *Harriman Retraced* comprises then and now essays, the words of the voyage participants interspersed with Litwin's own accounts of each stop. Lord's book is an impressionistic musing on the 1899 journey by one of Alaska's best-known nature writers.

Travels in Alaska, by John Muir

Alaska Days with John Muir, by S. Hall Young

The book that launched a thousand Inside

Passage cruise ships, and his companion's account of the same events.

Alaska: Saga of a Bold Land, by Walter R. Borneman

Alaska, an American Colony, by Stephen Haycox

Exploration of Alaska, 1865–1900, by Morgan Sherwood

Borneman's and Haycox's histories explain how the major events in Alaska since 1741 have molded the state and its people. Sherwood's recounts the men who made the first attempts to catalog the wonders of its vast territory.

The Life and Legend of E. H. Harriman, by Maury Klein

This magnificent biography devotes a full chapter to the 1899 expedition and places it in the context of Harriman's late-blooming career.

The Only Kayak: A Journey into the Heart of Alaska, by Kim Heacox

John Muir and the Ice That Started a Fire: How a Visionary and the Glaciers of Alaska Changed America, by Kim Heacox

Only Kayak intertwines the author's personal history with John Muir's accounts of his visits to Glacier Bay. *Ice That Started a Fire* examines Muir's time among Alaska's glaciers as a catalyst of

the American environmental movement.
Coming into the Country, by John McPhee

The book that almost every Alaskan recommends when asked for suggestions, and for a good reason: no piece of writing (by an Outsider, no less) better captures the forty-ninth state's uniqueness and ethos of rugged individualism.

SELECTED BIBLIOGRAPHY

Askren, Mique'l. "From Negative to Positive: B. A. Haldane, Nineteenth Century Tsimshian Photographer." M.A. thesis, University of British Columbia, 2006.

Berton, Pierre. *Klondike: The Last Great Gold Rush, 1896–1899.* Toronto: McClelland and Stewart, 1987.

Brinkley, Douglas. *The Quiet World: Saving Alaska's Wilderness Kingdom, 1879–1960.* New York: Harper, 2011.

———. *The Wilderness Warrior: Theodore Roosevelt and the Crusade for America, 1858–1919.* New York: HarperCollins, 2009.

Brooks, Paul. *Speaking for Nature: How Literary Naturalists from Henry Thoreau to Rachel Carson Have Shaped America.* Boston: Houghton Mifflin, 1980.

Cole, Dermot. *North to the Future: The Alaska Story, 1959–2009.* Kenmore, WA:

Epicenter Press, 2008.

Cruikshank, Julie. *Do Glaciers Listen? Local Knowledge, Colonial Encounters, and Social Imagination.* Vancouver: UBC Press, 2014.

Dall, William. *Alaska and Its Resources.* Boston: Lee and Shepard, 1870.

Dauenhauer, Nora Marks, and Richard Dauenhauer, eds. *Haa Kusteeyí, Our Culture: Tlingit Life Stories.* Seattle: University of Washington Press, 1994.

Dodge, Harry B. *Kodiak Island and Its Bears.* Anchorage: Great Northwest, 2004.

————. *Kodiak Tales: Stories of Adventure on Alaska's Emerald Isle.* Bloomington, IN: AuthorHouse, 2010.

Egan, Timothy. *Short Nights of the Shadow Catcher: The Epic Life and Immortal Photographs of Edward Curtis.* Boston: Mariner, 2012.

Emerson, Ralph Waldo. *The Essential Writings of Ralph Waldo Emerson.* Edited by Brooks Atkinson. New York: Modern Library, 2000.

Emmons, George Thornton. *The Tlingit Indians.* Seattle: University of Washington Press, 1991.

Fagan, Brian M. *The Little Ice Age: How Climate Made History, 1300–1850.* Boulder, CO: Basic Books, 2000.

Fortuine, Robert. *Chills and Fever: Health and Disease in the Early History of Alaska.* Fairbanks: University of Alaska Press, 1989.

Fox, Stephen. *The American Conservation Movement: John Muir and His Legacy.* Boston: Little, Brown, 1981.

Goldsmith, Scott. "The Path to a Fiscal Solution: Use Earnings from All Our Assets." Anchorage: Institute of Social and Economic Research, 2015.

Griggs, Robert F. *The Valley of Ten Thousand Smokes.* Washington, DC: National Geographic Society, 1922.

Grinnell, George Bird. "The Harriman Alaska Expedition." *Forest and Stream,* February–June 1900.

Haycox, Stephen. *Frigid Embrace: Politics, Economics, and Environment in Alaska.* Corvallis: Oregon State University Press, 2006.

Henry, Daniel Lee. *Across the Shaman's River: John Muir, the Tlingit Stronghold, and the Opening of the North.* Fairbanks: University of Alaska Press, 2017.

Hussey, John A. *Embattled Katmai: A History of Katmai National Monument.* San Francisco: National Park Service, 1971.

King, Bob. *Sustaining Alaska's Fisheries:*

Fifty Years of Statehood. Anchorage: Alaska Department of Fish and Game, 2009.

Kizzia, Tom. *The Wake of the Unseen Object: Travels Through Alaska's Native Landscapes.* Lincoln: University of Nebraska Press, 1998.

Kolbert, Elizabeth. *Field Notes from a Catastrophe: Man, Nature, and Climate Change.* New York: Bloomsbury, 2006.

Krakauer, Jon. *Into the Wild.* New York: Villard, 1996.

Lord, Nancy. "Glacial Gospel." *River Teeth* 16, no. 1 (Fall 2014): 47–53.

Marino, Elizabeth. *Fierce Climate, Sacred Ground: An Ethnography of Climate Change in Shishmaref, Alaska.* Fairbanks: University of Alaska Press, 2015.

McGinniss, Joe. *Going to Extremes.* New York: Alfred A. Knopf, 1980.

Miller, Don J. "Giant Waves in Lituya Bay, Alaska." U.S. Geological Survey Professional Paper no. 354-C, 1960.

Molnia, Bruce. "Glaciers of Alaska." U.S. Geological Survey Professional Paper no. 1386-K, 2008.

Muir, John. *Edward Henry Harriman.* New York: Doubleday, Page, 1912.

———. *The Cruise of the Corwin.* Boston and New York: Houghton Mifflin, 1917.

———. *The Mountains of California.* New

York: The Century Co., 1894.

————. *My First Summer in the Sierra*. Boston and New York: Houghton Mifflin, 1911.

————. *Our National Parks*. Boston and New York: Houghton Mifflin, 1901.

————. *The Story of My Boyhood and Youth*. Boston and New York: Houghton Mifflin, 1913.

Nash, Roderick Frazier. *Wilderness and the American Mind*. 5th ed. New Haven, CT: Yale University Press, 2014.

Ott, Riki. *Not One Drop: Betrayal and Courage in the Wake of the Exxon Valdez Oil Spill*. White River Junction, VT: Chelsea Green, 2008.

Punke, Michael. *Last Stand: George Bird Grinnell, the Battle to Save the Buffalo, and the Birth of the New West*. New York: Smithsonian Books/ Collins, 2007.

Raban, Jonathan. *Passage to Juneau: A Sea and Its Meanings*. New York: Pantheon, 1999.

Reiger, John. *American Sportsmen and the Origins of Conservation*. Corvallis: Oregon State University Press, 2007.

Ross, Ken. *Pioneering Conservation in Alaska*. Boulder: University Press of Colorado, 2006.

Scidmore, Eliza. *Appletons' Guide-Book to Alaska and the Northwest Coast: Including the Shores of Washington, British Columbia, Southeastern Alaska, the Aleutian and the Seal Islands, the Bering and the Arctic Coasts.* New York: D. Appleton, 1893.

Sides, Hampton. *In the Kingdom of Ice: The Grand and Terrible Polar Voyage of the USS Jeannette.* New York: Doubleday, 2014.

Sterling, Keir B. *Last of the Naturalists: The Career of C. Hart Merriam.* New York: Arno Press, 1977.

Tarr, R. S., et al. "The Earthquakes at Yakutat Bay, Alaska, in September, 1899." U.S. Geological Survey Professional Paper no. 69, 1912.

Wendler, Gerd, and Martha Shulski. "A Century of Climate Change for Fairbanks, Alaska." *Arctic* 62, no. 3 (November 2008): 295–300.

West, Michael, et al. "Why the Great Alaska Earthquake Matters Fifty Years Later." *Seismological Research Letters* 85, no. 2 (March 2014): 245–51.

Wolfe, Linnie Marsh. *Son of the Wilderness: The Life of John Muir.* New York: Alfred A. Knopf, 1946.

Worster, Donald. *A Passion for Nature: The*

Life of John Muir. New York: Oxford University Press, 2008.

ABOUT THE AUTHOR

Mark Adams is the author of the *New York Times* bestsellers *Meet Me in Atlantis* and *Turn Right at Machu Picchu.* A writer for many national magazines, including *GQ, Men's Journal, Rolling Stone,* and *New York,* he lives near New York City with his wife and children.